THE PROBLEM SOLVERS

Books by E. J. Kahn, Jr.

The Problem Solvers: A History of Arthur D. Little, Inc.
The Staffs of Life
Jock: The Life and Times of John Hay Whitney
Far-flung and Footloose: Pieces from The New Yorker,
  1937–1978
About The New Yorker *and Me*
Georgia: From Rabun Gap to Tybee Light
The American People
The China Hands
Fraud
The Boston Underground Gourmet (with Joseph P. Kahn)
The First Decade
Harvard: Through Change and Through Storm
The Separated People
A Reporter in Micronesia
The World of Swope
The Stragglers
A Reporter Here and There
The Big Drink
The Merry Partners
The Peculiar War
Who, Me?
The Voice
McNair: Educator of an Army
G.I. Jungle
The Army Life

THE
PROBLEM SOLVERS

A History of
Arthur D. Little, Inc.

E. J. Kahn, Jr.

LITTLE, BROWN AND COMPANY   *Boston · Toronto*

HC

Designed by Patricia Girvin Dunbar

*Published simultaneously in Canada
by Little, Brown & Company (Canada) Limited*

PRINTED IN THE UNITED STATES OF AMERICA

Contents

Author's Note

This book has been written with the cooperation and support of Arthur D. Little, Inc., but the selection and use of the material has been exclusively my own. The company is, of course, an institution, but over the years it has been more than anything else a collection of people — thousands of them, who have worked on a multitude of missions for a host of clients. It would be nice, but obviously impossible, to mention in the pages that follow all those who have been associated with the company. Many who no doubt deserve to be cited have perforce been overlooked, or their accomplishments too meagerly recorded. To the missing, my apologies, and to those present, my thanks for having shared with me recollections of the experiences and achievements that have kept ADL going for a century and have kept me interested in it.

— E.J.K.

THE PROBLEM SOLVERS

I *From Little Acorns*

Industrial research is the lifeblood of industry, and upon it
we must rely for that continuance of industrial progress
without which our growing population cannot hope to raise
or even maintain that standard of living for which our
country has been distinguished.

— Dr. Arthur D. Little, 1933

On Monday, October 1, 1984, ninety-eight years to the day after the founding of a two-man Boston firm from which they sprang, the twenty-five hundred employees of Arthur D. Little, Inc., and its subsidiaries were engaged in a variety of chores that, for most of them, typified their run-of-the-mill activities. This is what a few of them were up to.

Robert Kirk Mueller, who had joined the professional staff of ADL, as it is known, in 1968 after thirty-three years with the Monsanto Chemical Company and in 1977, somewhat to his and everybody else's surprise, had become the chairman of ADL's Board of Directors, had jet lag, having just returned from leading a seminar titled "The Role of Top Management and the Board in Enhancing Innovation" in Stockholm. Mueller arose at 5:00 A.M., played tennis at 6:30, and in the course of a working day that ended twelve hours later, presided at corporate headquarters in Cambridge over a seminar on the use of artificial intelligence to build a personal financial-planning system for a commercial bank, and discussed a new partnership-licensing agreement with a London-based Iranian consortium interested in worldwide development of a new ADL process for extracting soybean oil. When Mueller finally went home with a bulging briefcase at 6:30, he was too tired to practice on his bass fiddle.

3

Stephen W. Ritterbush, the president of Arthur D. Little Far East, Inc., which had opened for business in Singapore that spring, flew from his headquarters there to Hong Kong to confer with, among others, the president of a major American manufacturing company that wanted ADL to develop a strategy for penetrating the Indonesian market for marine engines; and a businessman interested in how ADL had been advising Japanese companies eager to get into the oil fields services business in China. Ritterbush had no chance that day to demonstrate his fluency, unique among ADL employees, in Samoan.

Stanley H. Werlin, of ADL's Government Marketing Group, had traveled with three ADL colleagues from Cambridge to Brooks Air Force Base, in San Antonio, to attend a conference of the American Defense Preparedness Association on the nation's chemical and biological warfare defense progress.

Alma Triner, vice-president for Public Relations, was in Cambridge preparing her remarks, in case a television channel should solicit them, in defense of an ADL nerve-gas-testing program that had got the company a lot of unwanted publicity for the better part of the previous year. After a ten-and-a-half-hour day at her office, in the course of which she also reviewed the text of a proposal to reorganize the telephone system of Thailand, she had just about enough strength left, by the time she got home, to feed her daughter, her dog, and herself.

J. Michael Younger, another vice-president and the head of Management Consulting in the London office, on Berkeley Square, learned to his delight that after six worrisome months of competitive negotiations, ADL had been awarded a contract to make a study to identify means of revitalizing Scotland's engineering industries. He also had to pacify some members of his staff who, after an expansion of their branch, didn't like the locations of their new offices.

Alfred E. Wechsler, senior vice-president and general manager of Professional Operations, had so many conferences in an eleven-and-a-half-hour work day (much of it spent in reviewing company plans for 1985) that he could allocate only fifteen minutes for lunch. He had a ham and cheese sandwich, lemon yogurt, and iced tea.

Phillip W. Hawley, a petroleum economist who was vice-president, Energy, for Europe, Africa, and the Middle East, had gone from his office in London to Angola, where ADL had been involved in oil activities for nearly fifteen years with both the Portuguese colonial government and, later, the independent socialist government. In Luanda, he was advising his clients — the Angolan government and Sonangol, the national oil company — on their negotiations with Gulf and Chevron over contracts involving more than $1 billion worth of new investments in offshore exploration and production.

George R. Gagliardi, an electronics systems specialist, was flying from Boston to Minneapolis to give a seminar to a major food company on CAVI, computer-aided visual inspection.

Bruce Williams, in charge of European telematics, was one of the several members of the London office who had lunch with Charles J. Kensler, ADL's senior vice-president for Life Sciences, who had flown over the night before from the States. Later, Williams arranged some slides for a presentation on telematics (a blend of computer and telecommunications technology) that ADL was going to make the next week to a prospective Norwegian client in Oslo.

Richard de Filippi, the president of Critical Fluids Systems, Inc., a wholly owned ADL subsidiary manufacturing industrial extraction systems, was in Cambridge, Massachusetts, having lunch with a venture capitalist who de Filippi hoped would invest in the firm. De Filippi had to dine at home alone because his son, with whom he normally ate, was in France picking grapes.

Harland A. Riker, Jr., senior vice-president and head of international operations, stayed in Cambridge. With Anthony J. Marolda of Management Counseling and Frank M. Yans of Resource Consulting, he spent a good part of the day meeting with the vice-president for corporate planning and development of a big Swiss aluminum company, for which ADL was hoping to be asked to develop a diversification strategy program for new business activities in the United States.

Santhanam C. Shekar of ADL's Wiesbaden office, who had overall market responsibility for Austria, was there in Linz discussing with Chemie Linz — that country's largest chemical and pharmaceutical company — the results of a strategic analysis ADL had made for its pharmaceutical division.

L. Ray Kelly, who from London supervised ADL's Middle East operations, was in Riyadh on his ninth trip of the year to

Saudi Arabia. Between a 7:00 A.M. breakfast conference with Dermot McMeekin, the chief ADL representative in a joint venture enterprise with the Saudi Consulting House, and a late afternoon flight to Jidda, Kelly met with (among several others) the chairman of the Saudi Investment Banking Corporation and some executives of Petromin — the state petroleum and minerals organization, and a longtime client — to discuss an ADL organization plan for that company's manpower development information systems.

William Reinfeld, vice-president for Development Economics of Arthur D. Little International, dealt with Thailand (negotiations on a $400,000 job to look into the privatization of transport), Egypt (a study of a proposed Luxor Visitor Management Center), Tunisia (an export strategy study), Taiwan (identification of foreign investment opportunities, especially in Panama), and Panama (a possible ADL role in advising a committee considering construction of a second Panama Canal). By the time Reinfeld got home, he was much too weary to remain awake until the end of Monday night football.

Christopher E. Ross, manager of ADL's Houston office, spent a good part of the day on what he considered fairly routine tasks: worrying, for instance, about the impact of acid rain on the eastern coast of the United States, and about fuel oil indexation in Papua New Guinea.

J. Ladd Greeno, an environmental specialist, took a Mississippi Valley Airways flight from Chicago to St. Joseph, Michigan, where he had an appointment to conduct an environmental audit of the Allied Corporation's foundry and automotive brake plant.

Roberto E. Batres, head of the Mexico City office, was in Istanbul working on a microcomputer-based project control system for a Turkish heavy construction company patterned on one ADL had previously set up for a large Brazilian contractor.

W. David Lee, manager of the Engineering Sciences Section, after a predawn, five-mile single-sculls race on the Charles River, presided over a meeting with ten representatives of the army and the air force who wanted to review the hardware specifications for an innovative ADL concept of air-conditioning based on devices called scroll compressors.

Michel d'Halluin, managing director of Arthur D. Little in France, spent most of the day in Paris with a government official and an investment banker who were trying to figure out a way of restructuring an old company with twenty-five hundred employees that, because of faulty management, had gone into receivership.

Senior Vice-President Samuel C. Fleming, while he was not completing arrangements for a trip to Montreal the following day, had ten separate meetings in Cambridge (one with a client over from Switzerland) that covered, among other topics, health care, information technology, environmental problems, internal budgeting and organization, and — this last his specialty — the strategic management of chemical companies.

Robert M. Tomasko, senior consultant in the Washington office, flew to Cambridge to prepare a report on the social responsibility of American companies operating in South Africa (that is, implementation of the Sullivan Principles) and to teach a course on organization and strategy at ADL's own degree-granting graduate school, the Management Education Institute.

Richard A. Stephan, a specialist in oil company reorganizations, was en route from Bogotá, Colombia, to Lima, Peru, where he planned to spend the following week advising the president of a petroleum company about the effect carrying out a recently completed ADL study would have on its future.

Anne J. Neilson, a senior consultant in the Chemical and Food Sciences Section, was getting set to depart that evening for London and Dublin, where she was going to talk to some English distilled spirits companies about an ongoing project to measure the flavor and chemical stability of a new spirit they were thinking of putting on the market; and to Irish Distillers, a longtime client, about modernizing their sensory measurement capability.

David W. Wheat, a senior consultant specializing in agricultural biotechnology, had lunch with a young Harvard graduate who was seeking guidance in making the transition from the academic community to the business world. Wheat was happy to be of service. "We all got our careers started with help and advice from others," he said afterward, "so we are glad to talk to those following similar paths."

Yoshimichi Yamashita, president of Arthur D. Little (Japan) Inc., spent most of the morning in Tokyo recommending to the chief executive officer of an American computer company how he could best break into the Japanese market, and a good part of the afternoon in the new town of Shinjuku celebrating the tenth year of ADL operations in Japan with an old client from Florida.

Richard E. Heitman, a senior vice-president, spent much of the day on the affairs of two more ADL subsidiaries: Pilgrim Health Associates and Delphi Associates. He took half an hour off from company duties to use some computer software he had developed himself to print a check to the United Way.

Jeffery C. Lapham, director of the Strategy Consulting Group of the Los Angeles office, was in San Francisco with executives of the Crowley Maritime Corporation, the world's biggest tug and barge company, going over strategy plans ADL had drawn up for recommendation to an imminent meeting of the company's board of directors.

Jerry Wasserman, manager of the Information Industries Unit of the Information Systems Section, was in Rochester, New York, reviewing with Eastman Kodak executives a scheme for developing a new administrative support system for their photocopy operations.

Andrew Sivak, vice-president of Biomedical Research and Technology, went to Richmond, Virginia, to discuss strategic planning for research and development work with an industrial client, from Knoxville, Tennessee, where he attended a meeting of the Society for Risk Analysis, the chair of whose liaison committee he was yielding after a three-year term.

Gerald J. Michael, the robotics practice leader of ADL's Computer Integrated Manufacturing Section, was en route from Chicago to Puerto Rico, there to assess the possible use of robots to improve an industrial client's productivity.

Lois C. Dreiman, a senior editor, ran into her office because her phone was ringing. A colleague wanted a hand in putting together a proposal to support NASA's efforts to launch a national space transportation system in both the domestic and international commercial markets. Later in the day, she checked some galley proofs on ADL's final report to the New York Metropolitan Transportation Authority on the technical and cost aspects of alternative automatic fare collection system concepts, and edited an article being submitted to the *Harvard Business Review* titled "Planning for Computer Integrated Manufacturing."

Nicholas Steinthal, vice-president in Europe, caught an early morning plane from his headquarters in Brussels to Frankfurt and proceeded thence, accompanied by two members of the ADL Germany staff, to Darmstadt for a four-hour conference with a multinational pharmaceutical company on a strategic development plan for its activities worldwide.

John J. Clancy, a specialist in graphic arts, paper, and security in the Product Technology Section, discussed with representatives of the U.S. Bureau of Engraving and Printing the preparation by ADL of a handbook covering future production equipment for U.S. postage stamps. He also worked on a proposal for devising a method of authenticating an allegedly hundred-year-old Peruvian bond.

Paul Damon Littlefield, senior vice-president and chief financial officer, spent most of the day in Boston, as a member of the finance committee of the New England Medical Center, trying to figure out a way to reduce hospital rates in 1985.

Sarah W. Fuller, president of Arthur D. Little Decision Resources, divided her time between ADL's Cambridge headquarters and its Burlington, Massachusetts, outpost. Most of her day was devoted to writing a final presentation on how a client company might, over the next ten years, triple its size. Between 5:30 and 9:15 P.M., she attended to her two sons, one of them three years old and the other two months; and from 9:15 to midnight she labored over a report for a client who had initially given ADL six weeks to complete it but now wanted it in five days.

Irwin Miller, the chairman and chief executive officer of the Opinion Research Corporation in Princeton, New Jersey (which ADL had bought in 1975), was at Middlesex Industrial Park in South Plainfield, New Jersey. His job today was wrapping up negotiations for a new Opinion Research facility that would open in 1985 and would double its telephone-interviewing capability.

Kamal N. Saad, a vice-president stationed in Brussels, was in England helping ADL's London Energy Group put together a paper, for a forthcoming European chemical industry meeting in Amsterdam, on changing trends in strategic thinking. He also helped the London Management Consulting Group get ready for a sales meeting with the senior officers of a big chemical company on innovation and the strategic management of technology.

John F. Magee, president and chief executive officer of Arthur D. Little, Inc., was at the Cambridge headquarters, where he con-

ferred with Lewis Rambo, his vice-president for Personnel, about
the sudden death that morning of a member of the staff and what
could be done for the bereaved family; discussed the future of yet
another subsidiary (since sold), The S. M. Stoller Corporation,
which dealt with nuclear energy; and had a chat with William
Reinfeld about the history and geography of Nepal. It was a relatively easy day for Magee; he was able to get away from the
stand-up desk in his office at 6:30 and go home, sit down, and put
the finishing touches on a model boat he'd been building, when
he could find the time, for the past two years.

The headquarters at which these far-flung and in many instances largely uncoordinated peregrinations were eventually recorded was an enclave on the western edge of Cambridge in a
dowdy neighborhood otherwise notable for a bowling alley, a
motel, a new suburban station of the Boston subway system, and
at least one nesting area for wild turtles and woodcocks. The
Arthur D. Little, Inc., citadel, a cluster of red brick structures that looked like a minimum security prison and was thought
by some of its inmates to have not a few characteristics thereof,
was called Acorn Park. Its founder was fond of the Latin phrase
Glandes sparge ut quercus crescant — in loose translation,
"Great oaks from little acorns grow" — and for many years a
winged acorn was the company's cherished symbol.

A buzzing hive of offices and laboratories, Acorn Park was the
home base for about half of the firm's employees, who by 1985
included representatives of most of the principal physical and social sciences, as well as engineers, technicians, and practitioners of
such occult contemporary specialties as strategic planning, management information systems, hazardous waste disposal, and risk
assessment. There was, for a time, even a resident philosopher.
The story went that he ran afoul of a disputative computer one
day and left in a huff. The philosopher's office space, according to
one natural scientist who likes to tell the tale, was soon usurped
by an expert on artificial intelligence.

Dr. Little once said, "Never mistake an organization chart for
an organization." Over the years, the successor administrators of
his company have tried manfully to come up with charts that re-
alistically portray their organization. When one employee made a
stab at that in the 1980s, his finished product had so many inter-

secting lines and crisscrosses that it resembled a Mondrian over-laid by graffiti. A company geochemist thought that a valid representation could be achieved only on videotape, with three dozen or so tiny squares and circles scuttling about on a screen like images in a PAC-MAN game. Every so often, the company would reshuffle its various groups, divisions, and sections into new entities, but the neatly structured chains of command would soon get tangled up, and unfortunately Acorn Park no longer enjoyed the unraveling services of a management consultant who had once succored a tea company by figuring out a way to keep the strings of the tea bags from getting all messed up when they were plucked from a box. (A lot of tea was consumed at that time by staff members who'd initially been asked to help separate clumps of bags they'd yanked out of packages.)

In the summer of 1984, Senior Vice-President Alfred Wechsler, who held a variety of other imposing titles, told an acquaintance, "I just found out that I was chairman of Arthur D. Little International." President John Magee once professed not to be perturbed by such seeming confusion in his ranks. "The only way to manage this company is not to manage it," he said. A detached social historian, Sherman Kingsbury, had written in 1965 in an article, "Arthur D. Little, Inc. — A Small Society,"

> ADL is a small society, committed to definite — even if partially unstated — objectives. Its members have certain common values which reinforce and are reinforced by the work organization, the administrative organization, the systems of formal and informal rewards and sanctions. Its problems and its strengths are derived from its values and traditions and from its interactions with other social systems surrounding it. As is true with any other society, anything said about it is only partially true. No description or chart is adequate to convey the whole experience of membership in the society or to make clear how it actually functions.

Later, a visiting Englishman, in a treatise titled "Impressions of ADL," wrote, "The structure is that of a collection of entrepreneurs who subcontract work to each other." There was no central direction or planning that he could perceive, "a curious situation for a company which advises others on corporate planning."

Among other things, Arthur D. Little, Inc., is a company that can give advice in an extraordinary variety of languages. One of its personnel officers — whose responsibilities do not normally encompass the hiring of professional members of its staff — reckoned in mid-1984 that ADLers (as members of the company family are informally known) were conversant in sixty-one languages, including Afrikaans, Amharic, Gujarati, Igbo, Kannada, Konkani, Latvian, Marathi, Sindhi, Swahili, Telugu, Urdu, Yiddish, and Yoruba.

In English, in which most of them can make themselves reasonably well understood even to laymen, they describe their institution in a variety of engaging ways — according to a long-standing member of the ADL Board of Directors, as "a halfway house between a university and a business"; according to a Harvard M.B.A. who spent a recent summer there, as "a kind of kindergarten, where everybody is playing with his own blocks or finger paints or crayons"; according to its chief executive officer, as "a network of professional people who manage change"; according to a staff nuclear physicist, as "a gathering of two thousand people, all of whom think that their CEO is doing a terrible job and that nobody else could do it better"; according to its chief counsel, as "a kind of zoo, with remarkably intelligent animals"; according to the overseer of most of its international business, as "a crazy place that's also a supermarket of expertise"; according to the chairman of its board, as "a floating flea market"; according to still others, as an oriental bazaar, a blind man's conception of an elephant, a medieval kingdom populated by jousting dukes and barons, a collection of cottage industries, a coordinated chaos, and a consumers' union. "You want to buy a chain saw, a pocket calculator, a stereo, or a pair of tennis shoes?" one ADLer said to a visitor. "Somebody here will be sure to know all about it." One of the charms of ADL, a listening colleague piped up, "is that I fit in here and I'm not a normal person." (ADL's own house organ, *The Little Paper*, runs classified ads. One published in 1985 for some Maine real estate — ocean view, blueberries — was phrased in a manner calculated to appeal to that special readership: "Ideal solar location. Excellent percolation test for septic tank and leaching field.") ADL has described itself, more staidly, as "the last place on earth where private enterprise really works."

Most outsiders are content simply to describe Arthur D. Little, Inc., as a consulting firm. Consulting is a time-old, and sometimes time-honored, occupation. Dr. Arthur D. Little, the company's founder, had a high opinion of Belshazzar, not only because he had called in David as a consultant on handwriting but, what was equally commendable, had paid him on the spot for his special services. "Belshazzar may have been a poor king," Little once wrote, "but he was an ideal client."

Much of ADL's annual business — by 1984, that amounted to a robust $213,363,000 — comes from clients it has served more than once, and one ADLer steeped in the classics is fond of pointing out that this was the case also with another legendary consultant, the Delphic Oracle. "Her customers would come and pitch tents near her throne and bring fancy gifts," he says, "and, through her acolytes, request an audience. If and when they finally got it, they weren't allowed to look at her answer to their questions till they got home. These were usually so incomprehensible that they were obliged to return, with even fancier gifts, to obtain an interpretation of the first answer."

Latter-day consultants were not always so highly esteemed. Until about the era of the Second World War, *consulting* was often a nasty word, deemed to be connected with, if not integral to, industrial espionage and like chicanery. Even today, its practitioners are sometimes viewed with cynicism or downright snideness. "Consultants are people who can tell you how to tie your laces better" is a typical remark. ADLers themselves are apt to enounce, after a couple of tongue-loosening drinks, such pejorative definitions of the typical consultant as "Somebody who is too lazy to work, too proud to beg, too nervous to steal, and with alcoholic tendencies." One ADLer who was about to retire after thirty-odd years in the consulting fold was asked what words of wisdom he would like to leave behind. "There are four levels of consulting," he said after a reflective pause, "grunting, humming, singing, and meditating." No less an authority in the field than the *Consultants News*, the industry's very own trade journal, was not above publishing this heretical characterization: "A consultant is, more often than not, someone brought in to find out what has gone wrong, by the people who made it go wrong, in the comfortable expectation that he will not bite the hand that feeds him by placing the blame where it belongs."

Be all that as it may, in the United States alone there exist today thousands of consulting firms, ranging in size from big ones like McKinsey & Company; Booz, Allen & Hamilton; SRI International; and Battelle Memorial Institute (the first two determinedly profit-oriented, the latter two nonprofit) to small, specialized consulting and one-man shops that, as one ADLer has said scornfully, "are apt to be nothing more than spare rooms in the overmortgaged homes of middle-level business executives out of a job." The *Financial Times* of London once proposed that *mckinsey* deserved a place in dictionaries as a verb meaning "to shake up, reorganize, declare redundant, abolish committee rule. Mainly applied to large industrial companies but also applicable to any organization with management problems." The word *little*, of course, has long been in dictionaries. ADL has occasionally attempted to capitalize on that. Once it had some promotional lapel buttons made up bearing the legend "Think Little."

It has been said of consultants that their burgeoning success is attributable to the circumstance that many corporate executives and government officials are incapable of independently managing their own affairs. "Consultants keep going because their clients want independent and preferably objective sanction for doing what they were going to do anyway but not trusting their own judgment," one ADLer says. Consultants sometimes go out of their way, out of kindness and prudence, to give their clients the impression that whatever new ideas consultancy may have generated were actually conceived by the clients themselves. "You have to be careful not to take too much credit when you help somebody out," says one ADLer whose habitual working garb includes a striped shirt and a bow tie, and who has groomed his facial hair into strikingly odd configurations. "Somebody's nose is always out of joint when a consultant is hired. Why, the guy down the line wonders, did my bosses have to bring in these wild guys with striped shirts and bow ties and funny beards to tell me what I'm doing wrong? The best thing you can do in such cases is to mollify the guy with his nose out of joint by giving *him* credit for whatever you do to save his neck."*

---

* When traveling on business, that particular ADLer customarily takes along a tennis racquet. "Almost all people who run manufacturing plants," he says, "like old cars or play tennis. I can play tennis or talk cars. I prefer playing tennis to downing eighty thousand martinis. Once I took my wife along, too, but that can be dangerous. We were in La Paz, in the early nineteen-seventies, and suddenly found ourselves in the middle of a revolution. My wife looked out of our hotel window one day and asked me why truckloads of men were coming up a hill. I'd been all over the world. Without even looking out, I said, 'They're probably getting ready for market day.' 'But why,' she asked, 'are they all carrying guns?' "

One ADL client, who owns a building materials company in the Midwest with annual sales of around $400 million, says, "You use consultants for their depth of knowledgeability and objectivity and also because they can save you a lot of time and money." Over one twelve-year stretch, that client estimated, he had enriched ADL's coffers by $1 million. "Some of their advice wasn't worth beans," he said, "but they played a pivotal role in our acquisition of two subsidiaries, each for thirty-five million, and those two had a big impact on a quarter of our annual sales afterward — that was a hundred million a year. Not a bad return, as I see it, on our consulting investment."

Some observers of the business scene believe that corporate executives gravitate toward consultants purely because everybody else seems to be doing it, that they are victims of a fashionable epidemic and are comparable, say, to flag-wavers at the Olympics. C. Roland Christensen, of the faculty of the Harvard Business School, has been a member of the ADL Board of Directors since 1960 and has a different viewpoint. Christensen thinks that there is a genuine place for consultants in the economic sphere. "The fundamental product of a consultant — advice giving and problem solving — can be important to organizational life," he says. "Indeed, in a substantial number of instances, the views of disinterested outside experts can be crucial."

For a company that evolved from two chemists nesting hungrily in a sixth-floor Boston aerie, hoping to hear the creak of the stairs outside that meant a client was approaching, it is appropriate that Arthur D. Little, Inc., is sometimes described as a catalyst for change. "Other people's troubles are our business," a 1907 advertisement for the firm proclaimed, and that sentiment was echoed in a much more recent ADL contention: "Hardly anything is none of our business." Today, 30 percent of that vigorous business can be loosely categorized as management consulting, 45 percent as technical consulting, and 25 percent as industrial research. Of all that work, 44 percent is done for private business clients in the United States, 26 percent for customers abroad, 21 percent for the American federal government, and 9 percent for state and local governments at home. President John Magee, in a 1981 speech titled "Our Management Values and Systems," tried to respond to the question, What business are we in? and his answer went, in small part,

We undertake research — in our laboratories and in the field — to find new answers to clients' questions.

We provide information. . . .

We manage intellectual properties. . . .

We help people in adversary or negotiating situations. For example, in the early decades of the company, assistance to clients in defending or challenging patents was an important part of our business and today we assist in all sorts of lawsuits, regulatory actions, and negotiations over the purchase or sale of businesses.

There is one thing we can say about "our industry" with certainty. It is essentially impossible to set bounds on it.

Another ADL officer has said of the company's boundless activities, "Our work defies any brief description, other than that it is to give a client, for a consideration, advice which he may either accept or reject." ADL frequently has no idea which alternative a client may adopt. It considers its staff's time one of its most precious assets; and because hours or even minutes spent following up on a completed case cannot be charged to that client or anybody else, ADL can sometimes only guess how fruitful its efforts have been. ("You pay us for an hour and we'll give you an hour" is the overriding philosophy.)

That lack of hot pursuit has been prevalent for decades. In 1930, long before environmentalists put a stop to such carryings-on, the Campbell Soup Company, which had a plant in Camden, New Jersey, got to brooding about its traditional practice of dumping wastes from the manufacture of tomato soup into open sewers that ran into the Delaware River. The refuse amounted to just 0.7 percent of the weight of the raw tomatoes gobbled up in the soup-making process, but even so that represented a mountain of mash. Could the stuff, Campbell's asked ADL, conceivably be dyed green and used in lieu of cottonseed hulls for fairway turf on the miniature golf courses that were then much in vogue? Did ADL have any other ideas?

A "Utilization of Tomato Waste" study was soon under way. The Little men assigned to it rejected the golf proposition: A dyed tomato-waste carpet would be too smooth, for one thing, they concluded, and for another too expensive. But what about chicken or animal feed? ADL had one hundred tons of seeds, skins, and cores diverted from the river and sent to a Boston feed company, which decided that such a product would contain three or four times the amount of fiber ordinarily desirable for their customers. How about mulch? Fertilizer? Tomato puree? Tomato juice? "While we appreciate there are some very definite objections to the conversion of any portion of this waste to a food product for human consumption," ADL reported, "we believe this is the only course by which you are likely to realize any profit above the total cost of processing this material." The report took months to prepare and cost Campbell's thousands of dollars; but there is no evidence that anybody at ADL ever bothered to inquire as to what course, if any, Campbell's elected to follow after all that time and trouble.

There was a time when clients of ADL gladly used testimonials from the company to promote their products. A 1913 advertisement for the Tileston & Hollingsworth Company of Boston, for instance, bragged that each package of its library paper included a certificate signed by Dr. Little confirming that its contents were 99 percent rag paper. Dr. Little's successors have never much gone in for self-aggrandizement and have professed to be horrified at the use or contemplated use of their findings in advertisements, publicity releases, or prospectuses for stock offerings. (The *Boston Globe*, in 1975, ran a feature story that said, "Somehow, when Arthur D. Little, Inc., reports on something, it becomes official." Years before, ADL was asked by Blue Cross of Boston to prepare a long-range planning study for the group. The consultants duly came up with one and expected Blue Cross to use it and take full credit for it. But Blue Cross wouldn't release it without an endorsement from a dispassionate outside agency. The health group asked ADL to furnish such an imprimatur. So ADL found itself in the odd position of giving its blessing to a plan that it had drawn up itself.)

However, for a 1984 convention of international flavor technologists in Anaheim, California, the company — a pioneering force in flavor technology — did unbend enough to install a small booth to call attention to its services. The woman staff member appointed to make arrangements thought it might be nice to have some souvenirs on hand to pass out. Her superiors gave her the nod, but only on condition that the gifts cost no more than a dollar apiece. She was able to obtain, for exactly that amount, one thousand magnetic paper-clip holders, with the company's name inscribed on each, and also the words "Throw a problem at us."

Problem solving has long been what ADL believes it does best. Since 1974, the company has been resolutely and rewardingly engaged in solving a problem for the government of Saudi Arabia: how to put together and make functional a $3 billion telecommunications system. Back in 1902, for a fee that probably did not exceed $100, Dr. Little had solved a vexing problem for the New England Telephone & Telegraph Company. The electrical contacts at the Milk Street station of its Boston operation were malfunctioning, and nobody could ascertain why. He had figured out the reason as neatly as Sherlock Holmes might have — by eliminating all other possible suspects until the only one left was the wind-carried drift, falling on the balky equipment, of ash particles resulting from a nearby restaurant's incineration of its outdated menus.

"We undertake commissions of all kinds," boasted the *Little Journal of Jocular Chemistry*, which the company put out on April Fools' Day in 1919. (Its editor was identified as Dr. A. Distinct Little.) "Nothing scares us. One of our trained staff will walk right into the cage and pat it on the head, and inside of a few minutes the most obstinate problem will lie down and roll over." It has not always been that simple. "When somebody comes to us with a problem," one contemporary senior ADL operative says, "we stay with it until we see the light at the end of the tunnel, but sometimes there are an awful lot of curves in the tunnel. In many instances, moreover, people don't know exactly what their problem is. They just know they have one. Our power, when you come right down to it, is the power of the question. The client may have, somewhere deep inside him, the seeds of awareness about what's bothering him, but these have to be nurtured and tended and brought to the surface. You have to be careful not to answer a client's question too fast. You may be doing him a much better service by suggesting, as tactfully as you can, that he is asking the wrong question. Then you can rephrase the question for him and, once you've got that far, begin to start searching for the answer."

It is not always a matter of questions and answers. Once, for instance, a naval research advisory committee commissioned ADL to study basic research in the navy — in other words, to do research on research on research. Another time ADL was called upon, once again at taxpayers' ultimate expense, to inspect the methods of inspection at the army inspector general's office.

ADLers sometimes grudgingly allocate a few hours of their treasured time to seek to identify and then to solve their own internal problems. A Long-Range Planning Committee that the company set up in 1958, for example, addressed itself to that issue and came up with the conclusion, among others, that its high-priority business goal should be the "application of research principles to solution of the problems of people who are willing to pay to have them solved." The committee wondered, though, "Is what we have proposed really enough of a vision? Solving other people's problems can be made to seem a rather dreary business. We think it can also achieve grandeur. We can imagine the future ADL as a key agency in the economy of the United States and the world, consulted on the really vital problems — technical, economic, and social — of the day, in the forefront of the application of new techniques, dealing always with those aspects of the economy that are changing and exciting."

By 1985, as Arthur D. Little, Inc., prepared to celebrate its centennial year, it had become pretty much that kind of agency. It might never wholly solve all of anybody else's problems, let alone its own, but it was — with some four thousand disparate projects simultaneously under way in sixty countries — the oldest and longest-lived consulting company in the United States and, perhaps excepting the Delphic Oracle, on earth.

II *A Boundless Curiosity*

*Chemistry is too often left like Cinderella sitting beside the
ashes of the laboratory furnace, while her two haughty sisters
drive away together to the industrial ball. But some day, not
far distant, her Prince will come and lead her forth to take
her proper place before the world.*
— Dr. Arthur D. Little, 1912

The year 1886 was an eventful one in many parts of
the world. In Singapore, the legendary-to-be Raffles
Hotel welcomed its first guest. In England, William Gladstone
introduced an Irish Home Rule bill. Among the notable publications of the year were *The Bostonians, The Strange Case of Dr.
Jekyll and Mr. Hyde*, Richard von Krafft-Ebing's *Psychopathia
Sexualis, Little Lord Fauntleroy*, and the first English edition of
Das Kapital. Auguste Rodin unveiled "The Kiss," and Georges
Seurat "Sunday Afternoon on the Island of la Grande Jatte." The
element germanium was discovered, the Pasteur Institute
founded, and the tracks of the Canadian Pacific Railway completed all the way out to Winnipeg. The Statue of Liberty was
unveiled in New York's harbor. Farther west, the Indian wars
ended when Geronimo was captured by federal troops and the
Navajos resignedly signed a peace treaty with General William
Tecumseh Sherman. Down South, Georgia pharmacist John
Styth Pemberton launched a syrup, the base of a fizzy headache
cure, that he called Coca-Cola.

On October 1 of that year, on the sixth floor of a dowdy brick
building at 103 Milk Street in downtown Boston, the firm of
Griffin & Little, Chemical Engineers, opened for business. The
premises it occupied were modest. There was a twelve-by-eight-

foot office and, adjoining it, a laboratory of the same cramped dimensions. The two principals, listed on their letterhead in an order that both thought reflected their relative importance, were Roger Burrill Griffin — tall, dark, full-bearded, aged thirty-two — and Arthur Dehon Little — short, clean-shaven but for a trim mustache, ten years Griffin's junior. Little had organized the partnership and had wanted to go into business in New York City, but Griffin, who had put in some time there, persuaded him that New York already had a surfeit of practicing chemists. So they had settled on and in Boston (population 400,000), where they felt comfortable, both having come from New England.

Not that Boston seemed at first to offer much more than New York in the way of commercial success. The city already had six similar firms scratching for a living. It was a time when patent medicines were in vogue, with all the suspicions these justifiably aroused. Much of the informed populace took a dim view of industry in general, and industry, for its part, was skeptical about science. Any manufacturer who put more than a mite of his profits into research and development would have been considered daft. "Industry and science were comparative strangers," Little would write nearly half a century later, by which time the two had become somewhat friendlier, "and industry had little desire for closer acquaintance. . . . In such a setting, the new laboratory stood like an outpost of pioneers in a forbidding land. For many years its essential business was that of blazing trails and inducing reluctant manufacturers to use them."

Among scientists in 1886, chemists rated not much more respect than numerologists or astrologers. The American Chemical Society, which had been founded ten years earlier, had just 241 members. Those chemists who, like Griffin and Little, had elected to hang out their shingles in Boston earned what frugal income they could largely by analyzing, for importers, shipments of foreign goods landed at Boston — sugar for candy manufacturers, nickel ore, ground shells, baking powder, spices from India, Ceylon, and Java. Some clients thought three dollars an ample reward for testing a sample, no matter how long that might take. Manufacturers were loath to spend even that much for analyses but felt they had to because their products would be suspect unless some presumably unbiased source would vouch for their reliability. Some chemists were glad to earn twenty-five dollars for a day's work or a night's work. Batches of raw sugar would be delivered to 103 Milk Street, for instance, at 6:00 P.M., and its consigners expected a report on their purity, or lack thereof, by 9:30 the following morning.

Griffin was a whiz at testing. He could vet forty samples overnight. The fee was seventy-five cents per sample. The Warren Powder Company imported sodium nitrate from British Guiana for gunpowder. Warren had its own in-house chemist, who regularly took a whole night to dissect each arriving batch. Griffin proposed matching that effort in two hours, and when he succeeded, Warren became a regular client — at three dollars a sample. (Testing water from local wells was more rewarding: The going price was five dollars.)

Early on, the firm won the approbation of a leather dealer who'd been paying eighty cents a gallon for a stain he especially admired and who, when the price was raised to eighty-five cents, got to wondering just what were the ingredients that made the stuff so dear. Griffin and Little analyzed the stain for him. It was 97 percent water, they were quickly able to inform him, and the rest of its contents could be picked up just about anywhere for a nickel. The leather man was astonished and his stain supplier outraged. Over the next century, the founders' successors would frequently be reminded that you can't please everybody all the time.

Arthur Dehon Little, the oldest of four brothers, was born in Boston on December 15, 1863 — just twenty-six days after President Abraham Lincoln delivered the Gettysburg Address. The boy's parents were Amelia Hixson and Thomas Jones Little — she an Englishwoman, he a scion of a New England family that had crossed the Atlantic in 1640. An artillery captain in the Civil War, Thomas Little had been wounded early during the conflict and assigned while recuperating to Fort Independence, a Boston harbor post established during Revolutionary days. Arthur (who, through his father, would eventually become a member of the Commandery of the State of Massachusetts Military Order of the Loyal Legion of the United States) was named after Thomas's good friend Arthur Dehon, a Civil War hero. When Colonel Fletcher Webster, son of Daniel Webster and the commander of the 12th Massachusetts Volunteers, was killed in August 1862 during the Second Battle of Bull Run, it had been Lieutenant

Dehon who had risked death himself by dashing out under fire and retrieving his fallen leader's body. (That middle name Dehon would in later years often be a stumper. The *Boston Globe*, in a single article about Arthur Little, once rendered it as both Dehan and Demon.)

After the war, the Littles — the paterfamilias by now a pensioner — moved to Portland, Maine. Young Arthur soon gave evidence of a restless and probing mind. A schoolteacher there reminded him many years afterward how another faculty member had "winked, blinked, and wondered at questions you asked and statements you made." The boy's curiosity seemed boundless. When Harvard University sponsored a contest for the best schoolchild essay on animal and vegetable life along the Atlantic seaboard, Arthur spent days prowling the wharves and piles of Casco Bay for specimens, and his report on his findings won him a second prize. Considering that many Harvardians of that era barely knew Maine existed, that was quite an accomplishment.

When Arthur was twelve, a schoolmate and he jointly invested a dime, or perhaps fifteen cents, in the raw materials for a chemical experiment. In the dimly lighted basement of the Little home, they stuck a glass tube through a cork, inserted the cork in a bottle containing some sulfuric acid and a few scraps of iron, and were pleased when, as they'd hoped, the acid bubbled and some hydrogen gas emerged from the top of the tube. Arthur's friend struck a match to get a better view of the phenomenon, and the whole contraption blew up — fortunately without injury to either of the perpetrators. "It was worth the money," Little reflected when he was fifty-eight.

At thirteen, he installed a makeshift chemical laboratory, better lighted, in the basement. His parents were not entirely happy about his persistent experimentation. For one thing, they wanted him to become not a chemist but a physician. For another, the whole house smelled. (Years later, Arthur elected to enshrine on a wall of his private office a picture of another boy washing glassware in a chemical laboratory of London's Royal Institution — Michael Faraday.) Young Little's parents became convinced that he deserved more advanced tutelage than Portland seemed likely to offer, and they somehow scraped up enough funds to send him to the Berkeley School in New York City for his high school diploma. A teacher there calculated, probably nonempirically, that the transplanted teenager already had a vocabulary of twenty thousand words.

In the fall of 1881, a few months before his eighteenth birthday, Little became a freshman at the Massachusetts Institute of Technology. M.I.T., which ever afterward would be intimately linked to him and to his company, was then located in Boston at 491 Boylston Street. Most of the courses that Little took were in chemistry, but he almost immediately also demonstrated an interest in and flair for writing. That November, he was one of four undergraduates who started up a campus newspaper, the *Tech*. A century later, Little's successors judged that he had been the "best and most stalwart writer of the founding fathers." He was also instrumental, in due course, in the inception of an M.I.T. alumni magazine, the *Technology Review*, to which he now and then contributed. In its December 1929 issue, he related how as a boy he had received what he called his first lesson in industrial economics: Climbing Mount Chocorua, in New Hampshire, he had come upon a commercial blueberry picker who had two milk pails full of berries alongside him but who was lunching on dry bread. Little had asked him — not very tactfully, the author conceded — why he wasn't eating some blueberries instead. "I can't afford to eat them," had been the reply.

In his junior year, Little became editor in chief of the *Tech*. He was by then being carried on the establishment's academic records as a special student "not in the full regular courses." The following summer, he studied papermaking in Amherst. He never returned to M.I.T. He had not graduated from his Portland high school either, but his classmates in Maine elected him president at their fiftieth reunion, in 1931. When, as an adult, he was put up once for membership in the University Club, that finicky establishment turned him down on the grounds that he had no university degree. M.I.T. was not so choosy. Degree or no degree, his fellow alumni picked him in 1912 to be their representative on the institute's governing corporation (of which in 1931 he became a life member), and in 1921 he was installed as president of the M.I.T. Alumni Association. By that time he had accumulated a gratifying assortment of honorary degrees: from Columbia University, Rutgers University, Manchester University in England, and M.I.T. itself. Even before he was thus ennobled, people had begun to call him Dr. Little — much as John Styth Pemberton, the Coca-Cola pharmacist, was honorifically known to his contemporaries as Dr. Pemberton. In Little's case, the technically unwarranted title had been conferred because he radiated authority and wisdom.

In the fall of 1884, his family by now unable to afford another year's tuition at M.I.T., Little went to work for the Richmond Paper Company in Rumford, Rhode Island, site of the first mill in the United States to convert wood pulp into paper by a sulfite process that had been invented in Philadelphia and perfected in Sweden and Germany. Little started out as a two-dollar-a-day journeyman chemist and file clerk. "I lost eight pounds in the first two weeks," he reminisced jokingly in 1929, "and as I weighed only one hundred and forty pounds it looked as though I would last just thirty-five weeks."

One thing that contributed to the arduousness of young Little's apprenticeship was that the two main functionaries at the company, a Swedish chemist and a German engineer, couldn't get along. After one particularly bristling argument, they both quit. Little, only six weeks on the job, found himself running the plant. He forthwith showed his mettle when his workers, nearly all of whom were far older than he, went on strike; he managed to cajole them into returning to work with their demands largely unmet. Once that was out of the way, he proceeded, with the absent plant owner's pleased consent, to overhaul the whole place, which seemed to have been operating up to then as much by chance as design.

He was lucky enough, moreover, to become acquainted with a visiting Japanese engineer who had investigated the use of sulfite processes all over Europe, and who was willing to impart to the American his considerable expertise. Little's own expertise was soon made evident: He devised and subsequently patented a digester vessel that markedly expedited the softening of wood pulp. Within less than a year, he was on an annual salary of $4,400, and his employer dispatched him to New Bern, North Carolina, to take charge of a paper mill that was being set up there. Little's replacement at Rumford was Roger Burrill Griffin.

Of Roger Griffin's background, far less is known than of Little's. Griffin's forebears had come to New England from Wales, and the family's coat of arms back there featured a griffin (more commonly spelled "griffon") — the monster, half lion, half eagle, that the ancient Greeks believed guarded the hoarded gold of Scythia. Roger Griffin was born in 1854 and, after studying chemistry at the University of Vermont, received his bachelor's degree in 1876. That same year, he became a charter member of the newly formed American Chemical Society. He put in a couple of years as an assistant to Dr. Edward R. Squibb, the pharmaceutical pioneer, and for another seven years performed chemical analyses at a New York laboratory before joining the Richmond company. Other chemists said of him, with awe, that he could handle as many as thirty analyses at once without getting them mixed up. It was this prowess that persuaded Arthur Little to invite Griffin — who was already thinking of leaving Richmond and had been offered a better job in Chicago — to join up with him when he decided, in August 1886, to strike out on his own. Griffin was amenable, provided suitable financial arrangements could be worked out. Soon they were. Little was to put up $1,500 for an office and laboratory, and to provide $1,000 in working capital. (That capital was all but used up at the outset; the laboratory equipment that the partners felt was essential to get under way turned out to cost $2,300.)

On August 29, 1886, Little sent his father, in Portland, a twelve-page handwritten letter. He wrote that Griffin and he didn't expect to have too much business in their first six months, "but are reasonably sure of a fair amount of work." They planned to concentrate on jobs for paper mills, the son said, because they were the only chemists in the country who specialized in that area. That should bring them $500 from the Richmond company, somewhere between $1,000 and $12,000 from other unspecified clients, and perhaps another $1,000 through a brother of Griffin's who taught chemistry in Illinois. "We shall be independent and permanently located," the son went on, confidence all but brimming over the pages. He added that Griffin "can do probably four times the work I can" ("at present," he added) but that the senior partner could probably teach the junior his tricks. Then came the matter of finances. Griffin "has no money and in order to go in with him on equal terms I have agreed to raise $2,500." Did his father know of anybody who might be interested? An Aunt Alice was mentioned. And finally — he was still only twenty-two —

"Suppose Mother will be glad to know that she is going to have a boy in Boston after all."

One way or another, the necessary $2,500 was assembled. A three-year copartnership agreement between Griffin and Little was duly executed. According to its terms, Griffin was to attend to the run-of-the-mill laboratory chores, for which he could draw thirty-five dollars a week from the firm's proceeds. Little, at twenty-five a week, was to be responsible for experimental (that is, not commissioned) laboratory work and for handling pulp and paper business. Also, he would do whatever traveling seemed prudent. The Milk Street building had an elevator, but it functioned erratically. Prospective customers were disinclined to walk up five flights to consummate a five-dollar deal. Accordingly, while Griffin hovered over his retorts and burners, Little, as he later put it, "pounded Boston pavements, first seeking minor technical assignments and then seeking even more minor payment for services."

Advertising didn't appear to help much, either, despite such glowing testimonials to their skills as the partners paid for in the *New England Grocer* that first fall: "Examinations of Chemicals, Drugs, Paints, Oil, Grease, Soap-stock, Soaps, Fertilizers and Fertilizing Materials, Minerals, Iron and Steel, Water Analysis, Analysis of Foods and Foods Products, and all kinds of general analyses made in the SHORTEST POSSIBLE TIME and at the lowest price compatible with Accurate and Reliable work."

Nor was the response especially heartening to a promotional letter the partners sent out on October 18:

Gentlemen:
Allow us to call your attention to the CHEMICAL LABORATORY which we have established at No. 103 Milk Street, Boston, where we are prepared to execute all kinds of CHEMICAL ANALYSES with ACCURACY and DISPATCH. . . .
Mr. Griffin and Mr. Little have had several years' Experience in the development of new chemical processes on the Commercial scale and are prepared to undertake, either in their own laboratory, or upon the spot, investigations for the improvement of processes and the perfection of products.
INVENTORS and MANUFACTURERS engaged in developing new ideas, can obtain from us full information upon any chemical

points involved and feel sure that their communications will be considered Strictly Confidential. . . .

The firm's first year proved to be a bleak one. The partners had hoped to gross $14,000. They took in $1,800. Their expenses came to $1,200. (Down in Georgia, Dr. Pemberton was not faring much better. In *his* first year, he peddled just twenty-five gallons of Coca-Cola syrup.) It did not much cheer Griffin and Little to reflect that a rival Boston chemist who'd been in business for twelve years had never yet cleared as much as $700 in any one of them. It took Griffin & Little seven years — by then they had agreed to split their profits evenly — before they netted as much as $2,200 apiece, or just about what Little had been getting paid at the end of his first year at Rumford. The partnership, another chemist reflected in 1931, "must have somehow found the means of endowing itself with a wonderful self-renewing quality of faith and optimism."

Things seemed to be looking up in 1887. Little was twice treated to European trips that year by patrons whom he had persuaded to let him investigate chemical processes he thought they might wish to invest in. The role of science — especially chemistry — in creating new and lucrative enterprises was something he cared deeply about and always would, though in practice he was never to profit much from what he preached. On his first venture abroad, on behalf of the S. D. Warren Company, the Boston papermakers, he was accompanied by a young Boston attorney, his friend Louis D. Brandeis. Still far down the road from the U.S. Supreme Court, Brandeis was in private practice and numbered Little among his clients. (One of Brandeis's law partners was related to the Warren family.) Reminiscing about that journey forty-eight years later, Brandeis — who rarely used first names in correspondence, but began letters to Little with "My dear Arthur" — wrote Little's widow, "Arthur's perception and charm illuminated much besides the chemical process." And Justice Brandeis told his old friend's secretary, "Those were joyous weeks Dr. Little and I spent together."

The purpose of that trip was for Little to look into and evaluate a paper-bleaching technique that European chemists, who were far ahead of their American counterparts in most areas, had developed. Little did obtain an option on the American rights to it, but all hands soon concluded that to try to take commercial advantage of it would be prohibitively costly. That November Little was sent back to Europe — a ten-day voyage each way at the least — this time to find out about a method of making straw board from a combination of stable bedding and horse manure. His sponsors already had an option to buy the American rights for that operation, at $75,000. Little visited a manufacturing plant in England that, in an era of horse-drawn vehicles, could readily obtain its raw materials from the London Omnibus Company. He then crossed the English Channel and, in a rented mill in Waterloo, Belgium, set up a pilot plant of his own, getting *his* raw materials from a nearby street-railway company. He didn't like the results. He advised his clients to shy away from the whole business, and the advice proved to be sound when the British company went out of business the next year, by which time the American rights fetched only £150 on auction.

Griffin & Little soon became recognized as a leading authority on the chemistry of papermaking. The partners were named official chemists of the American Paper and Pulp Association and, concurrently, of the Third Massachusetts District of the U.S. Internal Revenue Service. None of that was worth much. When, for instance, they were asked by a Vermont paint manufacturer to analyze a German process for keeping dried paint insoluble, they determined that the key ingredient was casein and that it could be made inexpensively from skim milk. The manufacturer was soon earning $2,000 a day from the sale of casein-based paints and living on Fifth Avenue in New York; but Griffin & Little, for its pains, received merely a flat fee of $725. Still, the chemists were becoming better and better known, and a book they finished in 1893, *Chemistry of Paper-making*, was for quite some time afterward a standard reference work for that industry.

Throughout all this, Roger Griffin was content to spend most of his time in the laboratory, while the junior partner plied the high seas and the hinterlands. In 1888, Griffin & Little had taken over the business of a chemist who wanted to retire and who had handled the testing of most of the bulk sugar that was imported into Boston. Over the following five years, Griffin, clearly a man of remarkable diligence and patience, was credited with analyzing no fewer than fifty thousand batches of sugar — at the usual seventy-five cents a sample — for a single chocolate manufacturer.

But Little was by no means a stranger to the lab. Once, for instance, he took on the job of analyzing some chicken feathers. The hens from which they had been plucked had won a beauty contest, and a rival breeder claimed that their foliage had been basely dyed. Little managed to extract enough dyestuffs from the suspect feathers to turn a skein of white worsted into a riot of color. He was addicted to morals and at once delivered himself of one: "Don't win prizes under false colors if there's a chemist in the neighborhood."

Then disaster struck. Little had found that appearing in court as an expert witness in patent litigations was a gratifying means of eking out the firm's meager proceeds — by 1893, Griffin's sugar work completed, they were averaging only about $375 a month, all but seventy-five dollars of that from two paper mills. He could make as much as ten dollars a day as a witness. (So eloquently and persuasively did he testify in one case that the lawyer who lost it at once hired him in another one.) While Little was thus occupied in a New York courtroom on April 13, 1893, back in Boston Griffin was doing an extraction involving some rhigolene in a flask of water, with a flame beneath the container. He noticed that the flask was leaking slightly and tightened its stopper. The flask broke, and he was enveloped in flaming vapor. Two laboratory assistants who were standing by beat out the blaze — one of them getting badly burned himself — but Griffin was beyond help. He died early the following morning. Not long afterward, the grief-stricken Little adopted a griffin as his company's first symbol.

The day after Griffin's death, the mail brought distressing news of a different order. The two pulp mills from which 80 percent of the firm's income had been anticipated both unexpectedly canceled their contracts. Little was about to call it quits. He started to pack up the office equipment, and he went back to New York to discuss a new job there, the nature of which is unclear. But he perked up after being invited to dine at the Union Club with his first boss, Charles S. Wheelwright of the Richmond Paper Company. (The moral that Little drew from *that* was: "No man should decide anything when he is hungry or thoroughly tired out.") One thing that encouraged him to carry on was the prospect of reaping some benefits from a trip he had made to an international exposition in Paris in 1889. There he had noted with interest a display of the work of the French chemist Count Hilaire de Chardonnet, who had converted cellulose into thread by treating wood pulp with nitric acid.

More important, Little also became acquainted in Paris with a thirty-four-year-old English cellulose technologist, Charles Frederick Cross. The son of a soap maker, Cross had started an analytical chemistry business — not unlike that of Griffin & Little — four years earlier, along with E. J. Bevan, up to then a chemist for a paper mill. Later they would be joined by another chemist, Clayton Beadle. The threads that de Chardonnet extracted from cellulose had one discouraging flaw; they were highly flammable. In 1892, Bevan and Beadle discovered that they could make a golden viscous liquid from cellulose — thus, in due course, the name "viscose" — by treating it first with an aqueous caustic soda and subsequently with carbon bisulfide. Then they regenerated the liquid into both film and thread, which were nonflammable. The implications for industry, Little realized as soon as Cross got word to him of the achievement, were profound.*

Griffin & Little obtained an option for the American rights to the viscose process, and Little, who would sometimes speak of "the destructive humility of chemists," went hat in hand to a number of New York money men — among them J. Pierpont Morgan, Bernard Baruch, and Frank Vanderlip — hoping in vain to get their backing. "While every chemist will admit he needs a banker," Little wrote later, "the fact that every banker needs a chemist is not yet recognized in financial circles." In 1928, Brandeis would write to Little from Washington in his characteristic nearly indecipherable scrawl, "What a change in the public's attitude toward Chemical Engineering in the forty-odd years since first you essayed teaching the obvious to armor-clad manufacturers."

Little did round up enough funds in 1894 to get a small plant under way at Waltham, Massachusetts, under the name of the

---

* Cross and Little shared a fondness for puns. One of Little's early associates, Wallace J. Murray, came upon a notebook of Cross's years later containing drafts of letters that the Englishman had sent to his American confrere. A postscript to one of these, written in 1893 shortly after the Earl of Dunraven's *Valkyrie II* had failed to win the America's Cup that October, went, "Dunraven will have 'done ravin' against his luck by this time and next year will no doubt use Viscose on his sails and improve our sails also."

American Viscose Company, but it soon foundered for lack of additional capital. (The following year, he was granted a patent for making cellulose acetate filters for incandescent lamps.) He did not give up trying. He persuaded a Philadelphia friend in 1899 to underwrite another business, the Cellulose Products Company (Little was named its chemical director), but that one ran out of money, too, and patents it had for nonflammable film and for artificial silk were bought by, respectively, Eastman Kodak and the Lustron Company.

With the downfall of that venture went the option to buy all American rights for the manufacture of artificial silk — the old English firm of Courtauld Ltd. had them in Europe — for, in Little's lonely view, a paltry $50,000. "Do you mean to say, Dr. Little," one prospective investor who spurned a chance to participate told him, "that man can ever produce fibers as good as those God has provided us?" By 1925, men other than Little were happily producing them at a clip of $81 million a year. "It was the scarcity of educated money in this country in 1901," Dr. Little wrote a quarter of a century afterward, "which caused the viscose patents for artificial silk to be sold at auction for $2,500, and which for many succeeding years diverted into English pockets the enormous profits of rayon manufacture in America."

By 1900, Little had a new Boston address — 7 Exchange Place, closer to the financial district than Milk Street — and a new partner. This was William Hultz Walker, a chemist six years younger than Little. Born in Pittsburgh, Walker had earned a bachelor's degree at Pennsylvania State University and a Ph.D. at the University of Göttingen, in Germany, a country where chemistry and chemists were held in far higher repute than they were across the Atlantic. Walker, who'd briefly served as a consultant to Cellulose Products, had been an instructor in analytical chemistry at M.I.T. since 1894. His students there credited him with such stimulating classroom observations as "An engineer who plays a moderately good game of pool has used judgment; if he plays an excellent game, he has wasted his time." The junior partner in Little & Walker would, it was understood from the outset, divide his time between teaching and business. When Walker died in 1934, his widow wrote to Little, "Will admired and respected you so strongly and has said to me many times, 'I owe so much of my success to the training I received from Mr. Little.' "

Little & Walker had a staff of only seven employees, but to make the firm seem more impressive, the partners invested it with seven departments: Analytical, Coal and Derivatives, Lubrication, Biology, Textiles, Engineering, and — papermaking still being the main source of income — Forest Products. In 1903, needing more space, the company moved again, this time to 93 Broad Street.

Toward the end of 1900, Little, by now thirty-six, decided he could afford to get engaged. He was emboldened to take that step when the new partnership was promised a retainer of $12,000 a year by one paper company. His fiancée, Henriette Rogers Anthony, received a letter from Roger Griffin's widow telling her she was getting an "ideal man." Mary Castle Griffin went on to say:

> I wish I could take your hand this morning and tell you all that is in my heart regarding Mr. Arthur Little, for while all must praise him, few, I feel, understand the perfection of his nature. As a former partner and as a friend, my husband admired and loved him above all men, and I realize how crude is all I may say compared with his greeting could it but reach you. Still I am sure that even my husband never dreamed of the depth of tenderness and loyalty, the rare unselfishness and sense of honor which he has shown to me. . . . Be good to him, my dear, for he is a rare man. I know not one to compare to him.

Arthur and Henriette were married on January 22, 1901, and, before settling down to housekeeping in Brookline, went to Florida for a honeymoon. That trip took a jarring turn when the bridegroom received a telegram informing him that the paper company whose retainer he'd been counting on had gone out of business.

The Littles never had any children. In 1911 they took in a fifteen-year-old nephew, Royal Little, whom from then on they treated like a son. Royal's father had died when the boy was four. His mother got remarried, to an itinerant printer. The family was living on a California ranch in 1911, and Royal was riding bareback to school on a mule. His uncle Arthur thought he needed a more urban education, and invited him East. He ended up, for better or worse, at Harvard University. As an adult, Royal would be extremely instrumental in the affairs of his uncle's company, though he was never associated with it full-time.

By 1911, Dr. Little had become a member in impeccable standing of the Boston establishment. He belonged to St. Botolph's and the Saturday Evening Club, and to The Country Club in Brookline. (He used the last largely for social purposes; on its golf course, he couldn't break 150.) He had highly placed friends. He had Louis Brandeis for his lawyer. His physician was the eminent cardiologist Paul Dudley White. He was a frequent guest at the Brattle Street, Cambridge, home of Wallace Donham, the dean of the Harvard Business School. Donham's young son Philip, who later worked for ADL, was as a boy as much in awe of Dr. Little as of A. Lawrence Lowell, the president of Harvard, who some Cantabrigians thought had practically a monopoly on arousing awe. "Dr. Little was so Victorian you couldn't believe it," Philip Donham said years later.

A fastidious dresser, Little was reputed among his acquaintances to be the sort of person who would put on a tuxedo after dark even while dining at home alone. An ADL house organ once suggested (the idea almost certainly came from the president's office) that Saint Loy, the goldsmith of Limoges, be designated the patron saint of chemists. "He was very handsome, as chemists should be," went the proposal, "and diligent, as they are these days, and wore fine apparel, as they do when they can." The only time Dr. Little was known to let his guard down was at a 1905 all-male reunion of the M.I.T. class of 1885 at Squam Lake, New Hampshire; he posed for a snapshot in a pair of bathing trunks that looked as if they were about to fall off. That was the year, incidentally, when M.I.T. was considering a merger with Harvard. M.I.T. solicited its alumni's reactions to that possibility, and Little, who was never at a loss for words, responded with a spate of them:

1. I do not regard the Harvard environment as the best one for the development of a great technical school.
2. Harvard influence would preponderate within a few years.
3. In the event of rupture the position of the Institute would be precarious.
4. I believe that the liberalizing influence which the Institute needs can be fully secured by methods less problematical in their outcome.
5. The Faculty constitute the working force of the Institute. To be efficient, their hearts must be in their work. They are, almost to a man, opposed.

6. I believe that if the step is taken the Institute will lose much of the interest or support of its alumni.

Little's clothes often smelled of tobacco. Dr. White's stern lectures about the evils of smoking notwithstanding, he was a chain-smoker, albeit an apparently guilt-ridden one. Once, his associates were putting together a photo montage to decorate the lobby of one of their offices. The best picture they could find of their boss showed him, though immaculately clad and sporting a patrician pince-nez, holding a cigarette. He ordered the exhibit dismantled.

He had a courtly, aloof air. None of Little's employees ever addressed him by his first name — nor, when it came to that, did they call his secretary by hers — and he used only their surnames. (He didn't care whether they called him Dr. or Mr.) Though his formal education had been limited, he was a voracious reader and had a ready flow of classical quotations at his command. A staunch believer in tidiness, he began each day conferring with his janitor about the state of cleanliness of his premises. He insisted that all outgoing letters be submitted for his inspection before any envelope was sealed, and he checked all packages to make sure they were neatly wrapped. He toured his laboratories daily, and if he spotted an unfolded newspaper, as if somebody had been reading it on the job, he would say, "No more of that!" and toss it into a wastebasket. One of his lab employees said that whenever he was summoned to the boss's office, he would first put on a jacket and tie and wash his hands.

Dr. Little said of himself that he was a "mouthpiece for science" and that he had "the simplicity to wonder, the ability to question, the power to generalize, the capacity to apply." He also had an eye, though perhaps no more than an eye, for attractive young women. Whenever a group photograph was taken of his staff, he would naturally be in the center of the front row; and more often than not he would arrange to be flanked by his most comely female employees. He insisted that one girl stop washing test tubes because it might roughen her hands. At one annual staff dinner, he attributed whatever success his company had enjoyed up to then, in practically the same breath, to a Ph.D. from M.I.T. "who picks eighteen thousand dollars out of the air" and "to Dorothy, who distributes the mail so prettily that it is a pleasure to receive even a bill from her."

There were still enough paying clients to keep the small staff fairly busy, but the work was hardly overwhelming. On a single day in 1902, Little & Walker dispatched two reports. One was to a company that had sent around a messenger with a sample of some fibrous material. The client had five tons of it in storage in the North End of Boston, an accompanying note said, and wondered what could be done with it. Dr. Little examined it at once and replied, "We have advised your messenger to have nothing to do with the material." The other report went to a Michigan outfit, the American Hulled Bean Company, which had shipped some hulls, wondering if they could be used for a cheap linoleum filler, or perhaps for cattle feed, or for fertilizer. "We greatly regret," was the verdict, "that our results have been so unfavorable to the material." It was not a fruitful day for the advancement of science.

And later that year, Little & Walker felt that they could not even charge the New England Shelled Nut Company after trying unsuccessfully to expedite the removal of shells from pecans by applying, in turn, nitric acid, bleach, chlorine, dilute sulfuric acid, concentrated sulfuric acid, aluminum chloride, charring, and slow pressure with a vise. The chemists had given up, they conceded, without attempting to remove the shells by tumbling them over sharp quartz, squirting compressed air at them, or attacking them with circular saws. "Our work on the matter," the turn-of-the-century problem-solving partners ruefully concluded, "has at least familiarized us with the conditions of the problem and brought home to us something of the difficulty of its solution."

Dr. Little was now beginning to make himself known not merely as an analytical chemist but also as a writer. Maurice Holland, in his 1928 book *Industrial Explorers*, would say of Little's prose, "He can explain how paper is made from wood pulp and do it so cleverly that the owner of a chain of newspapers . . . can understand him." To a 1903 journal, *Printing Art*, Dr. Little had himself contributed an article, "The Durability of Paper," which contained a definition of a sheet of paper that even most newspaper editors could probably understand: "essentially a web of felted vegetable fibers."

In 1904 the Little & Walker letterhead cited, among the services the firm stood ready to provide, "Analysis, Research, Advice, Expert Reports, Expert Testimony." (Their cable address was XYLEM, from the word meaning a tissue of plants and trees.) A Fairhaven, Massachusetts, woman friend of Little's that year sent him a sample of her well water, which he analyzed without charging the customary five dollars — perhaps unwilling to ask for a fee because he was constrained to notify her, as gently as he could, that her supply left much to be desired. "The probabilities are that a little sewage gets into it now and then," he wrote. The stuff was adequate for cooking, he went on, "but if you can get a better water for drinking I think I would try to do so."

Walker decided in 1905 that he couldn't do justice to either M.I.T. or the firm by splitting himself in two, so he returned full-time to the university, where he was soon named director of a research laboratory in applied chemistry that was being organized. When it finally came into being, in 1908, Dr. Little was the principal speaker at the dedication ceremony, and he said,

> Any moral or spiritual uplift must find its basis in the increased efficiency of the worker, and in this stage of our industrial development no agency is more directly available for increasing this efficiency than that afforded by chemistry as applied to industry. Every waste that is prevented or turned to profit, every problem solved, and every more effective process which is developed makes for better living in the material sense and more wholesome living in the higher sense.*

So Little was once again on his own. He was elated, in 1906, when an official of the U.S. Forest Service stopped by and asked him to look into the possibility of making paper pulp from kinds of wood not previously known to be useful therefor — among them, spruce, white fir, scrub pine, and loblolly pine. His conclusion that they had some promise led to the establishment, two years later, of a new national research center, the U.S. Forest Products Laboratory, in Madison, Wisconsin. (In 1908, Little advised the American Paper and Pulp Association, in his capacity as its official chemist, that it ought to think about making paper from

---

* The American Chemical Society gave Walker a gold medal that year for his work on the corrosion of iron and steel, and he was celebrated also for his research into the recovery of turpentine from wastes.

waste flax straw, marsh hay, bamboo, wild hemp, and cotton stalks.) Even so, those days — twenty struggling years after the business was founded — were difficult. Little liked to spend whatever time he could spare with his family in Maine, and he was up there in February 1907 when his assistant Hervey J. Skinner (like nearly all the staff, an M.I.T. graduate) wrote him, "The total amount of money received today is $44." And what Skinner, who was a member of what Little wistfully called his Progress Committee, had to report two days afterward was hardly indicative of progress: "Miss Bass says there is only about $20 in the bank as we have had to pay Davis's expenses and we have had to draw some for Olmstead to go to New York. Hope there will be something on Monday."

The previous year, 1906, had been marked by the death from an earthquake of a thousand Californians in San Francisco and, on the next day, of Pierre Curie in a street accident in Paris. Dr. Little, in an article for *Science* magazine, agreed with an editorial in the *Boston Herald* that had wondered if the two calamities might not have been of about equal loss to mankind.

III The Birthplace of Industrial Research

In the past the world suffered grievously from lack of knowledge; today it suffers from its rejection.

— Dr. Arthur D. Little, 1924

*F*or the company that would thenceforth be known by but a single name, 1909 was a watershed year. A new employee joined its ranks in January: Roger Castle Griffin, the son of Dr. Little's first partner. Despite — or perhaps because of — his father's ghastly death, Griffin *fils*, who had been nine years old at the time of the laboratory explosion, had resolved to become an analytical chemist himself, after receiving both a bachelor's and a master's degree from Harvard. Until his retirement in 1949, he played an increasingly important role in ADL's affairs. A brochure put out by the company in 1923 led off with the proud assertion:

> In our laboratories, as an indispensable adjunct of the broader phases of our work, thousands of analyses and tests of raw materials and supplies ... are made each year. Arthur D. Little, Inc., has co-operated with the American Society for Testing Materials in the establishment of standard methods, and we have also assisted in the revision of the Pharmacopoeia of the United States. For the benefit of the profession at large we have published our own approved methods, and the book is now in its fourth printing (TECHNICAL METHODS OF ANALYSIS, edited by Roger Castle Griffin, Director of Analytical Department.)

By 1909, the professional staff had increased to twenty-two. Dr. Little decided it was time to incorporate. The necessary

39

papers were drawn up by Louis Brandeis and executed at his office on May 7. The twenty-two-year-old company, it was thereby disclosed, had $2,178.16 in cash, $7,496.40 in accounts receivable, and furniture and laboratory apparatus valued at $11,565.18. One of the first acts of the newly designated Board of Directors was to sign Dr. Little to a contract, under the terms of which he was to be paid $12,000 a year for five years. He also got all of the common stock — 1,250 shares of it worth, at least on paper, $125,000. Right off, he returned $40,000 of that to the company, to be sold, if it so chose, to its employees. Roger Griffin, in a gesture of confidence, bought 30 shares for $3,000.

Brandeis, who charged $47.96 for preparing the articles of incorporation, proved in retrospect to be a better judge than he was a lawyer. Before Arthur D. Little, Inc., could go public in 1969, it was obliged to produce for the secretary of state of Massachusetts (the incumbent was Kevin White, later the mayor of Boston) its sixty-year-old incorporation papers. White was surprised to perceive that these were flawed: They were supposed to provide evidence that the company had $10,000 in capital assets, but Brandeis had somehow accounted for only half that amount. White informed ADL that, technically, it had never legally existed. However, in view of all the time that had elapsed and the fact that by 1969 (when the firm's annual sales were $46,282,000) it could be presumed to be worth $10,000, he would ignore the oversight.

Now that ADL was a full-fledged corporation, Dr. Little sought to enhance its internal structure by adding to its Progress Committee a Research Committee and, above them both, an Executive Committee. It was a measure of the company's still relatively modest scale of operations that the Research Committee was not empowered to spend more than five dollars on any piece of research without the authorization of the Executive Committee. The Research Committee did contrive on its own to disburse fifty cents for the acquisition of several bottles of carbonated water deemed necessary for an inquiry into a cheap substitute for the sheet cork used in beer-bottle stoppers.

By 1910, the company had a new and even more imposing roster of departments: Textile, Fuel Engineering, Gas Engineering, General Laboratory, Research, Electrical Engineering, Electric Railway, and Paper and Pulp, with A. D. Little in personal charge of the last. The firm was advertising the availability of its services in such journals as *Engineering News, Power, Metallurgical and Chemical Engineering*, the *American Machinist*, and M.I.T.'s student *Tech*, where its principals could meaningfully be identified as A. D. Little '85, president; H. J. Skinner '99, vice-president; H. S. Mork '99, treasurer; and F. A. Olmstead '03, secretary. The year before that, Dr. Little had placed an ad in the *Paper Trade Journal* that proclaimed, "Our Paper and Pulp Department" — his very own department — "has solved the most closely guarded secret of the paper trade, the method of manufacture of ENGLISH BIBLE PAPER."

In 1911, a substantial new client materialized: the United Fruit Company, which wanted to know if there was any chance of making paper out of bagasse, the thitherto discarded waste fiber from sugarcane harvested on its plantations in Cuba. Dr. Little believed there was indeed, and he designed and had built a papermaking machine that ADL later bought from United Fruit for further experimentation with cellulosic materials and that eventually ended up in the possession of, to the company's profit, the Crown Zellerbach Corporation.

Along its circuitous path to that landing place, the machine was used by the Great Southern Lumber Company, which under Dr. Little's tutelage began making paper from sawdust, stumps, and other previously ignored offshoots of its pine forests in Louisiana. Moreover, after studying Great Southern's modus operandi for eighteen months, Dr. Little was able to point out to its proprietors that the material they had been habitually throwing away could readily be converted into a daily yield of 794 tons of paper, 60 tons of resin, 6,000 gallons of turpentine, and 12,000 gallons of ethyl alcohol. In addition, he noted, the receipts from the sale of merely that output of paper would eclipse those routinely accruing from lumber itself. Throughout his life, Dr. Little was concerned about the wastefulness of his fellow Americans. He once wrote that "The United States is an aggregation of undeveloped empires, sparsely occupied by the most wasteful people in the world." Another time, he calculated that the United States, in those years before the First World War, annually wasted 150 million tons of wood, 1 million tons of flax straw, 365 billion cubic feet of natural gas, and 13 million board feet of lumber just from the trashing of old pencil stubs. So far as is known, nobody challenged the accuracy of that arithmetic.

Even today, technological research services account for about half of ADL's total revenues. Research and development were, in Dr. Little's view, crucial to the progress of industry, and he had frequently been astonished, back in the 1920s, by the inability of many American businessmen to comprehend what seemed to him so self-evident. He would often tell about one paper manufacturer of his acquaintance who stoutly maintained that all the scientific advice he needed could be provided by a son of his, a student at Yale University, who would come home every ten days or so and share with his father what he had learned in a freshman chemistry course. Similarly, Dr. Little would say, he had once asked an American scientist returning from a prewar tour of a German industrial laboratory whether they had better equipment, brains, and knowledge over there. The American had said they didn't. Then what did they have? "It was money — money willing to back such activity, convinced that in the final outcome a profit would be made." (It had to be "educated money," Dr. Little had added, allocated to vision rather than daydream.)

And in the same connection there was an article, titled "Let the Chemist Pay Your Bills," that he would write for *Collier's* in 1922, in which he told of a steel company's informing the superintendent of one of its mills that it was going to send over a chemist to help it out. That worthy is said to have replied, "Send down someone who can play the violin. We can stand his damned nonsense in daytime if he will amuse us at night." Dr. Little's bitterness about manufacturers' closed minds was unstemmable. "They rarely understand chemistry," he wrote on another occasion, "and, in proportion to their ignorance of it, they resent the suggestion that the chemist can teach them anything about their business. . . ." Their employees' attitude was "commonly one of militant skepticism. . . . [They] often pay less regard to the laws of nature than they do to city ordinances."

Yet another time, Dr. Little declared,

> The laboratory has become a prime mover for the machinery of civilization, and there is a direct obligation upon industry to support research with the generosity of an enlightened self-interest, for research is the mother of industry . . . and may even dispute with necessity the parentage of invention. Though invention may often seem to precede research, the essence of invention is the application of knowledge to new and presumably useful ends, and each advance in knowledge becomes a starting point and an incentive for invention.

And, as he put it in the *Atlantic Monthly,* "The price of progress is research, which alone assures the security of dividends." Little, whose shareholders once tried to ease him out of his own company because its stocks weren't paying any dividends, went on:

American manufacturers must be made to understand that we are in the midst of an industrial revolution, in the course of which many established businesses will find their balance sheets deeply dyed with red unless those charged with the responsibility of management can learn to direct the course in the flood of new knowledge pouring in from the laboratories.

"Research serves to make building-stones out of stumbling-blocks," Dr. Little said. Historians have held, for want of any more precise date, that organized research got under way in the United States in 1832, when the federal government contracted with the Franklin Institute in Philadelphia for a study of the causes of boiler explosions on steamships. As late as 1920, there were no more than seven thousand people employed in industrial research in the entire country.

Another significant date was February 7, 1911, when the responsible management of the young company called General Motors called on Dr. Little. The upshot of that fortuitous visit was the establishment later that year in Detroit of the first GM laboratory, designed and initially manned by Arthur D. Little, Inc. For a while, ADL had seven of its staff stationed there (altogether, they received $1,150 a month) to analyze and test materials destined to be made into motor vehicles. ("The Research Laboratory has become an important adjunct to all up-to-date manufacturing concerns," an ADL advertisement was proud to state the following year.) A possibly apocryphal story had it that not long after enough GM in-house employees had been trained to take over the Detroit laboratory from the ADL operatives, somebody said to Dr. Little, "You silly fool! Now you've gone and done it! They don't need you anymore!" and that he retorted, "The more research they have, the more they'll need me, because I'm the only one who can talk to them about it."

His own company's daily proceeds, however, still came largely from analytical testing — a dollar, for instance, for each sample of milk, with a 25 percent discount on ten samples or more. The Massachusetts State Board of Insanity was a steady and welcome patron; it retained ADL, for a flat fee of $4,000 a year, to analyze six hundred of whatever items it sent over (mostly foodstuffs); for any tests beyond that, the board would pay an extra six dollars apiece. Court appearances as expert witnesses helped meet the payroll, yielding twenty-five dollars a day or fifteen dollars a half-day, as a rule.

Now nearly thirty years in business, Dr. Little was becoming — in no small part because of his flair for self-promotion — increasingly known nationally. He was named official chemist to the American Institute of Metals. In 1912, he was elected to a two-year term as president of the American Chemical Society. The presidential address he delivered at Rochester, New York, on September 9, 1913, titled "Industrial Research in America," was printed in the *Journal of Industrial & Chemical Engineering* and the *American Brewers Review*. (The latter, in deference to its readership, ran it in both English and German.) The author had reprints made up, in English only, and sent them to practically everybody he could think of — to George Eastman and Gifford Pinchot; to the chief chemist of the National Canners Association; and to the presidents of M.I.T., GM, Lackawanna Steel, the New York Central Railroad, the Buffalo Foundry & Machine Company, the American Wool Company, the Empire State Society of the Sons of the American Revolution, and the United States of America. Woodrow Wilson's reaction, if any, is unknown, but Frank G. Ryan — the president of Parke, Davis — praised Little's "dignified and eloquent style" and added, "Here is an engineer who not only knows his subject, but can present it in worthy English." The district attorney of Massachusetts, Joseph C. Pelletier, said he had been about to throw the article away but changed his mind and read it, after which he passed it along to others. He wished every banker would read it, he said, instead of grousing about conditions. One banker who did read it, Frank Vanderlip of the National City Bank, had been lukewarm toward Little's overtures twenty years earlier, but now he wrote to him, "The picture you paint of industrial development is wonderful and the inventions that have brought it about amazing. We do not often stop to think of the mechanical and chemical fairyland about us, and it is distinctly interesting to do so occasionally."

Dr. Little's promotional efforts bore fruit. He was asked to contribute to the magazine *Youth's Companion*.

In 1914, ADL began to put out the first in what would be a long series of company publications. This one was the *Little Journal*, not a word of which went to press without Dr. Little's approval. Many of the words were of his own composition. The publication was addressed to chemists, engineers, and managers, and it aspired "to reflect the progress of scientific research through its columns in such a way as to be easily understood by the manufacturer, the banker, and in fact the average business man." One article warning all of them against bay rum and other products containing wood alcohol said, "See to it that your barber uses only the best toilet articles, and that the ginger ale you drink is one that does not contain this poison."

The *Journal* appeared only sporadically. There were no issues after that first year until 1917, conceivably because its principal contributor was too busy to meet deadlines. (He was preoccupied during part of 1915 with setting up his first branch office: a two-room outpost in New York City housed, appropriately, in what was and still is the Chemists' Club building, at 50 East Forty-first Street.) When publication was resumed, one of the first offerings was an anonymous poem, "Father Gander" — the poet was almost certainly Dr. Little — which went:

> There was a man in our town
> And he felt wondrous wise.
> "The men of science are," he claimed,
> "Poor fools who theorize."
> But when his business went to pot,
> With all his might and main,
> He called a chemical engineer,
> To set him straight again.*

Dr. Little himself had made several trips to Europe, of course, and at home he had sent employees as far afield as Louisiana, Michigan, Indiana, and North Dakota; but the bulk of the com-

---

* Two years later, there was another unattributed poem, its similarities in style suggesting the same versifier:

> How doth the little busy bee
> Improve each shining hour?
> By physics and by chemistry
> We learn to know its power.

> How doth the little silkworm win
> Its product from the tree?
> Because it is proficient in
> Its colloid chemistry.

pany's work was centered around New England. In 1916, though, he was asked by Lord Shaughnessy, the president of the Canadian Pacific Railway, to undertake a survey of Canada's natural resources. Little, traveling elegantly via the private Pullman of the general manager of the railroad, rode from Toronto west to Vancouver, collecting data all the way. That May, Arthur D. Little, Ltd. — "a corporation organized and equipped for the service of Canadian industry and the study and development of Canadian resources" — opened an office in Montreal. Within seven months, it had produced 165 reports, on the recovery of gasoline from natural gas in Medicine Hat, on the production of paper (it was almost a foregone conclusion *that* would be on the agenda) from waste flax and cereal straws, and on "other important matters." The Canadian government formed an Honorary Advisory Council for Scientific and Industrial Research to help implement the ADL findings.

"We are proceeding on the broad assumption that whatever benefits or develops Canadian industry or advances the interests of the Dominion must react to the benefit of the railway," Dr. Little had told a Montreal audience of educators early on. The assumption proved well founded. On ADL's recommendation, the Canadian Pacific bought some virgin land in Trail, British Columbia, and that turned out to be a real bonanza. The site was rich in minerals, and from it sprang the Consolidated Mining and Smelting Company.

For a secretarial job at Arthur D. Little, Ltd., Dr. Little hired a young Québécoise, Helen Bernice Sweeney. Sweeney moved to Boston in 1918, bringing with her a Canadian flag from the by-then closed Montreal office (she never embraced U.S. citizenship), and she became his private secretary. She had gone to Vassar College but knew no shorthand and had only a fleeting acquaintance with scientific terminology. Often, after Dr. Little dictated a letter to her, she was obliged to go to somebody else on the ADL staff and ask what in the world he was talking about. Why, for instance, had he written to one client that he was shipping some experimental alcohol in, as she understood it, ten-gallon "cowboys"? "Carboys," she was relieved to be told: large glass bottles. Sweeney stayed with the company until she retired in 1951. In the spring of 1984, not long after celebrating her hundredth birthday — the only ADLer known to have passed that milestone — she told a visitor, "Dr. Little had high standards, and he made you keep up to them."

In 1916, thirty years after his firm was founded, Dr. Little switched from the griffin that had been its symbol for nearly two decades to the winged acorn. He had adopted a winged maple leaf for the Canadian subsidiary and wanted the parent company to have something similar. In the 1950s, ADLer Charles B. Moore, who went on to become chairman of the Langmuir Laboratory, did a good deal of high-altitude balloon research for the navy. Moore had an alate acorn painted on his aviator's helmet. His colleagues promptly dubbed him the Flying Nut. (Moore had read in one version of Exodus that, contrary to the popular belief, lightning more often preceded rain than followed it. He was delighted, on one ADL research excursion to New Mexico, to have the biblical sequence confirmed when a bolt of lightning, with no aqueous warning, barely missed him and struck a nearby tree.)

From that time on, ADLers were much obsessed with oaks and acorns. Employees who put in twenty-five years with the company were rewarded with a gold lapel pin in the form of the flying acorn. Staff members who constructed some experimental devices for making abstracts of indexes of scientific abstracts called them Associative Content Retrieval Networks — so they could be acronymically referred to as ACORNS. The head of one contemporary division, letting other members of the professional staff know that his people had earned the firm some agreeable profits, conveyed the good news by saying, "We've been building up a cache of acorns." Whenever a new tree is planted on ADL turf, it is more often than not an oak. An English oak was added to the ADL arboretum a few years ago and was soon infested with gypsy moths. To solve that problem, a committee of resident Ph.D.s was hastily formed — dendrologists, entomologists, hydrologists, soil specialists, and a couple of computer programmers who volunteered to analyze the others' data after they were collected and verified. A building and grounds employee who had never made it through high school examined the ailing tree while the others were huddled in erudite session, and he at once took care of it. He sprayed it.

In the spring of 1916, Arthur D. Little, Inc., placed a full-page advertisement in two magazines, *Engineering* and *Metallurgical and Chemical Engineering.* The ad consisted of a reproduction of a letter to ADL — with "By Permission" above it — from Henry G. Powning, the president of B. A. Corbin & Son Company, makers of Corbin, "the Shoe Durable." The letter stated that the shoe company had just analyzed the cost of its raw materials ("Are your materials standardized?" was one of the questions that had been asked of prospective clients in an ADL ad in *Engineering* a couple of months previous) and that

> You may be interested to know the only items that do not show heavy advances are materials simplified and standardized by your laboratory. In fact — these costs are considerably less than two or even three years ago. One product in particular has been for over two years, and even now is showing an average weekly saving equal to your entire charge for research work. We sincerely wish more of our problems might come within your scope for solution.

Permission to reprint that letter cannot have been difficult to obtain. Henry Powning was a Brookline neighbor of Dr. Little's and a close friend. His company, located in Marlborough, Massachusetts, was the oldest manufacturer of men's shoes in New England. Powning also owned a second Marlborough concern, the Koehler Manufacturing Company, which made miners' lamps. As a client, he was grateful to ADL for having concocted an adhesive that kept rubber soles from falling off shoes, and for having solved one problem that had long plagued his workers: Some of the white shoes they made turned pink. (ADL discovered that the rubber soles of *these* shoes were being vulcanized with a poor choice of chemicals.) In the 1930s, Powning turned over his businesses to two sons and devoted himself almost exclusively to the affairs of Arthur D. Little, Inc. He was its treasurer, a member of its Board of Directors for more than thirty years, and, for much of that time, also in effect one of its chief executives, though he never took any salary and never had an office. He operated from a corner table in the library. Dr. Little, who had good reason to appreciate Powning's helpfulness, once wrote testimonially of "the superhuman dexterity and precision of American shoe machinery."

When for a while ADL was so strapped it couldn't obtain a loan from any bank, Powning put his own substantial credit on the line for it. He did not, however, countenance extravagance. He was so much of a penny-pincher that he insisted employees writing drafts of reports use both sides of every piece of paper. He took personal charge of the distribution of pencils. When somebody brought a stub to his library table and asked for a new pencil, he would measure the old one, and if he didn't think it was short enough, he would insist that it be further employed until it was stubbier. Few hard-pressed companies can have had a more conscientious treasurer. Powning would sometimes spend his Thursdays, when he could have been relaxing at the Boston Boot and Shoe Club, rushing around the city dunning laggard clients, because Friday was payday.

For the thirty-odd years since he had attended M.I.T., Dr. Little had remained singularly attached to the university. Most of his staff had gone there (the Griffins, father and son, being notable exceptions). William Walker was back on the faculty. Dr. Little lectured there on papermaking from 1893 through 1916, and after that he would periodically make an instructional appearance. (A January 1930 headline in the *Tech* went, "PRESIDENT STRATTON REQUESTS ALL FRESHMEN TO HEAR WIDELY KNOWN ALUMNUS AND SCIENTIST.") From 1912 on, there has almost always been an ADL executive on the M.I.T. Corporation and an M.I.T. dignitary on the ADL Board of Directors (since 1978 the latter has been Paul E. Gray, the university's president). By 1977, M.I.T. had an Arthur D. Little Memorial Lectureship, an Arthur D. Little Postgraduate Fellowship, and an Arthur D. Little Research and Innovation Fund. For a while, ADL and M.I.T. had a telephone tie line; the story went that one mischievous ADLer, by calling back and forth from one place to the other, managed somehow to get both switchboards hopelessly scrambled up.

Dozens of M.I.T. faculty members, over the years, have augmented their modest academic pay by moonlighting as consultants for ADL. A few of them received annual retainers from ADL merely for agreeing not to do consulting work for anybody else. Often, in reciprocation, they would recommend to their most gifted students that after graduation they consider employment at ADL. "It seemed to me," Helen Bernice Sweeney recalled in her one-hundred-and-first year, "that all the men at the company came from M.I.T. That was right. That was as it should be."

Dr. Little had been on M.I.T.'s visiting committee for the departments of chemistry and chemical engineering since 1912. The establishment by the university of a separate school of chemical engineering practice was one of his long-standing ambitions. He wanted chemical engineers, for one thing, to serve internships at factories, like medical students at hospitals. By 1915, he was chairman of the visiting committee, and that December, with war already under way in Europe, it delivered a report to M.I.T.'s president, Richard C. Maclaurin, which said in part:

> The training of chemical engineers involves many problems of unusual difficulty and complexity. The demands upon the members of this comparatively new profession are extraordinarily severe and varied and there is at present no place in the world where a training adequate to these demands may be secured. In this profession, more truly than any other, one needs to get into the water to learn to swim.
>
> The last few years have been prolific in discussion of how the chemical engineer should be trained. There seems to be a general agreement that this training must provide some actual close contact with large scale operations. This contact is not furnished by more or less perfunctory visits to a few plants. The chemical engineer must not only be well versed in chemistry and its laboratory methods and the general principles and broader practice of engineering. He must possess practical first-hand knowledge of the means and methods of handling and reacting upon materials in the large way, whether there are solids, liquids or gases, under pressure or vacuum, at high temperatures or far below zero. . . .
>
> At no time within the history of our country has public attention been so focused upon the development of our chemical industries as it is today. Never has the demand been so insistent for chemical engineers competent to develop and direct these industries.
>
> Partly because of the demand for munitions and partly as the result of failure to receive customary supplies from Germany the prices of most chemicals have increased several hundred per cent and are in some cases even ten times the normal figure. The market is bare of even such fundamental chemical supplies as sulphuric acid, bleach, alkali, phenol, potash, acetic acid and many dyes. Our present problem is to produce these things and many others at any price and there is a general determination to make our country as nearly as possible industrially independent as regards really essential chemical products. Peace will bring new problems arising from competition.

We must then produce at lowest costs. Our present prosperity and future industrial development will be determined largely by the ability of American chemical engineers to cope effectively with these industrial problems.*

President Maclaurin thought the visiting committee's proposal for a school of chemical engineering practice was splendid. It would cost $300,000 to implement. The man most likely to give M.I.T. that sum was George Eastman, the unpredictable Kodak man (who eventually committed suicide). At Maclaurin's urging, Little visited Eastman in Rochester, New York, and had a sympathetic hearing. Eastman wrote him on February 23 that the $300,-000 would be forthcoming, if details could be suitably worked out, and that his offer was good until June 1. Little wrote back that "the success of the new project for teaching industrial chemistry and promoting industrial research is very close to my heart, and the large measure of support which you have given it brings it for the first time well within the probability of attainment." (That same month, an ADL advertisement in the *American Wool and Cotton Reporter* said, "Inventions — improvements — are seldom made by the men on the job. Elias Howe was not a seamstress, Eli Whitney was a teacher, Alexander Bell was a doctor, Samuel Morse was an artist. The greatest improvements in your mill will not be made by your overseers — but rather by someone outside your organization, perhaps by the chemical engineer.")

Eastman sent along his check for $300,000 on June 2. He wanted the gift to be anonymous, but everybody who knew anything about M.I.T. and its benefactors was aware who "Mr. Smith" was. (All in all, when the truth came out after Eastman's death in 1932, he had enriched M.I.T. by nearly $20 million.) Nothing could have pleased Dr. Little more than to have his favorite academic institution set up a department specifically to teach his favorite subject. In 1919, after the new school had successfully got under way, Dr. Little was happy to be able to say, in a speech to the American Institute of Chemical Engineers, "It

* Forty-four years later, Dr. Warren K. Lewis, professor emeritus of chemical engineering at M.I.T., wrote: "Little was the first to recognize and emphasize the fact that undergirding all the techniques of the chemical industry is a basic structure of scientific principles, not involving new laws of nature but new aspects and applications of old and well-recognized laws — applications unfamiliar to physicist, chemist, and mechanical engineer and at that time ill-understood by the chemical engineer himself."

may, therefore, be truly said that Boston, always a pioneer in education, affords today within her metropolitan area opportunities for training to the chemical engineer which cannot elsewhere be obtained in the entire world."

Dr. Little wanted his company to be as close physically to M.I.T. as it had always been in spirit. When he had heard in 1910 that the university might build some new facilities in the Fenway area of Boston, he bought some property there himself. And, after M.I.T. decided instead in 1916 to move to Cambridge, across the Charles River, Little changed his plans accordingly. He felt reasonably secure at the moment; the Canadian Pacific was paying the company a retainer of $1,000 a month, exactly equal to his salary. He issued and contrived to sell new stock in the company worth $150,000. With the proceeds, he bought some land at 30 Charles River Road and put up a building. M.I.T. was right down the road, and it cheered Dr. Little when some of their neighbors — among them were Lever Brothers' corporate headquarters and a Filene's warehouse — started referring to ADL as M.I.T. East. The area began to be known as Research Row; a later president of M.I.T., James R. Killian, Jr., once hailed it as "probably the greatest concentration of scientific, engineering, and research talent in the world."

The new Arthur D. Little headquarters comprised three stories and a commodious basement. Dr. Little called it a research palace; others who had less confidence in him than he did called it Little's folly. The winged acorn was featured in ornamental ironwork above the front door and also on iron stair rails inside. At the entrance, carved in marble, were the words "Dedicated to Industrial Progress." The cornerstone of what Dr. Little proudly described as the "best commercial laboratory in the world" was laid on May 8, 1917. He likened the occasion to the christening of a baby. He had embedded in the stone his calling card and photograph, a set of 1917 vintage coins (penny, dime, quarter, and half-dollar), and copies of the *Little Journal*, the *Boston Herald*, several of his professional articles, and his "Paper Makers Trouble Book," a booklet.

Designed by the local architectural firm of Kilham and Hopkins, the building was, according to an ADL brochure of the day, to be "removed from . . . the thumping and disorder of . . . commerce . . . and industry," and "it must contain a chemical museum, to explain things." (Years later, the Boston Museum of Science would house an Arthur D. Little Discovery Room, sponsored by the company, the purpose of which was to introduce children to the physical sciences, in part by letting them actually perform simple experiments.) Down in the basement, there was a small-scale but fully operative paper mill, and also one room, sheathed in copper to keep out radiation, that was euphemistically known as the Gold Room. ADL has sustained its interest in paper and paper products to this day, though it is more apt to be concerned with using chemical artistry to render bank notes and lottery tickets foolproof against the depredations of counterfeiters.* That would surely have pleased Dr. Little. He might have been less gratified to know that by 1984 ADL was boasting that, for a large food-store chain, it had come up with a "new implementation plan with necessary support system to reduce the time and cost and almost eliminate use of paper in the ordinary invoicing system in the grocery industry in the U.S." On the other hand, he might have observed, with his never-ending worry about waste, that doing away with paper invoices — and, who could say, perhaps paper grocery bags as well — would certainly cut down on the nation's consumption of trees.

As the birthplace of industrial research, the ADL building was designated a National Historic Site by the Department of the Interior in 1977. This was done despite the reservations of the historian of the Historic Sites Survey of the National Park Service, who had said the previous June that he couldn't ascertain the identity of the architects and that, anyway, "The structure is not noted in architectural surveys of important Cambridge architecture and it does not appear to be of architectural significance." The facade fronting on the Charles River had been handsomely sheathed in brick and limestone; to save money, part of the rear had been finished in corrugated iron. When a young chemical en-

---

* For the U.S. Treasury, a latter-day promotional booklet stated, "We undertook a program to evaluate an experimental currency paper. That paper had been intended to embody an exclusive property that would be detectable only by a secret process, and which would thereby make it secure against sophisticated counterfeiting. Our task was to try to discover, by analytical examination of a limited number of specimen notes, what the special identifying property or material was, and to prepare samples of simulated currency which would effectively duplicate that special property. We were able to identify a number of significant compositional differences between the experimental paper and conventional currency paper, any or all of which might have been intended to serve as the exclusive identifying 'tag.'"

gineer, Roger H. Doggett, was starting at the company in 1936, he happened to remark one day to the austere Henry Powning, as they both stood near the iron wall, "Gee, that looks like hell." "Who asked you?" Powning replied. Doggett retired in 1984, after nearly half a century's dogged service, in the course of which, on behalf of a bathroom fixtures manufacturer, he helped construct a nonstop flushing toilet.

Dr. Little, who never learned how to drive a car and would arrive in style every morning in a chauffeured limousine, was justly proud of the edifice he had erected. He supervised the planning and decorating of every office, down to the location of each table and chair. To remind himself of his basic calling, he always had a mortar and pestle on prominent display in his own office, in the southeast corner of the ground floor overlooking the Charles River. The building had a kitchen and, for a while, a lunch room. That facility was shut down when Powning became suspicious that the cook was stealing eggs and taking them home: The company was being billed for half a dozen eggs per capita every day. A young chemical engineer, Walter J. Smith, was detailed to investigate the disparity.* Smith certified the problem of the missing eggs by sifting through each day's garbage, counting the eggshells therein, and subtracting the total from the number on the company's egg bill. The cook was confronted and, after confessing, fired; the lunch room was converted into a laboratory.

After the 1918 armistice, the riverside thoroughfare became known as Memorial Drive — to just about everyone except Dr. Little, who stubbornly used 30 Charles River Road as his business address until he died. The war had long been in progress in Europe, of course, when he set up shop there in 1917, and the United States was suffering from the deprivation of many chemicals — as Dr. Little's visiting committee had observed two years before — that it had normally imported from Europe, and especially from Germany. "The Germans have at least taught us the

---

* Smith's father had been an engineer at ADL in charge of its power plant. He died in 1924, penniless, just at the time his son was preparing to enter M.I.T. Walter paid for his education there by working at ADL from 5:00 to 10:00 P.M. for four years. When he wanted to continue at M.I.T. for a master's degree, everybody on the staff chipped in to lend him his tuition — $600 for two years. Smith had to take out insurance on his life and also agree to pay interest at the rate of 5 percent, so he wouldn't be receiving charity. Dr. Little and Helen Sweeney each contributed thirty dollars to the scholarship fund. Dr. Little got back $32.50 in the fall of 1932, when, with the Depression in full swing, he could probably have used it.

importance of the obvious," Dr. Little told a Canadian audience at the time. "They grew rich during the years of peace because they recognized and acted on their knowledge that science is only organized common sense, and as such had its place as the corner-stone of any business undertaking." Dr. Little was no less an ad-mirer of Teutonic efficiency in research and technology than was many another contemporary American scientist. "Krupp guns are the synonym of power and Krupp armor of inflexible resis-tance," the *Little Journal* had stated in December 1914.

That year, the United States found that it would have to make do without flongs — sheets used in making stereotype mats — which it had been getting all along from Germany. A New York flong importer named Benjamin Wood asked ADL to develop a homemade substitute. ADL did, and then it built and operated a South Boston plant for the Wood Flong Company. Whenever possible, Dr. Little liked to take an equity position in the busi-nesses his inventiveness helped create. Some of these enterprises were lemons. The Wood Flong Company was a ripe melon. In 1920, ADL sold back to it some stock it had received for its labors six years before and netted $68,000.

Most of the paper that was used for any sort of filtering pur-pose in the United States before 1917 came from Germany, and the curtailment of that supply became a crucial matter when America joined a conflict that involved gas warfare and required gas masks. There had been no Chemical Warfare Service in the army up to then; when the United States became a belli-gerent, gas masks were the responsibility of the Bureau of Mines. M.I.T., and particularly Little's former partner William Walker, were recruited by the bureau to work on gas mask filters, and Walker recruited Dr. Little. When the Chemical Warfare Service was established in 1918, ADL helped in its work on gas masks.

The company was also called upon by the government to fabri-cate dopes for airplane wings. A principal ingredient of these coatings had been acetone, derived from acetate of lime, which was in grievously short supply. ADL came up with two effective substitutes — one based on cellulose butyrate, itself dependent on kelp that could be obtained from the Pacific; and the other a solution of zein, the protein of the corn germ. The best charcoal for absorbing gas in gas masks, similarly, was conceded to come from coconut shells, but there was a scarcity of those. ADL helped solve that problem by substituting charcoal from cohune nuts, ivory nuts, peach stones, olive pits, and cherry pits. In an article titled "Natural Resources in Their Relation to Military Supplies," Dr. Little wrote afterward, "We made in all 5¼ million gas masks, and the failure in supply of such a thing as coconut shells might have lost the war. . . . The effective encouragement of science is the price of military efficiency."

As the war was nearing an end, the Germans started using diphenylchlorarsine as a weapon. It was not a source of poison gas, but of smoke gas. When detonated, it emitted smoke that, although not toxic, irritated noses and throats. The smoke could not be absorbed by charcoal. By then, there was an A. D. Little Unit in the Chemical Development Section of the Research Division of the Chemical Warfare Service. The unit took over the paper mill in the basement of the Charles River Road building. It soon came up with a filter that could absorb diphenylchlorarsine smoke. Wet pulp made from, among other materials, sugarcane pith, sphagnum moss, cottonseed hull fibers, and rope waste was sucked onto a wire frame, layer upon layer. After the filter thus formed had dried, the frame could be removed and the filter slipped onto a conventional gas mask and sealed with wax. The United States Shoe Machinery Company, a longtime ADL client, was assigned the task of producing what were called sucked-on filters, and it was tooled up to turn out one of them every six seconds — 14,400 a day — by the time hostilities had ceased.

Three of the men in the Chemical Warfare Service with whom Dr. Little worked on the sucked-on filter and other projects were Lieutenant Colonel Bradley Dewey, Captain Charles Almy, Jr., and First Lieutenant Earl P. Stevenson. Dewey and Almy went on, after the war, to form a chemical company for which ADL undertook many assignments, including the development of glues for labeling, sealing, bookbinding, and shoemaking.* ADL licensed its patents on those glues to Dewey & Almy (William Walker, after leaving M.I.T. in 1920, became a director of Dewey & Almy and the head of its patent department) and received a

---

* While the war was still on, shoe leather was hard to come by, and some manufacturers substituted animal skins whose use in peacetime would have been unthinkable. An article about that situation in the December 1917 issue of the *Little Journal* was headlined, bluntly, "RATS WANTED."

gratifying amount of its common stock in exchange. Bradley Dewey served for many years as a director of Arthur D. Little, Inc., and when in 1928 Dr. Little sent him an anthology of some of his articles, Dewey wrote him,

> How in the world do you ever have time enough to master such a field, much less write about it? ... Granting that it is basically a compilation, it is still a miracle to me that a man in your position, running the biggest business in the hardest field in the world, can also find time to do such a work, and in doing it, to do it better than could possibly be hoped for by anyone else. You are a wonder!

And to Little's widow, after her husband's death in 1935, Dewey would write that the world "will never again have so rare a mixture of scientific brilliance, imagination, business initiative and foresight, together with absolute honesty, good fellowship, and human understanding."

As for Lieutenant Earl P. Stevenson, he was destined to become the second president of Arthur D. Little, Inc.

IV *Who Says It Can't Be Done?*

The persistent difficulty has been to persuade men who are
without scientific background, how enormous is the extent to
which we are capable of helping them. The pioneer work
of enlightenment grows less as more and more laboratories
are established and engineers and others of technical
education are placed in control. But even so there is a
thousand times more work along the lines of physical science
waiting to be performed than had ever yet been attempted
— and here we are to do it!

— Dr. Arthur D. Little, c. 1921

*E*arl Stevenson, who joined Arthur D. Little, Inc., in
1919 and became its president in 1935, was first and
foremost a practicing chemist. Over the years he was granted two
dozen patents, including ones for recovering potash and borax
from brines, for extracting turpentine and rosin from pine wood,
and for molding plastics. Born in Logansport, Indiana, Stevenson
had come East to attend college at Wesleyan University, which in
1950 would name him the president of its board of trustees. At
the end of the war, he went to M.I.T., like so many other
ADLers before and after him, and got a master's degree there in
1918.

Stevenson had been at ADL only one year when, at twenty-six,
he was given the title of research director. His approach to research jibed with that of Dr. Little. Addressing the American Association for the Advancement of Science in 1925, Stevenson
said,

> The frontiers of science are further flung than those of industry; we
> must accept this fact and quicken our pace.... We have passed
> through a period of epoch-making discoveries; if we are to more com-
> pletely realize upon their potentialities our recourse is intensive re-
> search, wisely directed, adequately financed, and sustained in the face
> of obstacles. To better cope with this situation, more energy should
> be concentrated on the frontiers of our industries.

Stevenson was a no-nonsense man. When he became president, he insisted that all members of his staff answer their own telephones rather than use secretaries as intermediaries or buffers. He decreed that company travel, when humanly possible, be conducted at night, so nobody's daytime working hours would be frittered away in transit. He had a high moral sense, and he expected others to follow suit.* "We have to be gentlemen," he said. His hobby — not pursued, it goes without saying, on company time — was growing orchids.

The *Little Journal* bragged in 1918 that ADL's volume of postwar business had in one month equaled its first five years' total. There were echoes, in one job just completed, of the firm's earliest assignments: 556 separate analyses, on a rush basis, of the fat and moisture content of a whole shipload of cornmeal and wheat flour. More stimulating was a request from a farm products company to do something to alleviate a grievous situation that had arisen in grain fields: Crickets were chewing up the twine used to bind harvested sheaves. ADL sent a chemist and an entomologist to the scene of the crime. They soon determined that the parched insects were attracted to the twine because of the traces of moisture embedded in it, especially during protracted dry spells. The scientists advised their client, according to the *Little Journal,* to have the twine treated with "something that was more unpleasant than lack of shade, more offensive than drought, more horrid than thirst from the crickets' standpoint." There was no plan to butcher the crickets. "Men of research," the *Journal* explained, "are out after results, not revenge."

Yet another case involved actually running a manufacturing plant for an enamelware company in St. Louis. This firm wanted to insure chemical uniformity on its production line, and felt it could attain that only if ADL people would show its own people how to do so. (Stevenson was assigned to that still ongoing operation almost as soon as he joined the company, and for some months he spent more time in Missouri than in Massachusetts.) For all its industriousness — there was by now even a small office in Washington, D.C., to try to help corporations cope with a new

---

* Stevenson was outraged when, in 1937, he received an anonymous, typewritten note mailed in New York City and purporting to come from "Members of a Chemical Engineering Society." It asked, "Why do you keep Jews on your staff of consultant chemists to lower the prestige of your company and personnel? Respecting your standing, we protest." Stevenson passed it along, protestingly, to the American Institute of Chemical Engineers, but its source was never traced.

vexation, a federal income tax — ADL's gross revenue for 1919 was merely $55,109, and its net profit $4,456.

Just a year after Stevenson arrived, ADL took on another young hand, Raymond Stevens, who hailed from Nashua, New Hampshire. Like Stevenson, Stevens had been an officer in the Chemical Warfare Service; and he, too, would eventually become the company's president. Stevenson had the edge over Stevens in length of name, and he was also a few months older; as they both rose in the ADL hierarchy, Stevenson always ranked slightly higher. They were more respectful of one another than friendly. On Memorial Drive, their offices were at opposite ends of the ground floor, and they kept their distance. But they made a good working team. Stevenson was primarily a scientist. Stevens, though he had also gone to M.I.T. and knew his chemistry, was primarily a salesman. Like many salesmen, he was an extrovert — hearty, genial, gregarious. After he had been around for a while, he could scarcely go anywhere without running into some old acquaintance with whom he could, and would, pause to chat.

Dr. Little was fortunate in having his two new associates around, because some of the older members of his staff were becoming restless. They were exasperated at his carefree handling of ADL's financial affairs. On a personal level, his attitude toward money was simple enough: If you've got it, spend it. Once, at a time when his unpaid household bills were frighteningly high, he had come into a $25,000 windfall; on his way to the bank, he stopped off at an antique dealer's and bought a $20,000 Chinese vase. One curriculum vitae that he handed out to prospective clients said, "Have some knowledge of botany and forest trees and have studied Chinese porcelains."

"A professional man starts to fail the moment he permits money to shape his career," Dr. Little had written. Some of his associates were hard-pressed to concur. In 1916, the company issued some more stock, both common and preferred. Dr. Little got most of the common; only the common stock had any voting power. Moreover, not since the 1909 incorporation had any dividends been paid on any of the issues of preferred.

By 1921, the preferred shareholders had acquired more influence. They had two representatives on the Board of Directors. One of them, Carl F. Woods, was the corporate secretary, and a

crony of his, William W. Caswell, the treasurer. Caswell and
Woods had powerful allies among some of the veteran employees
who also owned some stock — Harry S. Mork, Gustavus Esselen,
and Hervey Skinner. Skinner dated all the way back to 1902 and
had been a vice-president since 1909.

Dr. Little's salary had risen to $25,000 by 1921. The disaffected
group made him a proposition: His salary would be doubled if he
would give the holders of the preferred stock some voting rights.
The offer was tempting, but he brushed it aside. At that, the dis-
sidents tried to brush *him* aside. The Board of Directors, then
five strong, convened to consider whether Little's own company
should fire him. He won, but merely by a three-to-two margin —
his own vote and those of Bradley Dewey and Everett Morss, an
M.I.T. classmate of Little's, formed the majority. Skinner, Mork,
Esselen, and a few other old-timers left in a huff and formed their
own company. Earl Stevenson was on enamelware duty in St.
Louis, and Dr. Little beseeched him, in a flurry of telegrams, not
to abandon ship with them. Stevenson remained loyal. He was
soon made a vice-president. Carl Woods was replaced as corporate secretary by Alexander Whiteside, a Boston attorney (Harvard '95, Harvard Law '98) who'd been associated with ADL for
five years. For another thirty years, Whiteside handled ADL's
legal affairs — until, at the age of eighty, he had an acrimonious
falling-out with Stevenson.

There was one last flurry of opposition. Toward the end
of 1921, the troubled company's books showed a net loss of
$77,031.61 over the preceding twelve months. At a special meet-
ing of the Board of Directors on October 5, the still-embattled
Caswell proposed that a special stockholders' meeting be called
for the purpose of dissolving the corporation and distributing its
assets. Woods seconded his motion. Everybody else present voted
against it. As a parting shot, Caswell and Woods moved that
every shareholder, common and preferred alike, be sent a copy of
the company's most recent operating statement and balance
sheet. The latter indicated that in less than fifteen months ADL's
surplus had shrunk from $120,267.11 to $23,349.61. That motion
was defeated, too. Caswell and Woods walked out of the meeting.
At the following year's annual meeting, Caswell, still a shareholder though emphatically not up for reelection to the board,
voted against the president's report, against the treasurer's report,

and against every act of the directors that was presented for ratification. That was pretty much his last gasp. Trying to shore up his sagging enterprise, Dr. Little reduced the staff's salaries by 10 percent and his own by 15 percent. The Memorial Drive building was mortgaged. Not long afterward, Henry Powning climbed aboard the foundering ship and got it back on a relatively even keel.

That otherwise bleak year of 1921 had two bright moments. First, Gordon Battelle, of the mining and smelting family, commissioned ADL to examine a new method of processing zinc ore in which his company was contemplating a heavy investment. ADL looked into it and judged it to be dubious. Then Battelle commissioned the company to devise a better process, offering a bonus of $40,000 for a practical one. In due course, ADL invented and had patented a way of treating the ore with a heated solution of ammonium sulfate and eventually converting it, after a few more intermediate steps, into zinc oxide pigment. That process was never adopted by Battelle's company, but he was impressed with the manner in which ADL had gone about its research and development. Although Battelle didn't pay the bonus, before he died two years later, he directed the executors of his estate to earmark most of it for the establishment of an "institute for encouragement of creative research, advancement of science, and making of discoveries and inventions useful to mankind."

The Battelle Memorial Institute came into being in 1929, in Columbus, Ohio, and half a century later it had evolved into a huge nonprofit consulting organization on its own. In the 1950s, the institute did much of the research and development work that resulted in the inundation of the business world by the Xerox machine. Before Battelle undertook that task, ADL had been asked by International Business Machines whether the newfangled copiers (developed by the Haloid Corporation, the precursor of the Xerox Corporation) were worth investing in. ADL, after perhaps too cursory an investigation, had advised IBM not to bother; there would never be enough of a market for them to justify the expense. The institute, on the other hand, was glad to tackle the job, and for its pains it ended up with a rewarding chunk of Xerox stock. Contemporary ADLers still wince at the memory of their predecessors' skewed judgment.

* * *

The July 1979 issue of an ADL in-house publication, *The Little Paper,* which had been inaugurated the year before, reprinted a Double-Crostic from "Dell's Official Crossword Puzzles." A dinner for two at an unspecified restaurant was offered to the first employee to turn in the correct solution. There was never an announcement of whether anyone had submitted the right quotation, from Daniel J. Boorstin's *The Americans* — " 'You can't make a silk purse out of a sow's ear' irritated Arthur D. Little in Nineteen-twenty-one. He secured ten pounds of gelatine manufactured from sows' ears. From this he spun an artificial thread, wove the thread into a fabric, and actually produced an elegant purse."

Dr. Little had not been especially irritated. He had merely had an idea: one that probably would focus more attention on his company, all things considered, than anything else it would accomplish in nearly a century; and one that, according to Willis R. Whitney, M.I.T. '90, the director of research for General Electric, would "long echo through the corridors of time." In resolving to achieve that legendary paradigm of impossibility, Dr. Little had aspired not only to demonstrate to skeptics the untapped capabilities of chemistry in general but, more specifically, to impress bankers who might want to invest, as he had been hoping they would for more than a quarter of a century, in artificial substitutes for silk. (At some point between 1905 and 1910, he had apparently made a "silk" necktie out of wood fiber, but that had generated little fanfare.) Once Dr. Little had concluded that it might be possible to bring off the sow's-ear-to-silk-purse trick, he delegated the work to two of his chemists: a senior one, Gustavus Esselen, whose last chore it would be before he departed after what was called the palace revolt; and a very junior one, Wallace J. Murray, who was not only an M.I.T. alumnus but had postgraduate credentials from both the University of Leeds, England, and the University of Geneva.

If Murray's first assignment at ADL may have to him seemed unusual, as for a Ph.D. in organic chemistry it no doubt did, that was in the ADL tradition. Many employees before and after him would be startled, if not dumbfounded, by their initiation into the company's modus operandi. A computer specialist, Everett T. Meserve, found himself on an airplane from Boston to San Francisco his very first day on the job in 1978, even before he had been processed for flight insurance; and he had only just checked into an ADL branch office in California when he was told to interview a prospective West Coast hireling. "Tell me what it's like to work at ADL," the interviewee said. "Well," said Meserve, "the last eight hours have been terrific." D. Reid Weedon, who became a senior vice-president of the firm, had a less frenetic baptism — after he enlisted, in 1946, it was several months before anybody gave him anything to do, and he just sat around reading old magazines. A young woman who arrived ten years after that *was* put right to work: She was given a platter of onions and instructed, as part of a project to develop a pill to combat bad breath, to chew them and breathe into a plastic bag.

Harland A. Riker, who had been hired in 1953, hung on to become head of ADL's international operations; but he came close to quitting in dismay and despair on his first day there. As Riker recounted:

> When I arrived, everyone was either shouting into telephones, talking loudly to be heard over the partitions, or scurrying from cubicle to cubicle with important-looking folders and flowcharts. The people I had already met were out of town that day and those in the office seemed distracted and not altogether sure what to do with me. Someone asked if I knew anything about Puerto Rico rum ... another asked if I was familiar with the principal manufacturers of greeting cards. Later, I was introduced to a mysterious group — any three people doing the same thing at ADL in those days called themselves a group — devoted to developing new consumer products. I was rather taken aback to find five or six people lying outstretched on mattresses on the floor scattered between benches, drawing boards, and machine tools. . . . It gradually dawned on me that they were working on new developments for a bedding company. [They] suggested that if I had some time available I could test [an] unoccupied mattress. I demurred on the basis that I was heavily committed to the future of the greeting card industry and quickly returned to the relative sanity of my cubicle with serious doubts that I would ever understand what people at ADL really did.

Wallace Murray at least didn't have to start from scratch when he was delegated to make a sow's ear into a silk purse. Dr. Little had already theorized that sows' ears (it was obviously futile to surmise that a single ear could be transformed into a purse), which consist largely of gristle and skin, could be rendered into glue, watered down, and then transformed with a bit of acetone and a touch of chrome alum into gelatin. If that residue were next filtered under pressure and squeezed through a spinneret perforated with holes of about a thousandth of an inch in diameter, and if the threads emanating from that could be spun into a fabric — presto!

Wilson & Company, a Chicago meat packer, was engaged to clip a hundred pounds' worth of ears from slaughtered sows — nobody ever counted the ear total — and pare that down to ten pounds of viscous goo. (In shipping that end product, Wilson obligingly sent along an affidavit to the effect that it was all of authentic porcine origin.) As it turned out, the threads that emerged from the spinneret were so brittle and frail that they couldn't be knitted or crocheted. So they were bathed in a glycerin solution to soften them, and then, on a specially constructed loom, they were gently woven into a silky material. Thence the purse — two purses, actually, each in two colors and of the dumbbell design fancied in medieval days by well-to-do ladies, with a gold silk container at one end for gold coins, and a silver silk container at the other for silver.

Dr. Little had a keen appreciation of and instinct for public relations. He knew he had something worth far more than its weight in precious metals when the first purse was produced for his scrutiny and approbation. A promotional booklet that he was quick to have prepared about his defiance of what had long been thought to be the laws of nature, titled "On the Making of Silk Purses from Sows' Ears," was soon available for circulation, although the printed version omitted a fairly hard-sell coda in his own handwritten draft:

> Does it not seem reasonable to you, dear Sir and Reader, that an organization which includes chemists that can make silk purses out of sows' ears, just for the fun of doing it, is also qualified to do other things? To solve problems for instance which hold back the progress of industry and ... prosperity because those who are scientifically blind repeat the heavy, dull, discouraging refrain: "It can't be done"? Who says it can't be done? Let's dig in and find out!

The first public display of one of the purses was on September 12, 1921, during a chemical industries exposition at the Eighth Coast Artillery Armory in New York City. The *Boston Tran-*

script commended the exhibit on its "fine weave and beautiful sheen." A correspondent for the *American Dyestuff Reporter* said a week later that

> this "stunt," of no *practical* value whatever, was in some ways as significant as anything else shown or told of in that booth, for it represented the chemists' shrill blare of defiance at worn-out tradition and the type of ignorance and mental inertia which compelled some early scientists to conceal their progress in the mastery of natural laws for fear of the stake. . . . The time and trouble expended in making the silk purse were distinctly worth while, and it is to be hoped that its lesson was not wasted upon the many lay brethren who flocked around it.

Interest in the silk purse revived in 1958 when Wallace Murray talked about it on the television program *I've Got A Secret,* after which Raymond Stevens presented one of the purses for permanent enshrinement in the Smithsonian Institution. Many ADLers got their first glimpse of the other one in 1977 — the same year in which the Kuwait Institute for Scientific Research was the site of an ADL lecture titled "You Can Make a Silk Purse From a Sow's Ear" — when, by that time insured for $40,000, the treasured clone was paraded around Acorn Park in the course of what was perhaps an inevitable aftermath of its creation: an attempt by latter-day ADLers to float a lead balloon.

ADLers, though they generally eschew frivolity in the company of clients, love to perform. When some ADL employees once formed an extracurricular acting group, they had no trouble picking a name for it — the Silk Purse Players. The managers of all the company's European branches convened in Cambridge, England, in 1981. A high spot of the get-together was a lively madrigal, the lyrics of which had been plucked from a sober statement of President John Magee in the company's annual report. Magee — who once jokingly said that sometimes he thought the company's business was "converting silk purses into sows' ears" — observed in a message he composed for the 1983 annual report that ADL had helped clients "find the fountain of youth." There is no evidence that anyone connected with the firm has ever essayed, on or off duty, to replicate that miracle.

"I think there's a lot of ham in all successful ADL people," said Clifford A. Bean, a telecommunications specialist employed there since 1972, who is also a card-carrying member of the Society for the Preservation and Encouragement of Barbershop Quartet Singing in America and the top tenor of the Outrageous River City All-Stars. "I once thought I was a schizophrenic, until I was chosen as a guinea pig during an ADL study of what makes people click. There were discussion sessions and homework, and then it suddenly dawned on me that I didn't have a split personality, that I was on center stage not only when I was singing but also when I was working — a ham all the time." Professionally, Bean was engaged in marketing strategy and market planning and diversification for cellular telephones. He was giving a talk on beeper systems at a San Antonio trade convention when he noticed that some of his audience was dozing off. He pulled out his pitch pipe (he always carries a pitch pipe), blew a shrill note on it, and rendered his finale in song. "It defied every image they'd had of ADL," he said afterward. The Outrageous River City All-Stars have worked cruise ships and ADL Christmas parties. A couple of years ago, the company put on a fancy dinner for its directors and their spouses at Dr. Little's onetime Brookline haunt, The Country Club. Robert Mueller, the chairman of the board, who is himself a barbershop quartet singer as well as a bass fiddler, asked the All-Stars to perform, and they inspired such bonhomie that one of the company's eldest elder statesmen, Charles J. Kensler, even took an ever-present cigar out of his mouth long enough to chime in.

Back in 1951, two ADL scientists — one was Howard O. McMahon, later an ADL president — had floated a lead balloon of sorts: a hollow lead sphere the size of a marble, which, by inducing an electric current into a magnetic field, they had levitated out of chilled helium. But that was in a laboratory. The notion of creating a much larger lead balloon that could fly out-of-doors was sparked in the late seventies by James D. Birkett, a playful Ph.D. in chemistry from Yale who specialized in hydrology and desalination. When he was involved in serious business, he spent his days advising Saudi Arabia on making its desert bloom or conducting studies on service behavior of large evaporation desalting plants for the Office of Water Research and Technology of the Department of the Interior.

Birkett had read an article in a regional monthly, *Boston* magazine, suggesting that ever since the sow's-ear caper, ADL had been a rather stodgy organization. A few days after that, he heard one colleague tell another, as he passed them in a corridor, "That idea has as much chance to fly as a lead balloon." Returning to his office, Birkett took out a pocket calculator, made some quick computations, and concluded that an object six feet in diameter, covered with lead foil about one millimeter thick and filled with helium, could conceivably be made airborne. He proceeded through channels. He sent a memorandum to Alma Triner, the company's newly installed head of Public Relations and its first female vice-president in any department, proposing "a jazzy little project to catch the public eye, to wit: ADL should construct and fly a lead balloon. . . . It would be a proud sight, flying over our corporate headquarters."

A Lead Balloon Committee was promptly formed. Birkett, naturally, was its chairman. Among the other members were a janitor, Triner's eleven-year-old daughter, Robert Mueller, and Gordon Conrad, a chemical industry expert who the year before, by coincidence, had had a play of his titled *The Lead Balloon* put on at M.I.T. This happened to be Mueller's first public performance since becoming chairman of the board at ADL, which he found refreshingly freewheeling after thirty-three years in the far more structured hierarchy of the Monsanto Chemical Company, and he celebrated his release by proclaiming, as the quest got under way, "There is no such thing as a free launch." The committee drew up rules: A balloon would not be considered a success unless it rose off the ground and stayed aloft "a convincing length of time." The company would underwrite "reasonable cost of materials." Any work done on balloons would have to be done on employees' own time.

Dozens of men and women thereupon devoted hundreds of free hours to the three balloons that were eventually constructed. One group hired an outside consultant. ADL itself obtained a set of current Federal Aviation Administration regulations on balloon flying and footed the bill for 125 pounds of lead foil eight-thousandths of an inch thick. Three balloons were prepared for takeoff on May 16, 1977 — after office hours — in the Acorn Park courtyard. One burst at the seams while being fueled. Another staggered upward and stayed airborne for about a quarter of a mile before collapsing. The third, a sausage-shaped contrivance fourteen feet long, soared up so fast that it snapped its tether. The effect on the cheering employees was not quite comparable to that at Lyons, France, on January 19, 1784, when Joseph Montgolfier and Pilatre de Rozier launched a lighter-than-air balloon and some of their spectators fainted while others fell to their knees in prayer; but it was profound enough for President Magee to acclaim the venture an "amazing triumph of engineering technology over common sense." The lead balloon was last spotted heading eastward over the Atlantic at 4,000 feet by a flabbergasted Delta Airlines pilot. The whole episode did so much to elevate the spirits of the ADLers who participated in it, one way or another, that some of them were disappointed, as the next few years went by, not to be urged to try to grow moss on a rolling stone.

V Tasting and Sniffing

*In any progressive civilization, industry is constantly pushing
its outposts forward into the new territory wrested from the
unknown by its advance guard, science. Science, however, is
merely information, so classified and organized as to be used
effectively and at once, and information, to quote General
Phil Sheridan, is "the great essential of success."*

— Dr. Arthur D. Little [n.d.]

*A*round the same time that Dr. Little got to thinking
about sows' ears and silk purses, he began inquiring
far more seriously into the potentials of petroleum. (In 1920, an
ADL publication had posed the questions, "All the world knows
that this is the Day of Petroleum, but what is the time o' day?
Does the clock mark forenoon, high noon, or afternoon?") A geologist surveying the future of the oil industry for the federal government had come to the gloomy conclusion that, unless vast new
reserves were found, "the oil industry of the past, with its uncoordinated wastefulness, must give place to a chemical coordina-
tion which will make the most of what remains of the petroleum
resource."

Plenty of oil remained, however; new fields were all at once discovered in East Texas. But any allusion to wastefulness, which
Dr. Little abhorred, was bound to get his imagination stirring.
Now that there was apparently to be a deluge rather than a dearth
of petroleum, he foresaw the emergence of a petrochemical industry on a scale never before considered possible. He collaborated in
1921 with Dr. Robert E. Wilson — then a professor at M.I.T. and
eventually chairman of the board of Standard Oil of Indiana
— on an article titled "Science's Future with Oil." Its thrust was
that the basic raw material of the chemical industry to come should

no longer be coal tar, as it had been for years, but petroleum.

Soon Dr. Little was approached by his friend Elisha Walker of the New York banking house of Blair & Company. Walker wanted him to look into the economic feasibility of a new vapor phase cracking process for petroleum. Accompanied by Earl Stevenson and Wallace Murray, Dr. Little went to Tulsa, Oklahoma, and made some tests. Another chemist who was on the scene said afterward, "Dr. Little had a real vision. He saw in the future a great chemical industry based on ethylene, butylene, propylene, etc. . . . [He] saw the possibilities of producing gasolines having definite properties adapted to specific uses instead of just taking whatever came off a crude still at about the right temperature."

The ADL team reported to Walker that it wasn't enthusiastic about the process it had evaluated, but that it thought it could come up with a better vapor phase distillation process. Blair & Company thereupon agreed, along with the Barnsdall Refining Company, to finance some preliminary research. When that produced promising results, they were joined by the National Distillers Corporation in underwriting a pilot plant, erected behind the ADL building on Memorial Drive, with a capacity of 25 barrels a day. A new business entity evolved — the Petroleum Chemical Corporation. Its most successful product was tertiary butyl alcohol, which could readily be converted into isooctane, or antiknock, gasoline. Petroleum Chemical built a much bigger plant, with a capacity of 250 barrels a day, in Tiverton, Rhode Island. Dr. Little thought he was going to strike it rich, but the company spread itself too thin. Instead of concentrating on the marketing of that single product, about which the Ethyl Gas Corporation, for one, was sanguine, it allocated too much of its insufficient capital to research and development of a whole slew of products. Its assets were eventually auctioned off, most of them being acquired by Standard Oil of New Jersey.

Once again, Dr. Little had shown himself to be better as a prophet than as a practitioner. His gift for prescience, though, continued to flourish. When in 1924, for instance, sound movies were looming on the technological horizon, he wrote in the *Atlantic Monthly*,

No longer is it necessary for our statesmen to tour the country. Their fences may be mended in the studio, and their constituents may simultaneously, in thousands of communities, view the candidate in a six-foot close-up as his argument is projected in a voice of twenty horsepower. It will handicap the senator who looks like a third-class postmaster.*

First-class stores nowadays often consider their most dependable customers to be members of old families who keep coming back generation after generation, and also moneyed Arabs. Ever since it began to operate on more than a shoestring, ADL has had satisfying relationships with both. It has worked rewardingly on a six-year industrial plan for Iraq, on a five-year agricultural plan for Oman, on a computer system for a Turkish construction company in Libya, and on a tourism development plan for Abu Dhabi. (Nearby Iran, whose people are mostly Persian rather than Arab, engaged ADL before the revolution for a long-range but short-lived national radio and television plan.) For Algeria, ADL has made studies on education, agribusiness, and, naturally, petroleum. When that nation's leader, Houari Boumedienne, addressed the United Nations General Assembly in 1974 and devoted much of his speech to a spirited attack on the imperialist world and its addiction to capitalism, his facts were based largely on material furnished him by ADL in an earlier study of the world economy and Algeria's place therein. It was through the recommendations of Algerian acquaintances that ADL was subsequently engaged by the emphatically noncapitalistic governments of Angola and Mozambique.

Some of the big American oil companies — themselves also ADL clients — were upset when they learned that ADL was trying to help out countries that had nationalized their thitherto privately owned petroleum industries, but ADL was not fazed. Its executives sometimes profess to view their participation in Third World ventures as ideologically irrelevant and, if not exactly on the level of missionary activity, at least akin to that of the International Red Cross. A major difference, of course, is that ADL is not an eleemosynary institution. "If our clients didn't know our work was expensive," one widely traveled ADLer observed, "our work wouldn't be as good."

Since the mid-1960s, no client has been more steadfast or re-

---

* No man is infallible. Dr. Little's crystal ball clouded when he said in the same article, "For long-distance travel overseas the airship will doubtless prove more available than the airplane."

munerative than the unwaveringly capitalistic country of Saudi
Arabia. Among its many other assignments there, ADL had
spent ten years drawing up plans and specifications for a huge
telecommunications network. When, in the late 1970s, the time finally arrived to start construction on what would be the largest
telecommunications job in history, three consortia put in bids.
Two were American and one European. The European group got
the nod. Not long afterward, Secretary of State Cyrus Vance ran
into the crown prince of Saudi Arabia and asked him, half chid-
ingly, why the American contestants had lost out on the enormous contract. "Why don't you ask Arthur D. Little," was the
reply. "They made the decision." ADL, which has had practically every branch of the U.S. government as a client at one time
or another, was persona non grata with the Department of Commerce for several months afterward.

As for longtime companionability with customers, 80 percent
of ADL's clients — among them nearly every company on the
Fortune 500 list — have used its services at least once before.
"Top executives . . . are drawn to Acorn Park like missionaries to
the Amazon," *Barron's* once somewhat giddily proclaimed. In
1984 an elderly client turned up who'd last been heard from in
1957. He wanted another job done, he said, much along the lines
of the earlier one, with which he'd been most satisfied. Nobody
who'd worked on that case was still around, and when ADL tried
to refresh its corporate memory by looking up what it was it had
done so apparently well, it couldn't find a copy of the twenty-
seven-year-old report — its files were in a more or less permanent
state of disarray. Fortunately, the client had one and was glad to
share it with its original source.

Over the years, some clients practically became members of
the family. Between 1930 and 1955 alone, for example, ADL carried out eighty-two separate assignments for the Owens-Corning
Fiberglas Corporation. ADL's relationship with a precursor corporation, Owens-Illinois Glass, went back even further; starting
in 1927, Owens-Illinois had put ADL on a $10,000-a-year re-
tainer for exploratory research on its behalf. (Charles Belknap, a
top executive of both glass companies, was later rewarded for his
fealty with a seat on the ADL board.) ADL scientists had a hand
in the development of fiberglass, an endeavor characterized by
some novel approaches to basic research: Employees at Memorial
Drive had to watch their step when they approached a certain

corridor, because Walter Smith was apt to be stationed at one end of it with a bow and arrow, shooting heated glass rods down the hall to ascertain how far they would stretch in flight.

Another faithful client was the Will & Baumer Candle Company, for which ADL solved a nagging problem. It stiffened the wicks in religious candles, which had had a lamentable tendency to sag. At one point, ADL engineers constructed a mechanical candle that burned nonstop, like an eternal flame, to probe the interrelationship during drips of wicks and waxes. Still another client many times over was Lever Brothers, whose patronage dated back to the early twenties and was the result of a neighborly sales call made down the riverfront by Raymond Stevens. For years afterward, ADL laboratories were all but awash in soapsuds. One newly hired graduate chemist, who had hoped on being admitted to Dr. Little's research palace to be put on some esoteric experiment that might lead to a Nobel Prize, found himself instead bent over a sink with eighteen cakes of Lifebuoy arrayed before him. He was instructed to wash his hands for exactly one minute with each cake, in rotation. The object was to discover the precise life span of a cake of Lifebuoy. The chemist had never had cleaner hands. By the time he was relieved of that duty and assigned to something more stimulating and less lathery, he was glad to perceive that he had any hands at all. An ADL publication edited by Stevens carried a lengthy history of soap in 1930, taking the cleanser all the way back to the Roman Empire. "As yet, the vogue of color in the kitchen and bathroom has had little effect on soap," the article went. "We may, however, expect to find a demand for the more delicate pastel shades, appropriately perfumed, in the near future."

Probably the most steadfast of all of ADL's early patrons was The Lane Company of Altavista, Virginia. Edward H. Lane and his family made cedar chests in an era when any self-respecting bride-to-be would no more have thought of being without one than without a fiancé. The Lanes became ADL clients in 1922 and remained so for more than thirty years. A mere index of the work that ADL did for them over just one sixteen-year stretch ran to twenty-five pages. Earl Stevenson embarked for the company on an in-depth compilation of cedar oil emission measurements. Of another Earl at ADL — Earl Stafford, to whom was delegated the responsibility of preventing bulges on the surfaces of chests accompanying families posted to the tropics — an in-house publication once declared, "His mission in life is to make brides happier."

ADL scientists went to prodigious lengths to keep Edward Lane happy. They investigated methods of creating beddings for dog kennels and henhouses out of cedar shavings. They persuaded the federal government to decree that no chests could be marketed as cedar unless they were fashioned of wood at least three-quarters of an inch thick. When Mr. Lane expressed curiosity about which kinds of cedarwood — red, white, or whatever — had the highest oil content, ADL dispatched a crew of foresters to his home state, had them fell four kinds of cedar in four areas, and then analyzed the trees' heartwood along with samples of the soil in which they'd been rooted. ADL pried into the intimate habits of cedar chests' most vicious enemies: carpet beetles, fur beetles, termites, and other vermin. One of Roger Doggett's first chores was to design a cedar-chest lock impenetrable by cockroaches. He imprisoned them in chests with different kinds of locks, stood guard outside, and meticulously kept count of the number of critters that escaped. He bred his own roaches. "I had no trouble finding them," he said. "There were plenty of them right on the premises." Dr. Little would have been shocked.

Another staff member bred clothes moths. Filene's, next door, borrowed some of these to gauge the security of its fur storage chambers. ADL performed countless tests with mothicidal chemicals, and at one point felt obliged to concede, with grudging admiration, that "clothes moths are very skillful in avoiding contact with any insecticide." In 1928, ADL proudly presented Mr. Lane with a scholarly dissertation (based on data from the zoological laboratories of Bonn University, Germany) titled "The Life History and Habits of the Clothes Moth," which said, in small part:

> The male moth, which is the one ordinarily seen and chased, is really a harmless, as well as a useless, creature. He lives on an average of twenty-eight days, during which time he neither eats nor drinks. In fact he continues to live until he dries up so much that life is no longer possible. . . . Courtship and mating are usually accomplished during the first day of his life — before he is seen flying about. It is really a kindness to the moth to kill him, to save him from a long lingering drying-up, but killing him is of no value to the householder. . . . The clothes moth appears to be without sense of smell,

and is a singularly dumb and senseless creature, particularly with regard to the welfare of the next generation.

The ADL employee who handled most of the company's cedar-chest work was a colorful chemist, Ernest Charlton Crocker, who, like Earl Stevenson and Raymond Stevens, had been in the Chemical Warfare Service. Crocker was only a private. He worked in a training program set up to teach soldiers how to recognize gases. He was one of the few enlisted men ever to have been assigned to the perfect slot because, despite being afflicted with hay fever, he had an exceptional sense of smell. That attribute was memorably historified when in 1951 the *Saturday Evening Post* ran an article about him (later abridged in the *Reader's Digest*) titled "The Man with the Million-dollar Nose."

Ernest Crocker, who joined ADL in 1922, was credited with being able to recognize nine thousand distinct odors. He enjoyed exhibiting his singular prowess. He would hold a silver-plated dish over a Bunsen burner at low heat, and as he received successive odors from it he would name, in the correct order, the steps involved in the plating process. One time the Coca-Cola Company was debating whether or not it should engage ADL for a certain job. Crocker rounded up a dozen or so Coke bottles of different vintages. He uncapped one after another, sniffed judiciously, and correctly announced the age of each. ADL got the assignment.

Crocker soon recruited, as a tasting and smelling associate, Lloyd C. Henderson, a colleague and roommate in the army. Together they reduced odors to simple arithmetic. There were, they told a meeting of the American Chemical Society in 1927, only four constituents of all odors: fragrant (as in the sweetness of flowers), acid (the sourness of vinegar), burnt (tarriness), and caprylic (goatiness, or putrefaction). Every odor could be described by a four-digit number, with the digits corresponding to the four constituents and each one expressing, on a scale of 1 to 9, how much of that element the odor contained. They worked out the mathematics for 244 aromatic chemicals and 115 natural odorants. Jasmine was 7643, clove oil 7563, coumarin 5114, natural peppermint oil 5226, phenyl isobutyl ketone 5555. Myrrh was 4174, but frankincense somehow never made the list.

Crocker and Henderson would play games with each other on

the phone, one of them rattling off four digits, the other being expected to convert them into an odor. A greeting of "6523" was their equivalent for saying "Hello"; that stood for the first rose they had ever smelled by the numbers. At lunch with his staff, or at parties at his home, Crocker liked to play what he called the Smelling Game. He would put liquids in small, dark, unmarked bottles and see who could, by nose alone, correctly identify the most of them. On warm spring afternoons, Crocker and Henderson would sometimes stroll through Harvard's Arnold Arboretum, conferring sets of digits upon various plants their alert noses encountered.

In those days, there was usually an ADL staff dinner at Christmastime. In his remarks at the 1927 gathering, Dr. Little said, "Mr. Crocker has earned a new M.S. degree — he has become a Master of Smells. He can analyze any smell and give it a numerical designation which discloses its components. I suppose it's the same way with dates and telephone numbers. It has its disadvantages — think of calling up a refined and attractive girl whose telephone number suggests a mixture of burnt leather and garlic with a little rancid fish oil and just a touch of coal gas. It isn't fair to the girl."

Ernest Crocker had been sniffing flowers for more than mere pleasure at the age of five, and at twelve — like Dr. Little before him — had installed a modest chemical laboratory in his home. As a teenager, Crocker operated a small but lucrative business providing lubricating oils to brass instrument players in his high school band. (As an adult, by way of demonstrating that his interests ranged beyond sight and smell, he made fireworks at home.) He worked for three years as a janitor at M.I.T. to save enough money to enroll there. After the war, he was hired by Dewey & Almy. He worked on can-sealing compounds, which gave him little chance to exercise his unique strengths. Dewey & Almy and ADL were close; Ray Stevens heard about the chap with the rare olfactory sense and, thinking ADL could make better use of it and him, hired Crocker.

That hunch was justified not long afterward when Stevenson learned that Lever Brothers was having difficulties with one of its perfumed soaps, which gave off a peculiar odor. Crocker was deputized to look into the situation, and after sniffing around like a bloodhound, soon solved the problem: The guilt could be pinned squarely on the copper surfaces of tables on which the soap was cut into bars. Soon after that, Crocker — now abetted by Henderson — determined that by using scents that were more durable than their traditional ones, Lever Brothers could save close to $1 million a year. Why, the two odor specialists reported to their client, 80 to 90 percent of the money that Lever Brothers spent on soap perfumes was dissipated before any of the soap was actually employed. "Possibly the 'blast' of perfume from a cake of fresh soap may have sales value and should properly be charged to advertising," they wrote, "but certainly it is of slight value to most users."

Lever Brothers executives must have been dazed by the flood of foamy prose that Crocker and Henderson poured out:

> Might not a smaller content of perfume be used in the cakes and a little be put on the wrappers and have the same or better effect and at great saving of cost? This is analogous to the case of Spearmint gum, where we understand the flavor is put on the paraffined inner wrapping where it is more stable than in the gum itself and where a much lower cost gives better general effect. . . .
>
> Fastidious smellers are able to approach a perfumed cake of soap gradually, and take in the various degrees of volatility more or less in order, and for their benefit, there should be a certain amount of odor interest in the character of the perfume as it runs the gamut. For instance, Lux perfume may begin with lemon or jasmine character, go through rose, through lily, and end in orchid or musk, and the effect will be very pleasing, yet if this is all smelled together rapidly, it will still be good.

Lever Brothers was nonetheless clearly pleased by this minute attentiveness to its problems, as it would later be by ADL's painstaking assessment of its doughnut-tasting methodology: It hired Henderson away from ADL. He would be only one of a number of ADL staff members who, after finishing a job for a client, would be invited to join its ranks. Years later, for instance, ADL was commissioned by a consortium of European wine merchants to study the prospects of starting a business in California. With an attention to detail that Crocker and Henderson would have ringingly endorsed, their successors at the firm examined such minutiae as the kinds of stakes and wire that ought to be used for grapevines. The venerable French firm of Moët & Cie liked the results, bought some land in the Napa Valley region of the state, started a company to produce a sparkling white wine that was at least a cousin of champagne, and, when it came time to choose a

president of the new concern, could think of nobody more qualified for the post than John Wright — the ADLer who had been a
co-author of the original report.

Ernest Crocker was not particularly easy to get along with. Although he was an accomplished performer and was much in demand as a speaker at meetings of the Association of Candy
Technologists and the Society of Cosmetic Chemists, he was also
something of a prima donna. He was accused by his colleagues at
ADL of capitalizing on their work: of, specifically, arranging to
have inventions of their devising patented in his name. "Crocker
had a nose for publicity," Roger Doggett said. But Crocker —
like those who worked with him — was highly esteemed by clients. The Wrigley chewing gum people were most grateful for his
furnishing them with a novel way of stabilizing oils and fats in
their products by means of licorice resins. (A visitor to ADL
would sometimes find three or four of its operatives simultaneously chewing gum and holding stopwatches in order to ascertain
the intensity of tastes and aftertastes.) Crocker's delicate palate
got him elected to the prestigious Wine and Food Society, whose
other members were probably unaware that he would have lunch
at a Nedick's even when traveling on an expense account. He was
as interested in flavors, professionally, as he was in odors. A 1945
book of his, simply titled *Flavors*, was highly regarded in its
genre, though a bit difficult for most laymen to comprehend: it
contained, in a chapter headed "The Physiology of Taste Perception," such passages as

> Those fibers that lead to taste buds in the two-thirds of the tongue
> nearest the lips are branches of the chorda tympani and lead even-
> tually by way of the seventh or facial nerve to the geniculate ganglion
> in the cerebral cortex. The taste buds at the third of the tongue at the
> back of the mouth are innervated by fibers of the internal laryngeal
> nerve, a branch of the tenth cranial or vagus nerve.

Crocker was an indefatigable writer. Whenever Raymond Stevens, the first editor of the *Industrial Bulletin* (a chatty, informa-
tive publication that ADL began putting out for its clients and
prospective clients in 1927*), was nearing his press deadline and
was short of copy, he knew he could count on Crocker to fill the

---

* It went in heavily for roguish headlines: "BARNACLE BELL" for a story about underwater telephone cables, "GEMESIS" for one on synthetic diamonds, "LET US SPRAY" for one
on aerosol, "THE LEI PUBLIC" for one on Hawaii, and, for one on electroencephalography,
"CODE IN THE HEAD."

gap with some such contribution as: "Smell memory is lasting. How we smile when we recognize a familiar pleasant odor! . . . The manufacturer is used to calling in experts to advise him concerning advertising, style, and other appeals to the sense of sight. He needs advice no less in matters concerning the sense of smell."

When it came to snacks, Crocker was fond of plugging up his nose and then chewing onions, which were deliciously sweet, he would assure anybody within earshot, if you couldn't smell them. He did a lot of research on refrigerators. He concluded that the worst smell exuders among items usually stored in refrigerators were ripe cantaloupes, overboiled cabbage, cut lemons, and boiled onions. The foods that had the worst records for absorbing smells were cottage cheese, cream cheese, mashed potatoes — and boiled onions. He also once asserted that, only ten seconds after injecting some vitamin B_1 into his arm, he could clearly taste it. It tasted, to him anyway, like peanuts. He was quirky about his work conditions. "It has been observed that loud noises completely prevent any smelling or tasting operations," he once observed. His last days were cruel. He suffered a paralyzing stroke, and while by almost superhuman willpower he got himself walking again, he was never able to recover his sense of smell.

Crocker's efforts in print, on the lecture circuit, and in the laboratory did much to drum up business for ADL in the general areas of taste and smell. When the federal government decreed that sassafras and safrole, which had customarily given root beer more than half its distinctive flavor, could no longer be used in its concoction, Hires appealed for help to ADL, which soon came up with an unexceptionable substitute. Walter Smith and three other longtime members of the ADL family — Howard Billings, Everett Atwell, and Benjamin B. Fogler, Sr. (later there would be a Ben, Jr., on the staff) — played a significant role in one historic triumph: the reduction in cooking time of Cream of Wheat from half an hour to five minutes. While they were at it, the ADLers consulted a knowledgeable outsider, Robert S. Harris, a nutritional biochemist at M.I.T. Professor Harris suggested that if they were going to reconstitute the old cereal, why didn't they go all out and fortify it with some of the ingredients in which it had been woefully lacking, especially iron and vitamins? Enriched 5-Minute Cream of Wheat was, for many a hard-pressed housewife, the happy outcome of that collaboration.

After Crocker was incapacitated, his work was carried on by a number of disciples he had trained. Prominent among them were Loren B. Sjöström, known as Johnny, among whose patents was one for improving the flavor of sardines; and Stanley E. Cairncross, who devised a tamper-proof self-sealing cylinder for Benzedrine inhalers. Sjöström came directly from Northeastern University with a B.S. in chemical engineering. Cairncross, a Columbia University Ph.D. in organic chemistry, arrived from yet another quite long-standing client, Bristol-Myers, for whom ADL did yeoman work over the years on Ipana toothpaste, Mum, Trushay, Minute-Rub, and Bufferin. Once, doing research on a paper they jointly presented to an annual meeting of the Institute of Food Technology, "What Makes Flavor Leadership?", Sjöström and Cairncross studied and tasted various brands of eight kinds of foods that seemed to have a clear-cut market leader: catsup, prepared mustard, salad dressing, canned luncheon meat, cola drinks, chocolate bars, peanut butter, and gelatin desserts — a heroic undertaking, it would seem, even for a teenager. The two men came through unscathed and told the institute, "Disagreeable aftertastes require something to wash them out of the mouth; it is more difficult to wash them out of the mind."

In 1947, the Upjohn Company appealed to Sjöström and Cairncross for help. Upjohn wondered why some of its medicines had to taste and smell so awful. When one of its multivitamin capsule bottles was opened, an odor emanated that could be likened to a blend of old gelatin, paint solvent, fish oil, and yeast. And the pills tasted even worse. What could ADL do about that? The addition of some aromatic chemicals and oils took care of the situation. Then along came International Minerals & Chemicals, which, under the trade name of Ac'cent, was marketing monosodium glutamate as a flavor enhancer but wanted to know just what effect MSG, as it was commonly known, had on the food to which it was added. Sjöström and Cairncross got onto that (first they had to study what effect salt had when it was added to food), and their studies evolved into a new concept called the Flavor Profile: an analysis of flavors and odors by means of the perceptual judgments of panels of trained specialists. Many companies soon had their own Flavor Profile experts; ADL ultimately trained 250 panels. All this research began in 1947, by which time Dr. Little had been dead twelve years. But it would not have surprised him; as far back as 1926, he had got to wondering about the potential uses of MSG upon hearing that in Japan it was a key constituent of soy sauce.

Still another longtime ADL client was Anheuser-Busch, which began to suspect that the Massachusetts group could be of service after a couple of ADLers were invited to a Newark brewery and confronted with twenty-eight bottles of Budweiser beer from a number of breweries. Twenty-eight glasses were filled. The ADLers didn't even bother to sip any of the contents. A few whiffs, and they singled out eight samples as being inferior. All eight, it turned out, had come from a single slipshod brewery. The Busches were impressed, and have retained ADL to do tasting ever since and to teach the subtle art to their employees. (It was thought for a while that blind people might make especially proficient tasters, and several groups of them came to ADL to be tried out, but it was regretfully concluded that they were no better nor worse than anybody else.)

No overt drinking is countenanced on ADL premises before 5:00 P.M., unless an important visitor is being treated to lunch in a secluded private dining room at Acorn Park (called, inevitably, the Oak Leaf Room), in which case sherry may be offered.* ADL's tasters are the exception to that stern rule, and they are sometimes the envy of their abstemious colleagues. Not only may — nay, must — the tasters do a good deal of sipping on their home turf (for instance, in the course of modifying Irish whiskey to make it more suitable for American throats), but they are sometimes dispatched on agreeable excursions. They have trained Pernod tasters on the Champs Élysées, rum tasters in the Bahamas, wine tasters in French vineyards. In Mexico once, they trained indigenes how properly to appraise a new beverage made from a distillate of cane sugar that a beer and brandy company had it in mind to market.

But mostly they taste beer: four times every working day, year in, year out. ADL tasters have been credited with being able to detect defects in bottled beer — the result, for example, of oxida-

---

* When Mimi Sheraton was the *New York Times*'s restaurant critic, she once expressed interest in ADL's food and flavor operations, and was invited to come by for lunch. Her hosts were afraid that she might end up writing something like, "How can these people charge for advice on food when theirs is so awful?" So they bypassed their own kitchens and had a caterer bring in a banquet: lobster mousse, duck and black mushroom salad, and more. Somewhat to ADL's relief, she never wrote about the lunch at all.

tion in the plastic liners of bottle crowns — even if the chemicals responsible for the trouble are present only in a tenth of a part per billion. No doubt to the delight of those they recruit, they sometimes call upon outsiders to supplement their sudsy research. In a 255-page promotional booklet that ADL once had printed up, titled "Qualifications for International Consulting," one entry among a couple of thousand went:

> An Arthur D. Little team consisting of staff from our Food and Flavor Laboratories and consumer marketers placed blind samples of three kinds of beer into some 40 college students' rooms or apartments. Beer was delivered to each student every other day for 12 weeks, and students kept diaries of the time, occasion, and numbers of beers consumed. A complex pattern of delivery was designed for the first weeks; consumer preference then determined the pattern. Statistical analyses pointed out some significant differences in beer flavor.

In-house beer tasting posed some problems for ADL. Most breweries, at least when it came to business operations, used to hold women in low esteem. Anheuser-Busch's two most important brew masters had male secretaries. Since 1949, one of ADL's principal tasters has been Anne Neilson, and when a beer company executive came to visit ADL, she had to be whisked out of his sight — as, indeed, was practically every other female around who couldn't be persuaded to grab hold of a mop. Neilson came straight to ADL from college and had to be trained herself. "All I knew about food when I landed here," she said, "was that I loved to eat."

ADL's current flock of full-time tasters numbers about a dozen, and they appraise not only beer but orange juice, cookies, and even dog food. They work in a small kitchen, which they call the Panel Room, whose starkness is alleviated solely by a poster depicting an Anheuser-Busch brewery wagon. Their kitchen has a dishwasher that is never used for anything except glassware. They had to order a new one a few years back; when they were trying to restructure Pernod, the old one got contaminated by traces of anethole, the ingredient that turns Pernod cloudy when water is added to it. The comments the tasters jot down on their score sheets would make a bartender blink: *astringent, medicinal, sour and bitter, rubber, dry wood, green wood, dry mouthfeel.* Another veteran taster, David Kendall, joined ADL in 1952, and over the ensuing thirty-odd years probably consumed more beer — nearly all of it in thoughtful sips — than many a long-shoreman downs in his wildest dreams.

ADL has earned a reputation for being reluctant to undertake any assignment unless it has reasonable hopes of being amply rewarded therefor; Kendall and Sjöström are rightly acclaimed in the company's annals for once having used their sensitive noses on a mission of mercy. A two-and-a-half-year-old boy had been admitted to Massachusetts General Hospital who had periodic acidosis and slipped into comas. His older sister had been similarly afflicted when she was his age, but she had got over whatever the ailment was. The children's mother said she could tell when an attack was impending because the children smelled peculiar just before they lapsed into unconsciousness. The doctors didn't know what to make of it. But one of them had heard about Ernest Crocker and the heirs to his expertise. The doctor called an acquaintance at ADL and said, "Can we borrow some of your noses?"

Sjöström and Kendall tossed aside some soybean sausage patties they'd been reflectively nibbling and rushed to the hospital. On entering the unconscious boy's room, they found five nurses and three doctors in it, along with an appalling assortment of pungent smells — lipstick and hair pomade and deodorant and tobacco and sweat and God only knew what all else. They shooed everybody out except the patient, flung open the windows, and waited for the air to clear. Then they began methodically sniffing the little boy, from head to toe and back on up. They knew all the normal human smells; what they were searching for was an alien odor. And soon they discerned it — a smell typical of that produced by an excess of short-chain fatty acids. With that crucial information to go on, the physicians were able to determine that the boy and his sister had both suffered from a genetic defect in their digestive processes, and a change in diet was all that was needed to solve that vexing problem.

This nonpaid performance was recorded in a 1967 issue of the *New England Journal of Medicine*, in an article titled "Isovaleric Acidemia":

> Olfaction is not usually considered to be a valued analytic tool in today's medicine. Yet it was two gentlemen from Cambridge (in particular from the Arthur D. Little Company) whose highly trained

olfactory sense astutely guided the medical investigators in their search for the offending metabolite. . . . Some future historian of medical progress should enjoy recording the wealth of experience and knowledge that solved the mystery of the children with the locker-room odor.

VI The Underlying Unity of It All

The laboratory is as much God's temple as the church.
— Dr. Arthur D. Little, 1924

*B*etween 1920 and 1940, ADL was mainly preoccupied with analytical testing; contract research, much of it in pharmaceuticals and petrochemicals; and product development, mostly in foods and flavors. The company was also trying to publicize itself, which was one reason for its having started to issue the *Industrial Bulletin* in January 1927. That journal was a monthly (except for one skipped midsummer issue), and by the mid-1940s it had a circulation of 32,000 and was available in four languages — English, French, Spanish, and German. In 1971, it changed its name to *The Bulletin*. It was only a bimonthly by 1976, and soon after that it drifted into limbo.

The *Industrial Bulletin* was dear to Dr. Little's heart, and when, soon after it began publication, ADL received a letter from a New York banker criticizing it for not dealing in more aggressive salesmanship, Little wouldn't let any subordinate reply but instead wrote back himself:

> After forty years of intimate contact with industry we think we can put out a bulletin dealing with industrial developments with somewhat the same authority that the bank deals with financial matters. We believe also that the type of people we want to reach are directly interested in early and authoritative news of developments that may affect businesses in which they are interested favorably or adversely.

Also as the scope of our business has enormously widened since many of our friends first knew us, we hope, by means of this Bulletin, to combat the impression remaining in some of their minds that we are still functioning chiefly as analysts or only along the comparatively narrow lines of our beginnings. We hope to be able, through the character of the articles in the Bulletin, to create a general and justified impression that we are broadly in contact with industry and that we view it from the coldly financial and managerial sides, as well as from the scientific and professional.

The *Industrial Bulletin* was not intended to be overtly self-promotional. The October 1931 issue, for instance, noted that "in the fifty-seven preceding numbers we have carefully refrained from references which might seem to exploit ourselves." (That was the year in which, although the *Industrial Bulletin* didn't brag about it, Dr. Little was awarded the coveted Perkin Medal of the Society of the Chemical Industry.) But the publication did manage to keep ADL's clients happy without being obvious about it. Thus, six years after The Lane Company had begun favoring ADL with its business, the *Industrial Bulletin* ran a story titled "Combatting the Clothes Moth," the conclusion of which went, "Recent improvements in the better grade of cedar chests, based on careful study of the physiology of the clothes moth, make them a dependable protection for well-cleaned goods."

Raymond Stevens was nominally the editor of the *Industrial Bulletin* at that time, but while Dr. Little was on the scene he went over every line of copy — all of it unsigned but much of it, like the clothes moth item, composed by Ernest Crocker — before it was released to the printer. Dr. Little liked to fill up odd spaces with quotations that he thought his readers might find applicable to their concerns: "There is nothing which can better deserve your patronage than the promotion of science" — George Washington; "Practice without science is a boat without a rudder" — Leonardo da Vinci; and "The way to end a depression is to fill it with foundations" — Arthur D. Little. (His successors at ADL continued that practice, citing such authorities as the Book of John, Mother Goose, and Bernard Baruch.)

The April 1928 issue, its publishers were proud to announce, was the first complete periodical (it was four pages long) ever to be transmitted by telephotograph. The text had been sent to New York and wired back to Boston. The *Industrial Bulletin*, which was not illustrated, acclaimed the potential of the innovative technology: It could be used for the expeditious circulation of X-rays, "Wanted" posters, and balance sheets. Moreover, "Mademoiselle attracts attention in a new bathing costume on the shore of the French Riviera. An American style scout dispatches a photograph by airplane to London and thence by telephotograph to California. That same afternoon Miss Los Angeles christens the re-created costume in the waters of the Pacific."

For the title of a speech Dr. Little had delivered at Philadelphia during the observance of the hundredth anniversary of the Franklin Institute, in September 1924, he chose "The Fifth Estate." Edmund Burke, he reminded his audience, had once pointed to the press gallery of the British Parliament — which harbored the first three estates in the form of Lords Spiritual, Lords Temporal, and Commoners — and had said, "There sits a Fourth Estate, more important far than all." Dr. Little wanted yet another genre added to the select group. "This 'Fifth Estate,' " he declared,

is composed of those having the simplicity to wonder, the ability to question, the power to generalize, the capacity to apply. It is, in short, the company of thinkers, workers, expounders, and practitioners upon which the world is absolutely dependent for the preservation and advancement of that organization we call "Science." . . . It is they who bring the power and the fruits of knowledge to the multitude who are content to go through life without thinking and without questioning, who accept fire and the hatching of an egg, the attraction of a feather by a bit of amber, and the stars in their courses as a fish accepts the ocean. . . . The "Fifth Estate" has recast civilization through its study and application of the great and fundamental facts of Nature and the laws of her operation. It has opened out the heavens to depths beyond imagination, weighed remote suns, and analyzed them by the light which left them before the dawn of history. It has moved the earth from the center of the universe to its proper place within the cosmos. It has read the sermons in the rocks, revealed man's place in nature, disclosed the stupendous complexity of simple things, and hinted at the underlying unity of it all.

It could readily be inferred that the speaker included Benjamin Franklin, Charles Darwin, Albert Einstein, Thomas Edison, and himself in the newly proclaimed estate, especially when, answering his own question — "What are the recompenses of the Fifth Estate?" — Little replied,

On the material side they have almost invariably been curiously inadequate and meager. It is incomparably more profitable to draw "The Gumps" for a comic supplement than to write "The Origin of Species." There is more money in chewing gum than in relativity. Lobsters and limousines are acquired far more rapidly by the skillful thrower of custard pies in a moving-picture studio than by the no less skillful demonstrator of the projection of electrons. The gate receipts of an international prize fight would support a university faculty for a year.

As was usual when he wrote something he considered felicitous, Dr. Little favored his business and social acquaintances with reprints of his remarks, and once again the response was gratifying. George Eastman praised "your facile and discerning pen." Herbert Hoover borrowed part of the speech for a speech of his own. A Czechoslovakian vice-consul in Mexico City had the address translated into a language he could comprehend, and was happy so to advise its author in a letter that was delivered (the world was smaller then) even though the envelope containing it bore merely Dr. Little's name and the words "Cambray, Mass., U.S.A."

The *New York Times*, an acknowledged spokesman of and for the Fourth Estate, editorially welcomed the emergence of the Fifth. Somebody promptly wrote the *Times* that the golf world had been called the Fifth Estate in a *Saturday Evening Post* article. Dr. Little, to whom slices and hooks had long been a heavy burden, retorted that he had got there first with the phrase and that in any event, "Good golfers are already replacing divots on so many fine estates that it seems ungenerous in your recent correspondent . . . to pre-empt for them also 'The Fifth Estate.' "

Dr. Little's close associates could sympathize with his rueful assessment in the speech of the comparative remuneration of professors and pugilists. His company's earnings were still pitifully small, totaling only $392,000 in 1930; the staff rarely numbered more than fifty during the twenties and thirties. It was not until 1944, nine years after Dr. Little's death, that the firm grossed as much as $1 million in a whole year. (In contrast, by 1984 Little's successors at ADL were disturbed when they didn't get at least $10 million worth of new business every month. There would be twenty-five hundred people on the payroll by that time.)

For a while in 1928, new vistas seemed to be looming far beyond the horizon. The Canadian Pacific excepted, ADL had done little work outside the United States. It did undertake a study in

1919 for a Bombay company on the possibilities of marketing paper made from bamboo, but that hadn't entailed any trips to India. And in 1922 Dr. Little had hoped, briefly and in vain, to become the agent in Germany for a Danish chemical company. Now, in October 1928, a letter arrived from the Amtorg Trading Company, which often represented the Soviet Union in foreign business transactions: Would ADL consider becoming its consulting chemical technologists for the entire petroleum industry there, and would it send somebody over to discuss details? Here finally, it seemed, was a chance for ADL to benefit from all the time and trouble and money it had lavished on the ill-fated Petroleum Chemical Corporation. Dr. Little deputized Thorne L. Wheeler, one of his principal executives at the time, to take on the assignment.

Wheeler, educated at Yale and M.I.T., was still another veteran of the First World War Chemical Warfare Service, where he had supervised the production of carbon and soda lime for use in gas masks. He was an oil chemist, and en route to Memorial Drive he had worked for a cotton oil company down South. At ADL he had, among other things, devoted himself to artificial silk, one of Dr. Little's celebrated interests, looking into the commercial possibilities of making it out of the corn protein zein.

Once he got the nod from Dr. Little, Wheeler set about preparing to leave for Russia. He got a passport. He had the necessary shots. It was wintertime, and he bought, at the company's expense, a fancy fur coat. But at the last minute it turned out the Russians didn't want *somebody* from Arthur D. Little, Inc. — they wanted Arthur D. Little himself. Since Dr. Little didn't feel up to making the long trip, the deal was off. Thorne Wheeler's fur coat was probably consigned to one of Ernest Crocker's cedar closets.

Dr. Little himself did go abroad once more: not to work but, in 1929, to attend a meeting in Manchester, England, of the august Society of the Chemical Industry, which had invested him with its presidency. While he was there, he received an honorary degree from the University of Manchester. He was sixty-six and was beginning to acquire the rewards of elder statesmanship. When Tufts University made him an honorary Doctor of Science in 1930, he was cited as a "Man of Vision, Prospector for Truth." The year after that, Columbia followed suit, and its president, Nicholas Murray Butler, hailed him as

Roger B. Griffin (1854–1893), cofounder and senior partner of Griffin & Little.

Arthur D. Little (1863–1935) at his desk in his Memorial Drive "research palace." (*Photo by George H. Davis*)

INDUSTRIAL BULLETIN

OF

Arthur D. Little, Inc.

Established 1886

January 1927 { CAMBRIDGE MASS. } *Number 1*

*A*NNOUNCEMENT *The purpose in issuing the Industrial Bulletins of Arthur D. Little, Inc., is to place before bankers, investors, and industrial executives early and authoritative information bearing upon the present status of industrial development or indicative of its probable trend. The Bulletins will be published monthly and mailed free upon request.*

NEW ENGLAND CONFERENCE

AT the second annual New England Conference, recently held in Hartford, Connecticut, research was stressed to such an extent as to dominate the proceedings.

The Council, which prepared the 1926 program, was probably as representative a body as ever convened in New England, and its findings are worthy of careful consideration by all those seriously interested in the prosperity of any section of the country.

The report of the Research Committee of the Council is specific in its recommendations. Copies may be obtained, at fifty cents each, from the New England Council, 201 Devonshire Street, Boston.

The Committee concludes that *"Above all things — New England needs research"* for the creation of new products, the utilization of wastes, the addition of new lines of manufacture, the extension of markets through the development of new uses for products — all to the end that the industrial base may be broadened and the slack time of its factories changed to running time.

CELL CONCRETE

A NEW and interesting type of structural material known as "Cell Concrete" has been developed in Sweden, where it has already found extensive application in side walls, roof and floor slabs, and as insulating material for cold-storage rooms, boilers and steam pipes. Cell Concrete is a light-weight concrete, made by mixing a tenacious foam into a mortar of cement, sand, and water, and is permeated with small, separate air bubbles. It is made in weights ranging from 18 to 75 pounds per cubic foot, the insulating capacity varying with the specific gravity, and becoming greater as the material is made lighter. In tests on heat transmission and fireproofness maintenance for an hour of a temperature of 1380° F. on one side of a slab 6 centimeters thick resulted in a temperature of only 130° F. at the other side of the slab.

ANTI-FREEZE COMPOUNDS

AS a consequence of open roads during the winter months, and the marked shift from open to closed cars, driving is no longer seasonal. This fact, coupled with the rapid increase in registration, has created a large market for radiator anti-freeze compounds.

Completely denatured alcohol has thus far almost monopolized this market, and the result is reflected in the increase in production from 42,033,824 gallons in 1921 to an estimated figure of 106,000,000 gallons for the fiscal year ending June 30, 1926.

Contrary, perhaps, to popular opinion, this demand for anti-freeze compounds is the largest single factor among those responsible for the growth of the industrial alcohol business during the last five years. The distribution of denatured alcohol for radiator use has risen in round numbers from 8,000,000 gallons in 1921 to 50,000,000 gallons for the 1925-26 season.

Further analysis of the situation shows, however, a healthy increase in the consumption by

Scientists and businessmen alike read Dr. Little's favorite journal, and the *Industrial Bulletin* was instrumental, in its day, in bridging the gap that had hitherto existed between them.

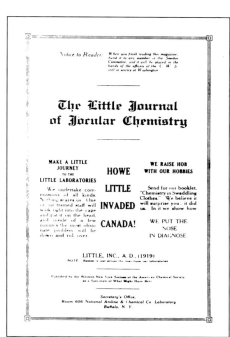

The Little Journal of Jocular Chemistry

Volume 1 Liter*   April 1, 1919*   Number **

Editor:
Dr. A. Distinct Little

Assistant Editors:
C. Horatius Herty, Epictetus Hendrick and H. Colorado Parmelee

Advisory Board:

C. Faraday Burgess	W. Dispersoid Bancroft
R. Freed Bacon	C. Clarence Baskerville
L. Hissutus Baekeland	M. Torique Bogert

Published at the expense of the Finance Committee.

The only publication of the American Chemical Society which has no back numbers.

No claims for non-receipt of this publication will be honored. "Missing from Files" is no alibi.

Special discount to imbeciles, criminals and minors.

Declared unmailable under Act of Congress of 1779.

All threats of revenge should be addressed to the Editor.

*Passages marked with an asterisk are jocular.

TABLE OF CONTENTS

A lighthearted approach to problem solving put out by the American Chemical Society on, few of its readers were surprised to perceive, April Fools' Day.

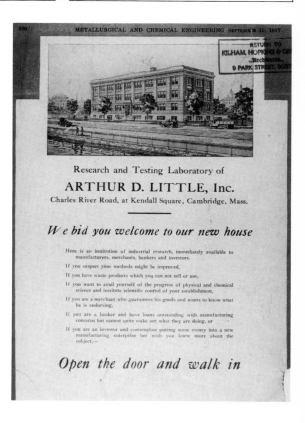

An early advertisement, in *Metallurgical and Chemical Engineering,* for the just-finished ADL building on the Charles River in Cambridge.

Dr. Little, dapper as usual, visiting one of his laboratories.

Ernest Crocker, the expert on flavor and taste who became known as the man with the million-dollar nose.

The 30 Memorial Drive building in Cambridge, headquarters for ADL from 1917 to 1954 and now a National Historic Site.

An aerial view of Acorn Park, in North Cambridge.

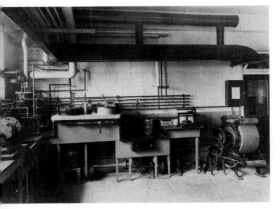

Then: At Memorial Drive, left and right, an experimental paper mill and a sample room for flavor storage.

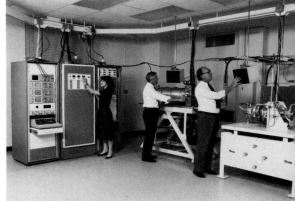

And now: At Acorn Park, left and right, research and development on molecular beam epitaxy and a rotary reciprocating refrigerator.

Two landmark events in ADL's long history occurred more than half a century apart. It was in 1921 that Dr. Little defied a long-standing and until then widely accepted cliché by making (above) a silk purse out of a sow's ear — or, at any rate, out of a number of sows' ears. And in 1977 his successors at ADL, not to be outdone, staged a contest to see who could best fly (below) a lead balloon.

A rare picture — taken in March 1977, on the occasion of General Gavin's retirement party — of four ADL chief executive officers en masse. Left to right, John F. Magee, James M. Gavin, Raymond Stevens, Earl P. Stevenson. (*Photo by Bruce Lederer*)

Howard O. McMahon, pictured alongside a liquid helium cryostat that he developed with his mentor and colleague, Samuel C. Collins.

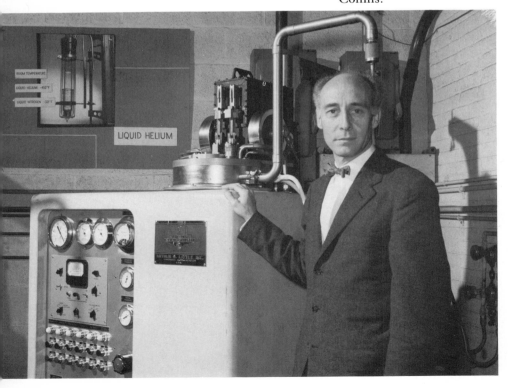

a captain in the organization and direction of research in the science of chemistry in all its manifold revelations; covering in his field of interest and influence almost every aspect of chemical engineering practice; fertile in invention, practical in application, and a genuine leader in the preservation and advancement of that organized body of knowledge which we know as science; one who, as even Sir Humphry Davy would admit, pursues science with true dignity.

For all that, Arthur D. Little, Inc., nearly went bankrupt in 1930. It staggered through largely because its executives — Earl Stevenson by now principal among them — could bring in as much as $150 a day by appearing as expert witnesses in patent litigations. The lifesaving bonanza was a $50,000 reward given to Stevenson by ADL's old client Lever Brothers after his testimony had manifestly helped that firm prevail in a patent infringement suit it had brought against Procter & Gamble. That bonus amounted to $5,000 more than ADL's net profit for 1931 — a year that ended with the distribution to all employees of a memorandum from Dr. Little ("Confidential and not to be discussed outside the organization") that went, in part:

> The major portion of our business comes from comparatively few clients, and we can only hope to retain them by serving them so well that they cannot afford to get along without us. It is, therefore, urgently necessary for each one of us to do everything within his or her power to increase the efficiency of our individual effort. . . . Small items of expense together make large totals, and no opportunity for savings should be overlooked. We have much expensive equipment, and its deterioration can be minimized by greater care in its use and in cleaning up after use.

At about the same time, ADL was advising its clients, established and prospective ones alike, that its admittedly small staff of fifty nevertheless had degrees from thirty-one universities, colleges, and technical schools — fifteen of these alone from M.I.T. One such notification said that ADL could be considered an "Industrial University" with a faculty "at your command as an effective adjunct to your own facilities."

More than two weeks before his seventieth birthday, Dr. Little celebrated the occasion, on November 28, 1933, at the height — or depth — of the Depression. Twenty-five colleagues and friends assembled at the Somerset Club in Boston to mark the event. The presidents of M.I.T. and Harvard, Karl T. Compton and James Bryant Conant, had to beg off because of previous engagements. Henry Powning was in England and, transatlantic travel being what it was in those days, couldn't get home in time. But Willis Whitney from General Electric was on hand, as were Harlow Shapley, the eminent astronomer; Everett Morss, the guest of honor's classmate at M.I.T. and an ADL director since 1920; and W. Cameron Forbes, once the governor-general of the Philippines and American ambassador to Japan, who'd been an ADL director since 1923 and whose fellow board members affectionately referred to him, as the Japanese had before them, as Uncle Cameron. Among the ADL luminaries on the invitation list were Roger Griffin, Earl Stevenson, Raymond Stevens, Thorne Wheeler, and the corporate secretary, Alexander Whiteside, who had sent out the invitations and played another consequential part: It was he who arranged with a bootlegger to provide the liquid refreshments. No women attended.

That otherwise barren year, the company's gross income skidded to $215,000, and instead of a slim profit, its books showed a net loss of $35,000. Retrenchment was the order of the day. Raymond Stevens was eager, like other regional salesmen, to join the local Rotary club, but the fifty-five dollars that would have entailed was judged an outlay that ADL could not afford. The company that by now had been in business for nearly half a century was gratified to be able to save seven dollars a month by using paper towels instead of cloth ones — except for six of the latter that were deemed essential for chemists' showers. There was another saving of $2.20 a month through reducing the use of floor wax by 50 percent. Everybody took a 10 percent cut in pay (15 percent for Dr. Little himself), which diminished the salary of Ernest Crocker, a pivotal employee by then for eleven years, from $5,400 to $4,860. At one point, Dr. Little was obliged to inform his staff — most of them still engaged in analytical chemistry, which from the outset had been the firm's forte, if not its raison d'être — that he could only pay them for two days' work a week. They didn't have much more than that anyway, but nearly all hands turned up every day notwithstanding. There was nothing else for them to do. The year 1934 was slightly better; the company's net loss was only $5,000. "What we need now," Dr. Little wrote in the *Industrial Bulletin*, "are more confidence men — men with enough confidence in the United States to start something themselves." A year later, in the hundredth issue of the *In-*

dustrial Bulletin, Dr. Little quoted a Parisian who, asked what he'd done during the Reign of Terror, had answered, "I survived." Dr. Little was glad to be able to observe that ADL had also survived — through Coolidge Prosperity, Hoover Depression, and Roosevelt Recovery. "Survival, in these times," he wrote, "is synonymous with success."*

During the seventieth birthday party at the Somerset, Dr. Little, called upon for a few pertinent remarks, had said, "Fortunately, the psalmist who fixed the span of life at three score years and ten had never met my family. The Littles generally lose their first youth at eighty and give up golf at ninety." His confidence in his own longevity was sorely misplaced, for his health was none too good. He had made no orderly plans for his own succession. No one was more concerned about that than his nephew Royal Little.

There had been a time when almost everybody connected with ADL had surmised, logically enough, that since the Arthur Littles were childless, the young man they had raised as a surrogate son would sooner or later take over from his uncle. But Royal had other ideas, some of them grandiose. (He once wrote a more or less autobiographical book titled *How to Lose $100,000,000 and Other Valuable Advice.*) On arriving in the East to live with his uncle, Royal had been enrolled in the Noble & Greenough School, in Dedham, and had entered Harvard in the fall of 1915. The boy had no money to fling around then; one of his letters to his uncle Arthur was a plea to have his allowance raised so he could buy enough coal to keep his dormitory room warm.

When the United States went to war, Royal joined the Harvard Infantry Regiment and then left the campus, along with many of his contemporaries, to attend officers training school in Plattsburgh, New York. He arrived in France as a first lieutenant in 1918 and was assigned to the 176th Infantry of the 42nd Division

* Dr. Little's very last contribution to the *Industrial Bulletin,* "Refrigerated Flies," appeared that June. It was a tribute to an unnamed but praiseworthily resourceful mushroom grower of his acquaintance. The mushroom man's piles of manure, used for fertilizer, attracted swarms of flies, which made him almost as much money as his mushrooms. These he captured, chilled, stuffed into milk cans, and sold to frog-raisers. Dr. Little compared him favorably with Professor Elihu Thomson, whom he also admired — in his case, for having destroyed male marsh mosquitoes by luring them into an electric furnace from which he had contrived to have emanate a hum of precisely the same pitch as that of a female mosquito.

(the famous Rainbow Division). Royal was an outstanding athlete all his life. In 1936, he helped organize the first ski club in Providence, where he eventually settled and became one of its most prominent and most philanthropic residents; he gave up skiing only at the age of eighty-one. He was adept at maneuvering white-water faltboats. He took up court tennis at sixty-two. (Royal's own longevity was phenomenal; he was still going strong, in 1985, at eighty-nine.) In France, he informed his Harvard classmates for one of their reunion reports, he had been the fastest man in his outfit with an entrenching tool.

In France, too, he may have saved the life of Douglas MacArthur. Lieutenant Little was in charge of a quiet sector of the front in the Argonne Forest. Quiet for the moment, that is; the American and German trenches were only a hundred yards apart, and the Rainbow Division was about to launch a drive across that narrow strip of no-man's-land. MacArthur, then a brigadier general and chief of staff of the division, turned up to inspect the lay of the land. He said he was going to walk out in front of the Allied trenches, in broad daylight, and look over the enemy fortifications. Lieutenant Little, whose assessment was that any such move would be suicidal, took a deep breath and told General MacArthur, "I'm in charge here, and I'm not going to let you go." MacArthur backed off.

Royal was discharged from the army in May 1919 and returned to Harvard to get his degree. He needed two-and-a-half more credits than he'd already earned. He got one in Conversational French when a well-disposed professor asked, *"Parlez-vous français?"* and he replied flawlessly, *"Mais oui, mon Professeur, je parle très bien."* He got another in Conversational German when a no less kindly faculty member asked *"Sprechen Sie deutsch?"* and he was able to respond, unfalteringly, *"Jawohl, Herr Professor."* The final half-credit Royal still needed came in a map-reading course. The accommodating professor in charge of that instructed him, with mock sternness, that the granting of a Harvard degree was nothing to be taken lightly, and that he would have to give a final examination. He pulled out a map of the northeastern United States. Little had been leading troops all over Europe and had spent more time with maps than with mattresses. The professor asked him to identify certain black lines that didn't meet. "Latitudes." And that black line from Boston to Providence? "The New Haven Railroad." And, finally, that big blue blotch? "The Atlantic Ocean." The professor beamed. "Young man," he said, "you just graduated from Harvard."

Then Dr. Little, who was still hopeful that Royal would join his firm, outlined what struck the older man as a reasonable preparatory agenda: two or three more years of graduate work at Harvard, next a Ph.D. in chemical engineering at M.I.T. Royal said he was sorry, but he had had all the formal education he could stomach. His uncle shrugged sportingly and said in that case, Royal should go into some business with a growth potential. Two of the most promising businesses he could think of were chemicals and synthetic fibers. Dr. Little arranged for interviews with both Bradley Dewey, who was on the ADL board, and another friend, Eliot Farley, who had founded the Lustron Company, which since 1914 had been producing cellulose acetate yarn — used in artificial silk — based on an old patent of Dr. Little's. Royal was fonder of Farley than of Dewey, but he announced that if he was going to end up in artificial silk, he ought to start off by learning about the real thing. So he apprenticed himself to Cheney Brothers, who wove genuine silk in South Manchester, Connecticut.

Royal did move on to Lustron, and after that company was taken over by the Celanese Corporation, Royal borrowed $10,000 and launched the Special Yarns Corporation in 1923. That evolved into the Atlantic Rayon Corporation and eventually into the Textron Corporation, which he nurtured into a conglomerate with fifty thousand employees at 150 plants and annual sales — of machine tools, flatware, golf carts, chain saws, and so forth — of more than $3 billion. Just before the Vietnam War, the first conflict in which helicopters figured significantly, he made an uncommonly shrewd investment: He bought the Bell Helicopter Company.

Royal Little — who, according to the *Wall Street Journal*, was "generally credited as the inventor of the modern conglomerate" — did not always endear himself as he prospered. He was hanged in effigy in Nashua, New Hampshire, after he bought and then closed down an old textile mill there. The general president of the Textile Workers Union of America told a Senate subcommittee in Washington that "Mr. Little is supposed to be a manufacturer, but on the record he is an undertaker. He buys mills in order to bury them."

Now and then, when contemplating an acquisition, Royal

would consult ADL, just like any other client — except that he had the advantage of also being a key member of its board. During one fierce New England blizzard, when only a few exceptionally hardy Bostonians kept appointments, those who made it to an ADL directors' meeting were surprised when a snow-covered Royal Little, then over seventy, hove into view. He had skied over.

On his way up the corporate heights, Royal Little had hit upon an effective way of impressing the proprietors of textile mills to whom he hoped to sell yarns. He took up flying, got his pilot's license, and began swooping down on customers, landing a light plane on fields alongside their mills. He gave up flying when he crashed on Long Island, in a fog, in 1939. ("I had got to the point where I started scaring myself making landings," he said years afterward.) By then, he had also become interested in parachutes. He was manufacturing them, and he saw no reason why he shouldn't try out his own product, all the more so when the Second World War began and parachutes assumed a much greater significance than ever before. In 1942, he persuaded John J. McCloy, then assistant secretary of war, to authorize him to make a jump at Fort Benning, Georgia, the army's main parachute-training installation. Royal betook himself there and presented a letter from McCloy to the commanding general, who said he didn't care what his superiors in Washington wanted: No military personnel over forty-two were allowed to jump, and he was damned if he was going to let a forty-six-year-old civilian set a preposterous precedent.

Royal persisted, and the general finally said he could jump — but only on condition that he first go through a grueling two-week training regime to which would-be paratroopers, many of them in their teens, were first subjected. One training exercise consisted of climbing to the top of a sixty-foot-high platform, attaching one's chute to a fixed hook, leaping off, falling free for about ten feet, being brought up with a jerk, and then sliding swiftly down a wire onto a pile of hay. Two youthful soldiers ascended to the platform with Royal, but they were apparently acrophobic. "I said to myself, 'Hell, let an old guy like me go first, maybe it'll encourage 'em,' " he later recalled. "But when I last saw them they were still clinging to the top of the platform. After that, there was nothing to it. I made my jump, qualified, and went home." He saw no reason ever to jump again.

In 1959, approaching his sixty-fourth birthday and feeling that it was time to try something new, Royal launched the Narragansett Capital Corporation, one of the nation's earliest venture capital firms. He turned that over to his only son in 1977, when he was eighty-one; with twenty-one boards and committees to serve on, Royal figured he had enough responsibilities to keep him occupied. He had already retired from the ADL board, in 1968, after forty-three years' service. When he was first a director, the going fee for attending board meetings was ten dollars a session. Royal believed that some corporations overcompensated their directors, and he was proud that in large part because of his insistence ADL was an exception to that practice. He did, though, agree to an arrangement whereby each director, after he retired from the board, was to receive a lifetime pension of twenty dollars multiplied by the number of months he'd served — $240 per year. In Royal's case, that added up to $10,320. By then, he didn't need it.

Royal had named his son Arthur Dehon Little. Young Arthur went to Stanford University, and on leaving college was not interested in going into any business — neither his father's nor his great-uncle's. He wanted to be a social worker. When, however, the executive director of one agency told him he'd never get far in that field without a couple of years of postgraduate study, he came around to his father and asked for a job at Narragansett Capital. That sideline company of Royal's, when its stock was repurchased in 1984, fetched $110 million.

Until the spring of that year, when Arthur took part in a series of seminars on corporate development that ADL sponsored, he never had much to do with the company whose name he bore. His parents had brought him around to ADL when he was eight, in November 1952, and an item in the *Little Acorn* reporting the visit said, "To many members of the staff to whom the name has now become a symbol, it was both pleasing and startling to see it personified in the guise of a schoolboy." The following year, when the company moved to its North Cambridge headquarters at Acorn Park, the nine-year-old boy was invited to dab some mortar on a cornerstone before it was set in place, and also to help Earl Stevenson's twin grandchildren plant an oak tree.

When Arthur was around seventeen, he earned one dollar from ADL by signing a document granting the company permission, if it ever felt so inclined, to drop the "Inc." from the corporate name and operate under his name. After he grew up, he had occasion once to call the company, and a kind of who's-on-first dialogue ensued: "I'm Arthur D. Little." "No, no, sir, *we're* Arthur D. Little, what's your name?" He felt better, not long afterward, when he heard about a Chicago businessman who'd told somebody, "I'm going to visit Arthur D. Little." The response had been, "Which one — the venture capitalist or the consulting company?" And the response to *that*, the latter-day Arthur was happy to learn, had been, "Of course, the venture capitalist. Is there a consulting company by that name, too?"

Late in 1934, Royal Little and the other members of the ADL board got to worrying seriously about what would happen to the company when Dr. Little was no longer at its helm. Royal urged his uncle to install Earl Stevenson, to all concerned the logical choice, as his successor. Dr. Little, who had started the firm when he was twenty-two, argued that Stevenson, at forty-one, was too young. "You'd better put him in while you're still around to see if he can handle the job," Royal told his uncle. Stevenson became president on January 24, 1935.

The staff was relieved, because Dr. Little had seemed markedly less inclined to handle the job properly himself. For instance, the company had been approached by the president of the Southern Railroad, who wanted Dr. Little to go to Washington, D.C., to discuss a potentially lucrative assignment. But Dr. Little had sent a neophyte employee, Harry B. Wissmann, in his stead.

Wissmann was an anomaly in what was still essentially an old Yankee firm closely affiliated with M.I.T. He was born in San Francisco, raised in Chicago, and ended up at the Harvard Business School, of which Dr. Little's old friend Wallace Donham was then the dean. Except for social occasions, though, ADL had had not much rapport with that school. That would radically change.* Over postprandial brandy and cigars, Dean Donham

* By 1966, Harvard Business School boasted a Royal Little Professorship of Business Administration, and six years earlier one of its professors, C. Roland Christensen, had joined the ADL Board of Directors, somewhat to his surprise. Royal Little and Earl Stevenson had walked into Christensen's office one day without knocking. They had decided to put a member of the Harvard Business School faculty on the ADL board, and the incumbent dean, Stanley F. Teele, had recommended Christensen. After having briefly introduced themselves and explained their mission, Royal had asked, "What do you have to offer as a director?" When Christensen had replied, honestly, "Damn little," Royal had said, "Okay, you're in," and had walked out. Christensen was still on the board in 1984, by which time John Magee, the incumbent chief executive officer of ADL, would say ad-

would now and then gently chide Dr. Little for having so many staff members from M.I.T. Why didn't his friend just for once take on somebody with some business training? he kept asking. Dr. Little said at last that if Donham could come up with someone who was also either a chemist or an engineer, he might be interested. Donham checked with a woman in his placement office. She found one such person in each category, but neither had an especially outstanding record. Then she happened to look into Harry Wissmann's folder. He had done very well scholastically and had at least taken an undergraduate chemistry course at the University of Illinois, where he was elected to Phi Beta Kappa. At Harvard Business School, moreover, he had written one paper, on the marketing of newly developed products, that had impressed the faculty members who'd read it. And so Wissmann was hired at $1,800 a year to be Dr. Little's personal assistant. For more than half a century afterward, he would figure importantly in ADL's ever more complex affairs.

When in 1935 an inexperienced Wissmann presented himself at the Southern Railroad offices in Washington, he was relieved to perceive that the assistant to the president of the railroad, to whom he was directed, was blind and couldn't tell how young he was. The first question the president's assistant addressed to him was, "Mr. Wissmann, what do you know about the South?" Aside from the outcome of the Civil War, which it seemed inappropriate to bring up, he didn't know much. But he had learned in his brief exposure to ADL that Dr. Little had a long-standing interest in the production of paper from southern timber, so he took a deep breath and began a lengthy and somewhat inventive discourse on that subject. He was soon interrupted. "Mr. Wissmann," the assistant said, "surely you don't believe that the future of the South is linked only to wood?" The Southern Railroad reacted much as the Soviet Union had a few years earlier: If it couldn't have Dr. Little in person, ADL wouldn't get the job.

Dr. Little was spending less and less time at his office. He pre-

---

miringly, "Chris has a sense of what this place is all about." When, later that year, Christensen was honored at Harvard by becoming its first business school faculty member ever to be given the lofty title of university professor, *Harvard* magazine, without identifying him as an ADL director, said that he was celebrated for conducting seminars which "lavish on pedagogy the same free-swinging, brainstorming energy that business consultants usually reserve for profit-and-loss statements."

ferred Palm Beach, Florida, in the wintertime, and Maine — his boyhood state — in summer. Moreover, his health was deteriorating, so much so that in the spring of 1935 he even had to forgo the fiftieth reunion, on Cape Cod, of his class at M.I.T. He was staying at a resort hotel in Northeast Harbor, Maine, on August 1, 1935, when he suddenly died — either of pneumonia (he had caught cold in New Hampshire, on his way north) or of a heart attack, or a combination of both. A *Boston Transcript* editorial said the next day, "The career that reached its end last night is truly one of the best which Boston has known." Raymond Stevens wrote his widow, "I feel that I have lost a member of my immediate family," and Roger Griffin, "I feel that for the second time in my life I have been left without a father."

At the next meeting of the ADL Board of Directors, on August 9, Mrs. Little was voted a stipend of $500 a month for the rest of her life — which wasn't long; she died fourteen months later — and Griffin was asked to prepare an appropriate memorial resolution for the company's records. "The word 'impossible' was not in his vocabulary" was part of that tribute. Royal Little, in an unpublished memoir, would later write that "we lost one of the greatest men of vision that this country ever produced."

Dr. Little naturally wanted the business he had created and nurtured for forty-nine years to outlast him. But he seemed not to be sure enough of his relatives or business associates to put it directly in their hands. In his will, after making provisions for his widow and a few others — Helen Sweeney, his secretary, received a $5,000 bequest — he declared of the company,

> Its beginnings go back to a time when there was no appreciation of the place of science in industry and for many years it was a pioneer in a hostile country. It has earned an enviable national and international reputation for the high quality of its professional service. It is, therefore, my strong desire to ensure the continuance of the corporation as an effective agency for benefiting industry through research and to provide for the maintenance of the standard of professional ethics which has governed its practice.

So he decreed that, once his wife had died, all of his holdings of Arthur D. Little, Inc., stock would go into a trust for the benefit of the one outside organization in which he had unswerving faith — the Massachusetts Institute of Technology.

VII Stills and Masks and Stencil Paper

Modern progress can no longer depend upon accidental discoveries. Each advance in industrial science must be studied, organized, and fought like a military campaign.
— Dr. Arthur D. Little [n.d.]

*I*n the last five years before Dr. Little's death, the average earnings of his company had come to a meager $6,230. And that figure could have been worse: From 1919 on, the deferred unpaid dividends on its preferred stock alone amounted to $340,000. In 1936, ADL was reorganized. The biggest asset on its books had been $306,000, for "good will." To make the company look better and stronger, on paper at least, that arbitrary figure was reduced to $72,898.04 — a result that may have been computed as much by divination as by science. All the outstanding stock was replaced by a new issue. These shares were put into a trust, and M.I.T. agreed not to dispose of its majority share of them for at least twenty years. The trustees were Royal Little, W. Cameron Forbes, and Horace Ford, the institute's treasurer — all three of them members of the ADL Board of Directors.

At the same time, President Stevenson reshuffled the operating chain of command. While Dr. Little had been in charge, and on the premises, everybody had had to report directly to him. Now, Stevenson established sections according to scientific disciplines and delegated more responsibility to his deputies than anyone had enjoyed theretofore. (Also, he set up a new entity, called Arthur D. Little Associates, for the purpose of giving key senior employees a share of the company's profits — assuming, that is, that there would be any to spread around.)

But what mattered even more, in Stevenson's view, was finding innovative kinds of work to supplement the routine analytical jobs that, despite occasional glamorous diversions, had always furnished the bulk of ADL's income. In 1936, fifty years after the company's founding, 20 percent of its work still consisted of four- or five-dollar laboratory jobs. The few contract research arrangements ADL had with big corporations like Owens-Illinois were more stimulating and, Stevenson hoped, would be more rewarding in the long run. Moreover, he and his senior associates may have been mindful of a statement — one which Dr. Little would have vehemently disputed — that had been made around the turn of the century by Sir William Crookes, the outspoken head of the British Association for the Advancement of Science (he had advanced it, for one thing, by discovering the element thallium): that no gentleman had ever made a living from analytical chemistry.

So the new administration took a deep breath and turned over all its analytical work to, ironically, a firm composed mainly of individuals (Hervey Skinner prominent among them) who'd left ADL after the so-called palace revolt of the early 1920s. Stevenson was pleased to be relieved of all that and to be able to turn his attention to appealing new chemical processes, even though they didn't always bring in money: the use of extractions of mangrove trees, for instance, as a toxic against barnacles and other annoying forms of marine life; the quick-freezing of fruits and vegetables with a sugar solution spray; and a pressurized blast furnace.

Julian Avery, a fraternity brother of Raymond Stevens's at M.I.T., had been working in the patent department of Union Carbide. Avery had read in a publication of the U.S. Bureau of Mines that three hundred to four hundred pounds of coke were wasted in the production of every ton of pig iron. Avery postulated that operating a blast furnace at slightly elevated pressure would decrease coke consumption and increase iron output. He obtained a patent on the process in 1938, but Union Carbide was not interested. So he approached Stevens and ended up by assigning the patent to ADL. During the Second World War a shortage of pig iron was encountered, and the War Metallurgy Committee studied means of alleviating the problem. The Avery invention was selected for trial, and a blast furnace at a Republic Steel defense plant in Cleveland was converted to high-pressure operation in 1944. The process showed promising results for about two weeks and then ran into mechanical problems. After the war, Earl Stevenson and Bruce S. Old, recently hired as ADL's first metallurgist, approached Republic and found its key people willing to experiment further, since improvements on Avery's process had been suggested.

A team from ADL, led by Old, worked at Republic's Cleveland and Youngstown plants in 1946 and 1947 in converting two furnaces and in monitoring their operation around the clock. Iron production increased between 10 and 20 percent, and coke rates decreased about 13 percent. Steel producers from all over the world came to marvel at the novelty, but few seemed eager to invest in it right away. The reason soon became clear: While a few moved rapidly to take licenses, the rest of the world waited for the basic patent to expire in 1955. As would frequently be the case, ADL was not unwilling to let a client take credit for what its own staff had achieved. Thus the ADL team members ghostwrote a paper to be delivered at the annual meeting of the American Iron and Steel Institute by the chairman of the Republic Steel Blast Furnace Committee. When the paper won a gold medal, he was allowed to take full credit for it.

In 1938, while Avery and his co-workers were perfecting their device, there was another heartening development. The New York investment banking house of Eberstadt & Company wanted to launch a Chemical Fund, whose assets were to consist exclusively of shares of chemical companies. But Ferdinand Eberstadt didn't think he or his staff had the expertise to judge which of the many companies around were the most promising. ADL was invited to serve as the new fund's technical consultant, and it functioned as such for more than thirty years. Leroy Marek, a chemical engineer who had many high-level responsibilities at ADL (for a while, he was in charge of most personnel and administrative matters), was the principal liaison with the Chemical Fund and became one of its directors. For a long time, the fund would not invest in any company until ADL — in effect, Marek — had looked into it and pronounced it acceptable.

Another important person in the era following Dr. Little's death was a Harvard Ph.D. in chemical engineering, Robert V. Kleinschmidt. He had been at ADL since 1926, when Dr. Little and Stevenson thought it would be useful to add to their staff someone familiar with thermodynamics. They had been told that Kleinschmidt, then an instructor at the Harvard Engineering School, had the right qualifications. But Little — with impeccable gentlemanliness that Sir William Crookes could not have faulted — didn't approve of trying to raid university faculties, and before even approaching Kleinschmidt had gone around to see A. Lawrence Lowell, the incumbent Harvard president, to obtain his consent. The only problem was that, after Kleinschmidt joined ADL, there wasn't enough thermodynamical work to keep him busy, and so he had left and taken a job with Du Pont. But he hadn't been happy there, and after a couple of years asked to return to ADL.

Not long afterward, Raymond Stevens was talking one day with some officers in the U.S. Navy, and they asked him, "What would be the best way to obtain potable water if you were on a tropical island with no fresh water supply and you could bring in only a minimum amount of engine fuel?" Stevens, who knew that Kleinschmidt had written his dissertation on heat pumps, put the question to him. Kleinschmidt mulled it over and reported back that he thought he could devise a compression still which would produce 175 pounds of fresh water at the expenditure of but a single pound of fuel — an efficiency ratio three times better than that of any existing machine.

But that was in 1936, and the peacetime navy, however interested it might be in outside research, seemed to have no funds to subsidize any of it. So Earl Stevenson took a chance and told Kleinschmidt that the company would underwrite the construction of a demonstration still in a second-floor corridor at Memorial Drive. Not even there, though, was enthusiasm wholehearted. As Raymond Stevens would later reminisce,

> Whereas there was general acceptance of the significance of this development if it were successful, there was equally general doubt and skepticism, approaching the sarcastic, about the possibility of achieving anything approaching the claims indicated. . . . The skepticism existed even within the navy and within members of the engineering staff of ADL, Inc., outside the group immediately concerned who had faith in Dr. Kleinschmidt's ability.

Nothing much happened until 1938, when the navy invited anyone who happened to have a still to demonstrate it competitively at Virginia Beach, Virginia. Kleinschmidt's prototype was dismantled, crated, and taken to the scene, where it outperformed its rivals so markedly that the navy's interest was finally aroused. ADL was commissioned to build a modest-sized one. When that proved satisfactory, two much larger ones — with capacities of one thousand and five thousand gallons, respectively — were ordered by the Marine Corps, which was judged likely to have some of its troops end up on the sort of arid islands that had been mentioned to Stevens at the outset.

ADL was still a relatively small concern, with only eighty-five employees overall, and had nowhere near the manpower nor the facilities to manufacture these stills, so it entered into an agreement with E. B. Badger & Sons to turn them out. Soon, when the chances of America's going to war loomed larger and larger, more orders came in. The first Kleinschmidt stills were installed on American submarines in the spring and summer of 1941, and more of them were on Pearl Harbor wharves, waiting to be placed aboard ships, when the Japanese attacked.

By 1941, Kleinschmidt, a naval reserve officer, had been called up for active duty. M.I.T. recommended to ADL that it replace him with Allen Latham, Jr., a mechanical engineer who had worked for Westinghouse, Du Pont, and, most recently, Polaroid. Latham took over the supervision of the Kleinschmidt stills and ran the program throughout the Second World War. (At one point, during hostilities, it was only with considerable difficulty that Latham was able to procure a much-needed lathe for further developmental work on the process. When the lathe finally materialized, the joy at ADL's usually fairly staid laboratories was so boundless that a bottle of champagne was also procured and broken over it.)

By the war's end, there were enough units in service — mostly on submarines and with Marine Corps task forces — to provide ten million gallons of fresh water a day, enough to satisfy the minimum daily needs of a million men. In the case of the submarines, not only was the availability of more fresh water than ever a morale booster, but because it could be used to keep the vessels' batteries functioning as well as for drinking and washing, it enabled those ships to extend their cruising time before having to return to port from forty-five to sixty days. And, inasmuch as it usually took fifteen days for them to get to an area of operations and back, their effectiveness was actually doubled: from fifteen days to thirty.

There were even hand-cranked stills specially designed for life rafts. Latham tested those at a fatigue laboratory at Harvard, and although the trial wasn't as rewarding as he'd hoped — he estimated that he barely managed to pump more water than he lost in sweat — he was pleased enough to take one by train to Washington (sharing an upper berth with it) and exhibit it there to Kleinschmidt, who'd been assigned to the Bureau of Ships. The inventor didn't want to have water, salty or fresh, slopped over his office floor, so the demonstration was adjourned to a men's room, to the astonishment of a couple of admirals who wandered in while it was under way.

In an article that Kleinschmidt wrote in October 1945, he said, perhaps a trifle optimistically, "Compression distillation is in its infancy. It has gone to war and made good. The same principles and techniques will be converted to peaceful use and will make pure water available practically anywhere on earth and for any purpose where real advantages would result from its use." That same month's issue of the *Marine Corps Gazette* contained another article, which recounted that by the tenth day after the marines landed on Iwo Jima, the Japanese there were "desperate for water" and that they "had nothing comparable to our mobile waterworks." There had been nothing comparable, either, in the history of ADL. Between 1941 and 1952, its share of the proceeds from Kleinschmidt stills amounted to $1,271,218.

Even before Pearl Harbor, Earl Stevenson had taken a leave of absence from his ADL duties to join the chemical engineering division of the National Defense Research Committee. He turned over ADL's management, temporarily, to a quadrumvirate: Raymond Stevens, Thorne Wheeler, Howard Billings, and Henry Powning.

Among Stevenson's wartime responsibilities was to furnish oxygen masks for pilots of high-altitude unpressurized planes; along the way, he recruited an anthropologist to design a mask that would snugly fit nearly every shape of face. Stevenson was also much involved in the development of incendiary bombs — specifically the M-69, which was so devastatingly used in a March 1945 air raid on Tokyo, when about 97,000 Japanese were killed, another 125,000 injured, and thousands of fires ignited all at once — some of them in fire stations. "It certainly is very gratifying to learn that all the time and energy which you people put into the old M-69 bomb paid off in the end," James Bryant Conant wrote to Stevenson in January 1946. Conant added parenthetically, "I am not one of those people who have an uneasy conscience about the strategic bombing of the Japanese!"

Stevenson kept in close touch with his colleagues back in Cambridge. Indeed, of ninety-five war-connected assignments that ADL undertook before V-J Day, twenty-one were for the National Defense Research Committee. One of the less destructive of these was the production of smoke clouds both for air raid protection and troop concealment. ADL technicians perfected an oil-based liquid with a vile odor that American troops in Europe, it was hoped, could spray at the enemy, and "make the person on which it was squirted," Raymond Stevens later reported, "a marked individual, highly unacceptable to his associates, immediately and for a matter of hours." (Johnny Sjöström worked on that project; when he went home at the end of a day in the laboratory, he was sometimes highly unacceptable to his family.) Whether the stuff was ever used in combat is moot; no one knows for sure, either, whether GIs ever got to squirt an even more repulsive variation that ADL devised for the war in the Pacific, a substance that Stevens described as "stronger and even fouler and more fecal in odor."

More benignly, ADL worked on laminated plastic body armor, and powdered milk and powdered eggs. It also composed a salvage operations instruction manual for the navy, in the course of which Wallace Murray once was sent underwater to examine the condition of the sunken ocean liner *Normandie*. ADLers even tried, without much success, to find a surefire cure for athlete's foot.

In one ADL laboratory or another, scientists helped refine a napalm fuel thickener. That job was supervised by Billings, who seemed the right person for it because he had once, in more peaceful times, contrived to thicken ink for A. B. Dick stencils. And when the Dick company, which before the war had imported most of its stencil paper from Japan, had that source blocked, ADL came to its rescue by prevailing on another long-time client, the Manning Paper Company, to fill the breach.

"Think what effect the lack of stencil paper would have had on the paper work avalanche needed to win the war!" an anonymous ADL historian burbled after hostilities ceased. Similarly, when Bristol-Myers no longer had ready access to the glycerine and some essential oils that had gone into its Ipana toothpaste, ADL's food and flavor people created a wartime Ipana.

It occurred to someone high in U.S. Army circles that inasmuch as baseballs were the objects that most young American men knew best how to throw, why not redesign hand grenades in that familiar configuration? ADLers rose to that challenge, though the war ended before their weapons could be tested in battle.* There was much work in the laboratories, too, on protective ointments and on wound-healing compounds.

Early in 1945, when an invasion of Japan still seemed probable and it was feared that Japanese soldiers with explosives strapped to their bodies might hurl themselves in kamikaze fashion upon American tanks, ADL came up with a device — called the Skink — by means of which sheets of flame fifteen yards long could be spurted from each of a tank's four corners. Like all new weapons, the Skink had to be tested. That was done — as was the testing of the wound-healing compounds — on pigs, whose skin more closely approximates that of human beings than does any other animal's.

ADLers had acquired a good deal of expertise with pigs; they had been using them for more than a decade in connection with Bristol-Myers hair and skin products. (Over the years, ADL research laboratories have also been visited, often sacrificially, by bats, beagles, frogs, rabbits, squirrels, hamsters, guinea pigs, fish, birds, monkeys, sheep, chipmunks, rats, and, at one time, forty thousand mice. The presence of these last must have had a profound effect on a couple of pet cats simultaneously in residence, who, though both were females, had been named Arthur D. and Little Inc.) During the war, twelve hundred pigs gave up their lives at ADL to help the Allied cause, some of them emplaced in sixteen-foot-high towers at the Boston Fire Fighters' School at a

---

* Once Ben Fogler, Jr., had to take a few of the newfangled grenades, then classified top secret, on a night train to Chicago. He cached them under a seat that, before he could retrieve them, was converted into a young woman's berth. Fogler didn't get much sleep: He didn't dare invade the lady's privacy, and he wasn't allowed to tell anybody what was in his luggage.

time when ADL was trying to figure out a way of protecting submarine conning towers from suicidal plane attacks.

Some of ADL's most imaginative wartime work was done on behalf of the Office of Strategic Services: a soluble paper that in emergencies could quickly be chewed and swallowed; a solution called Dog Drag, which when applied to shoes could throw bloodhounds off the track; and the Hedy, a panic-creating noisemaker (a fireworks company collaborated on that one) which simulated an artillery barrage and whose cover supposedly allowed friendly troops to advance with impunity while the enemy cowered in their bunkers. Before giving up the project as impracticable, ADL also spent some time trying to fabricate huge luminous animals that could be floated over Japanese lines at night for the purpose of frightening the troops encamped there and, conceivably, causing them to flee to the rear.

In 1941, one of the myriad concerns of Dr. Vannevar Bush, the head of the National Defense Research Committee, was how to make oxygen conveniently available to men on the battlefield, on shipboard, and in the air — for welding *and* breathing. Before the war, just about the only way to transport oxygen had been in 200-pound steel containers. Not only were these heavy, but steel was in short supply. Dr. Bush wanted a small container that two men could carry. Stevenson turned to two men he knew were eminently qualified to tackle the problem and who had a prototype ready for him in a few months — a gasoline-powered unit, weighing only 150 pounds, that compressed air and then cooled it and liquefied it, meanwhile isolating its oxygen content. One of the first places it proved useful was on the North African desert.

The two problem solvers were Samuel C. Collins and Howard McMahon. Collins, who died at the age of eighty-six in 1984, had joined the M.I.T. faculty in 1930 as a professor of mechanical engineering. McMahon had come to ADL in 1941, soon after getting his Ph.D. from M.I.T. in physics and chemistry. Eventually — from 1964 to 1972 — he would become the company president; and he would also be one of the very few Americans, all of them ADLers, to have their names enshrined on the moon.*

* Among the many chores ADL has performed for NASA over the years was the design and manufacture of laser retroreflectors. Small arrays of these stationary mirrorlike de-

Born in Canada, McMahon had gone to the University of British Columbia, and while still a student there was granted a patent for the invention of a bubbling Christmas tree candle, the first of thirteen patents he would accumulate. (A much more consequential patent was one he later acquired for inventing a so-called blood bomb — an eighteen-inch-long cylinder, five inches in diameter, for the preservation of blood and other biological materials in plastic encased in freezing water.) At M.I.T., Professor Collins had been McMahon's faculty mentor, and the two of them were close professional and social associates ever afterward. Between 1942 and 1944, they spent much of their time at Wright Field, in Dayton, Ohio, working on lightweight oxygen generators to be carried on B-29 bombers.

After the war, Earl Stevenson urged Collins and McMahon — the former back at M.I.T., the latter down Memorial Drive at ADL — to collaborate on a contrivance that would liquefy helium more expeditiously than any process previously devised. Collins, who would become known as the father of cryogenics for his work with temperatures down to minus 456 degrees Fahrenheit — only 3.67 degrees above absolute zero — built a prototypical helium liquefier at the university, and McMahon tinkered with and refined it at ADL. McMahon was the sort of absent-minded scientist who, when engrossed in his work, often becomes oblivious of time and everything else. He was laboring away at Memorial Drive at 4:00 one morning, far from a telephone, when he heard a commotion outside the building's locked door. It was the Cambridge police, rapping for admittance. "Your name McMahon?" they asked when he appeared. "Your wife's been trying to reach you. She's having a baby."*

---

vices were placed on the moon to reflect pulses of light from lasers on the earth back along their paths. By measuring the round-trip transit times of the pulses, scientists could precisely establish earth-moon distances and motions. There have been three arrays of retroreflectors on the moon since the manned lunar landings of the late 1960s. On the inside of the housings in which the individual reflecting elements are mounted, one of the ADLers who worked on them, Edward Boudreau, engraved the names of McMahon and a few colleagues.

* McMahon's acumen was vividly demonstrated by a memorandum he wrote just a few hours after the bombing of Hiroshima: "Many statements have appeared in the press describing the severity of the explosion of an 'atomic bomb.' Most of these are probably understatements because they refer only to the explosive effects of the thermal energy. The induced radioactivity produced in neighboring substances may well be an important factor in warfare."

The collaboration on a helium liquefier led to a host of other novel developments in cryogenic technology; and the Collins helium cryostat, as the first machine became known, would ultimately be installed in more than two hundred research laboratories across the globe. ADL itself built and sold more than fifty of them, for $25,000 apiece. A thumping stamp of approval for the pioneering efforts of Collins and McMahon came in 1979, when the Cryogenic Engineering Society of America conferred on McMahon its highest honor — the Samuel C. Collins Award.

In December 1951, ADL metallurgist Bruce Old received a phone call from the Atomic Energy Commission, with which he had been closely associated a few years earlier. He and a colleague, Roger S. Warner — a onetime chief engineer for the AEC — were asked to fly at once to Los Alamos, New Mexico, for an urgent consultation. A Virginian educated at the University of North Carolina and later, like so many other ADLers, at M.I.T., Old had worked for Bethlehem Steel before the war. While assigned to the office of the secretary of the navy during the war, he had become acquainted with Stevenson, who thought ADL should have an in-house metallurgist and offered Old that post. One of Old's many accomplishments at ADL was his invention of the jet tapper, a device for tapping open-hearth furnaces in steel mills by using an explosive to punch holes in them by remote control, instead of having men do that job — at considerable risk of exposure to molten metal — with sledges and wedges. The shape of the jet charge was exactly like that of an ice cream cone, and Old had got the idea for it while watching a son of his eat one. That invention turned out to be worth about $300,000 to ADL.

At Los Alamos, Old and Warner were informed that the United States was planning to explode a hydrogen bomb the following November. The AEC needed some tank trucks, called dewars (after a Scottish scientist who'd made contraptions for storing volatile liquids), and it wanted ADL to design, manufacture, field test, and operate them, for a consideration of $1.5 million. ADL had already teamed up with the Carrier Corporation of Syracuse, New York, on an AEC-subsidized project to make extremely high-efficiency filters that could screen out 99 percent of the particulate matter in the atmosphere. Now, early in 1952,

ADL and Carrier formed a new subsidiary called the Cambridge Corporation. Old was its president, Warner its vice-president.

The Cambridge Corporation rented a garage in Somerville, Massachusetts, next door to Cambridge, and for nine months had as many as four hundred people there, working in shifts around the clock, seven days a week, to get the dewars ready. Old, who has written four books on tennis, scarcely had time to swing a racquet. The dewars were very special vehicles, with aluminum-foil-lined bodies twice as thick as those of ordinary trucks.* There was only one hitch. The government was in a hurry to get the work done but annoyingly dilatory about paying for it. Although ADL knew it would get reimbursed sooner or later, it had little cash on hand, and to meet its suddenly swollen payroll it was obliged to sell its building to Harvard and to lease it back. (M.I.T., which already owned most of the company, couldn't buy it, for that would have constituted a conflict of interest.)

The finished dewars were driven out to Boulder, Colorado, where the National Bureau of Standards was producing hydrogen that ADL was supposed to liquefy. That done, the tank trucks were loaded up and very gingerly driven, with Howard McMahon aboard one vehicle, to Los Alamos for further testing before they were shipped out into the Pacific Ocean. McMahon and Warner were among some thirty ADLers engaged in one phase or another of the H-bomb work who went to Eniwetok, in the Marshall Islands, to help prepare for and witness the historic blast. McMahon was aboard a ship twenty miles from the epicenter, and when the sound waves created by the detonation reached him it felt, he would later say, like being hit in the belly with a two-by-four. Old was at J. Robert Oppenheimer's home in Princeton, New Jersey, when Oppenheimer received a cablegram relating the dimensions of the effect of the test. "The yield was so much higher than any of us had imagined," Old said afterward, "that we all almost fainted."

---

* The storage and transport of liquefied, highly inflammable gases is a worrisome business. In the 1930s, an entire neighborhood of Cleveland had been devastated when a tank of liquid methane broke apart. A generation after that, ADL engineers were able to help in the construction of tanks aboard an oceangoing vessel, the SS *Methane Pioneer*, which successfully crossed the Atlantic with a cargo of liquid methane.

VIII Analyzing Business Operations

Science is now advancing at a rate so rapid and with results of such far-reaching influence that no industry can hope to ignore research and live.

— Dr. Arthur D. Little [n.d.]

During the war, the Allied cause had been much aided by the emergence of operations research, a then-novel concept relating to the analysis of administrative and managerial options by means of the physical sciences. According to one peacetime definition, this new field was "the application of scientific and mathematical techniques to the analysis of a variety of business operations."

When the U.S. Eighth and Fifteenth Air Forces set up bases in Europe, for instance, and wondered what mix of high-explosive and incendiary bombs could most effectively be carried on each airplane, a half-dozen Americans — notable among them the ADL physical chemist Gilbert W. King — were dispatched to England at the urging of Earl Stevenson to study and analyze the performances of bombers of the Royal Air Force. Similarly, the U.S. Navy's efforts to search for and destroy German U-boats in the Atlantic were much enhanced by scientists (including the physical chemist George E. Kimball) who changed the navy's traditional methods of waging that particular kind of warfare. Previously, when an enemy submarine had been seen at point x at time y, it had been the practice to steam out toward that spot and start searching from there, even though that was probably the last place on earth, or at sea, the vessel was still likely to be found.

The scientists (with the help of some actuaries from the insurance business) persuaded the navy to substitute, based on probabilities, an expanding spiral of search; and whereas the navy had previously been wasting thousands of tons of depth charges in fruitless sorties, now there was a saving in explosives and a dramatic rise in the kill rate of enemy submarines.

Raymond Stevens, abetted by Gilbert King, believed there was a place for operations research in helping to solve the peacetime problems of ADL's clients. Also, being a salesman, Stevens saw operations research as a way of attracting new business to the company, which sorely needed it. One-fourth of ADL's commissions were coming its way through the good offices of M.I.T. (for example, a $65,000 job to advise the Army Service Forces how best to store a huge cache of surplus artillery matériel), and there were now 156 ADLers to be kept occupied. Stevens persuaded Stevenson to get ADL into operations research and to support that work, even if at a loss, for at least three years.

The first client to express interest was Sears, Roebuck. That company had asked ADL to advise it on an apparently highly profitable new method for making antifreeze. ADL had done some careful investigating, discovered that the process was a fraud, and saved Sears, Roebuck $1 million that it had been ready to invest. The big mail-order house was understandably grateful, and — largely on the initiative of one of its vice-presidents, Theodore V. Hauser, an M.I.T. alumnus and a friend of Stevens's — committed $10,000 toward some preliminary operations research studies aimed at making the distribution of its catalogues more efficient. Stevens invited Gilbert King to work on the project, and King brought in Kimball — at first part-time, so he could continue teaching at Columbia, and later full-time. King had already become interested in the use of computers to help science; one of his contributions to the company was to introduce programmed IBM punch cards. Kimball, along with Philip Morse of the M.I.T. faculty, would write the first textbook on operations research.

Harry Wissmann was put in charge of the new Operations Research Section. He needed a bright young assistant with a background in mathematics and economics, and he turned to the placement office of the Harvard Business School for help. He was given the name of John Magee, a twenty-three-year-old graduate of the business school who, as it happened, had never heard of either operations research or Arthur D. Little, Inc. Magee was offered a job, and accepted, and he not only ended up as president of ADL but president also of the Operations Research Society of America, which in 1978 conferred on him its highest honor — called, appropriately, the George E. Kimball Award.

Like Dr. Little, Magee grew up in Maine. In 1943, when he was sixteen and a high school junior, his father (a regional official with the Federal Housing Administration, an insurance expert, and a part-time professor of economics at the University of Maine) suggested he try to go to college early and get in a year before he was drafted. Logically enough, Maine was his first choice, but he was turned down because of his youthfulness. Bowdoin College was more receptive, and Magee went there until the navy got him and made him a Japanese language expert. After V-J Day, he finished up at Bowdoin, went to the Harvard Business School, and then briefly attended the University of Maine, which considered him old enough at last even to teach. He came finally to Columbia, for a Ph.D. in mathematical statistics. When Magee asked a professor there what career opportunities existed for a specialist in that field, his mentor replied, after a reflective pause, "Well, you can always teach mathematical statistics."

By now it was 1949, and Magee was getting married and needed a job. He was happy to be offered one at Johns-Manville, in New Jersey.* Magee spent a year there as a financial analyst in the building products division. (His hobby then and afterward was building furniture. His wife and he occupied an uncarpeted, upstairs apartment in Somerville. Their neighbors were not especially cordial, because all day long Mrs. Magee would walk on their bare floor in clicking heels, and next he would come home in the evening and start pounding away with hammer and nails.) When Harry Wissmann phoned to discuss a job at ADL, Magee was dubious but interested enough to go to Cambridge and hear more about the proposition. Raymond Stevens warned him that the operations research project was experimental, and that he might be unemployed at the end of a year. But when Magee's father-in-law, a metallurgical engineer, said he thought the risk was

* Years later, when Paul Littlefield was ADL's chief financial officer, Magee was astonished to learn that it was Littlefield's father, Joseph — at the time, the Johns-Manville controller for financial analysis — who had given Magee his start in business.

well worth taking — an increase in salary of $1,000 a year was one compelling reason — he moved to Arthur D. Little early in 1950.

Tall, gangling, slope-shouldered, soft-voiced, Magee was at first regarded by his new colleagues as something of an unsophisticated maverick: a small-town boy thrust into a big cosmopolitan environment. By the time he had risen to the summit of the ADL hierarchy, his self-assurance was unexceptionable. It was his wont to wander into the company cafeteria at lunchtime and sit at any table with a vacant chair. When President Magee one day joined a group of much lower level functionaries that included a cigarette smoker inadvertently seated at a table with a No Smoking sign on it, the chief executive officer, aware of his companion's craving, reached over and moved the sign out of sight. Another member of the assemblage muttered something about the prerogatives of power. "No, anyone else here could have done it," Magee replied. "It's not power. It's what everybody at ADL exhibits — lack of respect for authority."

The July-August 1953 issue of the *Harvard Business Review* contained what was for many business executives in search of excellence a watershed article. It was titled "Operations Research for Management." Its co-authors were John Magee and Cyril C. Herrmann, who had a doctorate from the Harvard Business School and was an assistant professor at the M.I.T. School of Management. Herrmann moved over to ADL the following year and stayed with the firm — representing it in, among other remote areas, Iraq, Egypt, Honduras, the Philippines, and San Francisco — until he started his own consulting company in 1982.

The *Review* article brought in new clients. Neil McElroy, then the president of Procter & Gamble — which had apparently forgiven ADL for helping it lose to Lever Brothers in their litigation twenty-three years previous — invited Herrmann and Magee to dine with him in Boston at the Ritz. A testimonial appraisal of operations research titled "How to Invent a Profession" was contributed to the *Journal of Industrial Engineering* by Alvin Brown, vice-president of finance at Johns-Manville. Magee, who if he had not invented operations research had indisputably popularized it, felt highly complimented because it was the first known notice his former boss had ever taken of him. Johns-Manville became an operations research client. So did General Electric, Westinghouse, Continental Can, and Johnson & Johnson. (Johnson & Johnson executives who received a couple of traveling salesmen from Memorial Drive were impressed with their devotion to duty when the ADLers insisted, to their hosts' astonishment, that they would prefer to work straight through a scheduled coffee break.) Some fifteen latter-day ADL activities, in such areas as Telecommunications, Information Systems, and Financial Industries, can all be traced back, in one way or another, to the birth of Operations Research.

Magee — one of whose favorite quotations is Eric Sevareid's "Most problems are caused by solutions" — was one of quite a few young people hired in the postwar years who, unlike their colleagues longer on the scene, were not primarily physical scientists. Rather, they were specialists in economics, management, organization, or planning. Their proliferation evidently even surprised their superiors. Around the mid-fifties, for example, Earl Stevenson asked Philip Donham, the son of the business school dean and himself a veteran of a decade's consulting at Booz, Allen, to study ADL's own internal organization. Stevenson wanted to know if ADL should switch its emphasis from technological research to management consulting. Donham had no compunctions about telling people what they did not expect to hear. As an ADL staff member later on, he twice advised corporation presidents that the best solution for their companies' problems would be to fire themselves. Now, he looked into ADL's activities for the preceding ten years and reported back to Stevenson that 30 percent of that work could be characterized as what he had been taught at Booz, Allen to call management consulting. Stevenson seemed surprised to learn that what he was contemplating doing he had in fact in substantial measure been doing all along.

Because so many of the new faces at ADL looked as though they hardly needed shaving, when a client came to call on them their immediate superior, Richard J. Coveney, would sometimes phone an older person at M.I.T. and ask him to rush over and sit in, to lend an air of seniority and credibility to the discussion. Coveney's Business Research staff formed — along with Operations Research, Industrial Economics, and Industrial Evaluation — the company's Management Services Division, which was run by Leroy Marek — one of whose chief postwar functions had been to appraise seized Axis-owned assets for the Alien Property Custodian — until Magee took it over in 1963.* By then, Management Services was accounting for 40 percent of the firm's gross income.

The kind of consulting work it did was exemplified by an experience of two subsequent enlistees in its ranks, Frank Seabury and Don W. Smith. A consortium of companies asked ADL to study a new engine that it was thought might have widespread potential, especially in long-haul trucking, and to compare it with existing engines and analyze its marketability. Smith, an electrical engineer with degrees from both M.I.T. and the Harvard Business School, built a mathematical model, a computerized replication of various highway systems and how trucks negotiated them. To make sure that the computer's findings jibed with reality, he and Seabury had researchers armed with stopwatches hitch rides on trucks traversing the Massachusetts Turnpike. These outriders were supposed to keep careful track of, among other things, how often and at what mileposts drivers shifted from one gear to another.

Eventually, enough data were assembled, by computer and by seat of the pants, to enable Smith and Seabury to predict with confidence what freight costs (including loading, unloading, and maintenance) would come to for the new engine compared with standard ones. Their findings were emphatically negative, much to the distress of the engineer who'd developed the new engine. "How can you say there's no market for this," he asked them plaintively at one meeting, "when I've spent five years of my life

* Magee was an organization man, in the better sense of the term. He construed it to be essential, if not crucial, to an understanding of ADL's evolution over the years to contemplate its sometimes convoluted solutions for its own internal problems. In 1960, when he was completing his first decade at ADL, the company had six divisions, with a vice-president in charge of each: Research and Development, Engineering, Life Sciences, Energy and Materials, Advanced Research, and Management Services. In 1970, there were seven divisions: one of them International, and three each under Technical (Engineering, Life Sciences, Research and Development) and Management Consulting (Management Services, Management Counseling, and Industrial and Regional Economics). In 1972, all the divisions were abolished, and more or less autonomous operating sections — Health Care, Energy, Environment, and others — substituted for them. By the 1980s, there were thirty operating sections divided, for administrative purposes, into thirteen groups, and the names of some of the newfangled sections reflected the changing breadth of the company's interests and activities: Biomolecular Sciences, Financial Industries, Organizational Development, Electronic Systems, Safety and Engineering Technology, Telecommunications Sciences.

working on it?" Smith and Seabury did a lot of their computer work at night. The operator of the machine they used was an Armenian woman. At first she irritated them somewhat because she kept bringing in stuffed grape leaves and dripping oil all over their printouts. But when they got stumped while talking about gearshifts and highway curves and elevations, she proved to be unexpectedly helpful because, as nobody had bothered to tell either of the men before, she had a daytime job, too — as a truck driver.

For all of its reaching out to explore new horizons, or at any rate truck stops, ADL did not forsake technology. It had been interested in and supportive of inventiveness from the outset. Back in 1932, when its library was still modest (as was its net income: only $47,000), it nonetheless boasted as one of its proudest possessions a complete file of the *Official Gazette* of the U.S. Patent Office, dating back to 1790. More than two thousand patents have been granted to ADL inventors over the years. In the old days, the rights to these were almost always passed along to the client for whose sake the work in question had been done; the inventors had to be content with a touch of glory and, after a while, a $100 pourboire presented to them at an annual ADL Patent Award Lunch. ("Our product is your creativity," Raymond Stevens intoned at one such celebration.) Later, in 1958, the company moved into invention management and shared with inventors, either in-house ones or outsiders, proceeds from their discoveries in return for developing and marketing them. ADL's most rewarding such collaboration was with Dr. John C. Sheehan of M.I.T., who devised a synthetic penicillin in 1965. The company had a 44 percent stake in it, and that turned out to be worth $15 million.

New products are rarely that remunerative. Back in 1917, ADLers attempted to make a charcoal briquette substitute out of peat. They gave up, after not inconsiderable out-of-pocket disbursements, when they concluded ruefully that it required more energy to create a peat briquette than could be produced by burning it. Two generations later, another task force of ADLers was much more successful when the Husky Oil Company invited it to try to make barbecue briquettes out of lignite. No fewer than eleven people were assigned to that mission, the completion of which entailed fabricating a briquette that would not fall apart, would not emit a sulfurous odor, and would burn with a clear and attractive flame; conducting a market survey to estimate its sales; designing a bag to package it in; tasting food cooked over it; and, finally, producing a fifteen-minute motion picture expounding on its virtues. Early on, the technicians involved in the complex enterprise stirred in an oxidant to accelerate the rate of ignition. That worked beautifully. Much too beautifully, it turned out: Several railroad cars loaded with experimental briquettes caught fire and were reduced to ashes. A house organ called the *ADL Review* afterward commented laconically, "We decided against using an oxidant."

At the request of Schenley Industries, ADL experts once fabricated both a cola-flavored wine and a collapsible waterproof cardboard champagne bucket; history does not reveal whether the two were judged compatible, or indeed whether either of them had much consumer appeal. For the Empire Pencil Corporation, ADL produced, after four years of intensive effort, a plastic pencil that looked like and could be sharpened like a conventional wooden one; it was hailed in graphic circles as the first consequential change in pencils in two hundred years. An automatic chemical dispenser to keep toilet bowls cleaner was an easier challenge; that took only two years.

Another time, when ADL was asked by American Home Products to make a flushable diaper, a house organ recounted after that battle was won, "In retrospect, the obstacles to devising an article which would have wet strength but which could disintegrate in a toilet seem so great that we are surprised we undertook the task." ADL ingenuity resulted in disposable T-shirts and bathing suits, too, and in a pill-making machine for which there was, lamentably, no commercial use because it could produce pills far faster than the pharmaceutical industry could sell them. Then there was a newfangled refrigerator for Frigidaire; on taking a prototype to Michigan to reveal the marvelous things its innards were capable of, its designers were cruelly upstaged by a rival demonstration. To show how sturdily another refrigerator had been built, somebody had arranged for an elephant to lumber up a ramp and stand on top of it.

From Dr. Little down, ADLers have exhibited a flair for the dramatic themselves through the years. The company was asked by the National Highway Traffic Safety Administration to construct an antitheft device for automobiles. ADL began by doing away with ignition keys; it ended up with a keyboard into which a code number had to be punched before an engine could be started. To demonstrate the contrivance's efficacy, the company called in a reformed car thief who deservedly had the nickname Tinker — he could steal any locked automobile in forty-five seconds. Tinker was briefed and shown blueprints of the new device. Even so, after trying for seventeen minutes to start up the vehicle to which it was attached, he gave up and said, "The only way to steal this car is with a tow truck."

Dr. Little was a golfer, albeit an inept one, and when in 1931 a new golf ball came on the market, the *Industrial Bulletin* took note of the event by saying, "It was hoped that the change would increase low and decrease high scores, and shorten the length of the drive obtained by the more expert, thus bringing the expert and the duffer closer together. . . . Experience with the new ball has not met expectations." A. G. Spalding was a longtime ADL client, and on its behalf ADL did a lot of work with sports equipment. Once when the U.S. Golf Association was pursuing its vain hope of keeping drives under 250 yards — a distance that most professionals in the 1980s would, of course, consider middling — ADL obligingly conducted some tests at Dr. Little's old turf, The Country Club. The association had built a driving machine supposed to replicate Byron Nelson's swing, which was deemed to be par. ADL borrowed it and catapulted golf balls of various sizes and shapes all over Brookline, trying, with the aid of stroboscopic photography, to determine the proper dimensions for an ideal ball.

After 1964, much of the sports work ADL took on was entrusted to Richard Stone, a physicist who had been a navy submariner and, after the war, had spent five years helping Admiral Hyman Rickover perfect nuclear submarines. ADL had hired Stone because of his expertise in electronics and nuclear power, but during the Vietnam War he became disenchanted with that kind of work. Fortunately, at that moment the U.S. Coast Guard came around; it wanted a study made of life jackets. The ones then in vogue would keep bodies afloat, all right, but not necessarily face up. Stone was put on that job because he knew what made submarines float. ADL built an indoor tank for him, ten feet in diameter and ten feet deep, and he had volunteers, men, women, and children, jump into it wearing various kinds of life jackets. Fishes float flat. Human, he quickly perceived, float vertically, like sea horses. Stone devised a jacket with the buoyancy built into the front of it, and an incalculable number of men overboard have ever since gratefully popped up to the surface like sea horses. (There was no patent involved, since his research was government-funded.)

Stone, who broke his back in 1980 and had to give up most sports except swimming, also discovered that, just as gymnasts perform best when they hit a trampoline a shade off center, so do tennis players when they hit a ball about one-and-a-half inches off the center of their racquets. Inasmuch as they were certain to try to hit in the center notwithstanding, he instructed a client to make a racquet — not yet on the market — with an imperceptible built-in distortion. Stone also once invented a machine to stitch baseballs and displayed it to Happy Chandler when he was commissioner of that sport. Chandler was dismayed. Stone wished to know why. "We have twenty nice old ladies up at Cooperstown stitching baseballs," Chandler told him, "and we don't want to have to fire them."

In the early 1970s, ADL was asked by both the government's Consumer Product Safety Commission and the National Swimming Pool Foundation to examine the matter of people's breaking their necks while diving into pools. Stone was the logical person to handle that. He and some patient associates began to amass statistics on at what speed and at what angles divers hit the surface of the water and how they behave beneath it. Most accidents, they discovered, did not result from diving off springboards but, rather, into shallow water. (Insurance companies sometimes urge motels not to embellish their pools with boards, but at least one motel has been sued because it didn't provide a board; the litigant argued that without one there was no way of ascertaining which was the deep end.)

Stone's own tank at ADL had by then been dismantled, but he had access to a pool at M.I.T. and, what was more important, to the divers on the university's swimming team. ADL affixed reflectors to the divers' bathing caps, wrists, and ankles, took stroboscopic photos as they leapt into the air and plunged downward, and from analyzing these were ultimately able to advise pool manufacturers on how to make their products as safe as possible, though with the caveat that nobody could expect a motel guest with three martinis under his belt to behave exactly the same as an intercollegiate varsity letterman. "We have the basic physics of diving in hand," Stone said afterward. "If we were instrumental in saving one broken neck we were also saving a family a lot of grief and saving society the millions it would have had to spend on a paraplegic."

After Edward M. Kennedy's car went off a bridge at Chappaquiddick in 1969, resulting in the death of Mary Jo Kopechne, his family commissioned ADL to determine — for possible use in an inquest or trial — how long one could be expected to survive in that car in that water. Along with another physicist, a meteorologist, and an oceanographer, Stone obtained the car and, usually working in the dead of night to avoid tourists who found that particular scene attractive, conducted underwater tests at the bridge. They concluded that the probabilities were that anybody trapped inside would have had no more than four minutes' supply of air. Coming up for air themselves after one long night's work, the ADLers were confronted at dawn by a busload of Japanese tourists, who wondered what they were doing. "We're forming a committee," Stone said. The Japanese nodded, smiled, and moved along.

Before such an entity as the Consumer Product Safety Commission existed, there was a public uproar about the danger of children's toys. The Toy Manufacturers of America, naturally disturbed at the association of such chilling words as *ingestion, laceration,* and *strangulation* with its products, commissioned ADL to make a study of toy safety and to help it develop some criteria for the industry. So deeply did ADL get involved in that line of inquiry that for several years one of its senior scientists, Derek E. Till, served as chairman of the Toy Manufacturers Voluntary Safety Standards Steering Committee. Later, in an effort to combat uncertainties about the specter of ingestion, ADL technicians made mathematical models of children's throats and swallowing muscles.

An Englishman with a degree in chemistry from the University of London, Till was himself a survivor of a high-risk experience; for five years during the Second World War, he had been an RAF bomber pilot. He came to ADL in 1951 — his father-in-law

knew a father-in-law of one of Earl Stevenson's daughters —
and he was assigned to Product Technology, working under
veteran ADLer Laurence R. B. Hervey, who created a flushable diaper that, as it happened, had not made it to the marketplace. "There are many technical triumphs that never become
articles of commerce," Till once sadly mused. Till and Hervey
were the mainstays of another aborted ADL undertaking in
the mid-fifties. A subsidiary of Bristol-Myers wanted ADL
to try to make some paintbrush bristles. Chinese hog bristles
had long been the favorite raw material (American hog bristles
were deemed inferior), but because of the Korean War they
had become tremendously expensive, when obtainable at all.
There was no synthetic known that had the required resilience
of natural protein and that could be tapered to a fine point.
ADL thought that a protein chemically akin to hog bristles
could be obtained from chicken feathers. Hervey and Till
figured out a way of extracting the protein and then extruding
it. One young woman working on experimental solvents — Dr.
Little would have been aghast — had a good deal of skin peeled
off her hands.

They set up a pilot plant in an abandoned supermarket in
Salisbury, Maryland, where there were so many chicken farms
that they could readily obtain a truckload or two of fresh feathers
every day; fresh ones were moister than others and smelled better, or at any rate less worse. That ADL outpost made a lot of
brushes, but before they could become articles of commerce,
three things happened: Somebody invented a process for converting chicken feathers, which the Salisbury plant had been getting practically for free, into animal feed so that they acquired
some value; the Korean War ended, and the U.S. government released a stockpile of Chinese hog bristles it had been hoarding;
and Bristol-Myers sold off its subsidiary and lost interest in the
whole enterprise. ADL was disappointed. It had had such high
hopes for its revolutionary paintbrush bristles that to call attention to them, one of its promotional people had evoked the at least
momentary interest of an assemblage at a trade show of the Associated Industries of Massachusetts by flinging a live chicken into
the audience.

One job that Till found especially invigorating came his way in
the late 1950s. The Sampson Cordage Company, an old New

England firm, made braided clothesline. In an effort to diversify, Sampson began making braided nylon polyester fibers, which most yachtsmen soon started using in lieu of conventional ropes. The company also convinced the U.S. Air Force that nylon braid would make an acceptable substitute for the piano wire it had been using for towing targets — usually made of polystyrene foam — in training exercises. The targets were generally five thousand feet aft of the planes carrying them aloft. The braid was unquestionably safer, since a plane's wing could be severely damaged by hitting a wire, but the ropes broke more often than the air force liked.

Sampson approached ADL for help. Till and his cohorts looked up all the available literature on the effects of airflow on wires and strings, and found to their surprise that most of it dated back to the First World War, when biplanes had struts. They knew that nylon stretched and that the degree of its extension was directly related to the stresses upon it. If they could figure out exactly how much a rope stretched in flight, then they could decide how thick and how long it should be to serve its purpose without snapping. So they took a five-thousand-footer and painted it with alternating black and white stripes, each six inches long. They attached that to a target and sent it aloft. Till, in another plane, flew alongside the towrope taking photographs of it; and the stripes enabled him later to calculate to what stresses it had been subjected. "It was nice to get back up in the air," he said, with characteristic British understatement.

Till became a naturalized American, but not before he had been working at ADL for several years; he wanted to make sure first that McCarthyism was not permanent. Another native Englishman at ADL, Dennis C. Jeffreys, also took out American citizenship, but — characteristic of the fiercely independent nature of many ADLers — he made a point of breaking out the Union Jack and flaunting it every Fourth of July. An electronic systems specialist, Jeffreys perfected an electronic coin recognition gadget to deter the use of slugs in vending machines.

One of the more picaresque innovators in ADL history, who arrived in 1949 as a protégé of Richard Coveney and stayed around for a few stimulating years, was William J. J. Gordon.

ADL had always been interested in trying to predict the shape and usefulness of consumer goods of the future; once, Raymond Stevens assigned a young employee to do nothing but read science fiction on the off chance that he might get some marketable hints. Gordon, who had studied physics at Harvard and philosophy at the Sorbonne, was put in charge of something called a Creativity Group, with, at one time, as many as a dozen groupies under his wing. He set up shop on the third floor of a onetime hosiery factory in Kendall Square, a few blocks from the Memorial Drive headquarters. Refusing to dress like a conventional consultant in white shirts and muted ties, Gordon preferred to sport T-shirts, khakis, and sneakers, often with a bright red handkerchief protruding like a flag from a pocket. He even had a secretary who came to work in knee socks at a time when they were considered daring. (Earl Stevenson did not seem to mind any of that. He would now and then tote a sandwich over to Kendall Square at lunchtime and say wistfully, "This is the way it used to be in the old days.") In summers, Gordon, who had independent means, would move his whole crew to an estate of his in Littleton, New Hampshire. Stevens once mildly complained. "My clients like it there," Gordon replied. "Boston's too hot." A short story he had published in *The New Yorker* in 1961 — it was titled "Director of Research" and couched in the first person — was about a consultant who thought that the ideal arrangement for fruitful research was ten good people in a barn.

It had been Gordon's crowd testing mattresses when Harland Riker was hired. Their accomplishments became legendary, though not always profitable. One man among them attained the dubious honor of causing the abolishment of ADL's traditional Christmas parties, held in a Cambridge hotel. In the course of a no-holds-barred dance, he landed feet first on a table around which Stevenson, Stevens, Leroy Marek, and their wives were sedately seated. Among the Creativity Group's achievements during business hours was the invention of a mattress turner, which at the flick of a switch could flip over a mattress as if it were a pancake. One time a potato chip company came to Gordon with a problem. It felt that too much of the space inside its containers was being wasted on air. Also, its chips broke in transit. Gordon, who liked to think metaphorically, got to brooding about wet leaves and how nicely they nestled together. He procured some potato flour, made a mold, formed chips in it, and packed these, neatly nestled, in a tennis-ball can. He dropped the can out of his third-story window, and none of the chips broke. When he took his discovery to the head of the potato chip company, that eminence said, Gordon recalled, "This is the greatest thing I've ever seen!" The only trouble was, he added a few minutes later, that Gordon's potato chips tasted like — well — wet leaves.

Once again to save air space, Gordon devised a way of compressing Kleenex tissues so that far more of them could be stuffed into a box than was the norm. A paper company executive betook himself to New Hampshire to observe the outcome of that effort, and to impress him the Creativity Group exerted more pressure than had been *its* norm — so much too much of it that when they opened an experimental box for the visitor, they discovered they had converted the paper back into wood. There was also a talking clock, an all-purpose tool, and a revolutionary can opener. In recognition of all that derring-do, Gordon — who was given to making challenging statements like "Why does a chair have to look like a chair?" — soon became known in ADL circles as Wild Bill. His tenure there happened to overlap for a while that of another William Gordon, who, though he was of no more discernibly meek disposition than most of his colleagues, became saddled with the nickname Mild Bill.

Wild Bill Gordon was the originator of a concept called synectics, which he described in a 1961 book of that name as "the joining together of different and apparently irrelevant objects [i.e., leaves and potato chips]. . . . the integration of diverse individuals into a problem-stating problem-solving group." He had begun thinking hard about creative processes during the Second World War, first for the British armed forces and then at Harvard's Underwater Sound Laboratory. While in the Royal Navy, he was a salvage expert, and he introduced a method of recovering stray, unexploded torpedoes by means of a device called a Golden Retriever: a string with a buoy or balloon attached to it that was automatically released from a spent torpedo when it slowed down.

After the war, Gordon was asked by the American navy to help it solve a vexing problem. Its new nuclear submarines could stay underwater so long that they had a lot of garbage to dispose of. It couldn't, of course, be allowed to float to the surface, where it could give away a sub's location; so the ships were obliged to allocate a good deal of their precious cargo space to bricks, which were used to drag the garbage to the ocean floor. Gordon's solution was for the submarines to make their own bricks, while in transit, out of the salt left over when they produced fresh water with their Kleinschmidt stills. In the course of that estimable research, he wrote a play called *A Ton of Bricks.* One of the characters in it felt that before submerging garbage it was necessary to learn all about garbage. He began buying the stuff, and suddenly garbage had real value. Before the play ended (on paper, that is; it never got produced), a garbageman was avidly reading the *Wall Street Journal.*

One of Gordon's Cambridge neighbors on Brattle Street was Al Capp, whose own inventiveness was unimpeachable. When scientists at Harvard were doing some experiments in the sixties on human genetics, Gordon was happy to supply Capp with a scenario for a comic strip: Harvard men produced a huge carrot that fell in love and eloped with a professor's daughter; to the couple's chagrin, a motel in Connecticut wouldn't admit them on their honeymoon. Capp graciously reciprocated by illustrating a synectical article Gordon wrote for *Fortune.* The "Li'l Abner" man provided a portrayal of how to solve the problem of getting a wheelchair up a flight of stairs: a goat butting a man perched atop a huge snake.

Over the years, as ADL's business very slowly grew — not until 1956, after seventy years of existence, did the company's net income pass the $1 million mark — its executives opened, and sometimes soon closed, small regional outposts around the country. There was an office in New York in 1936, one in Washington in 1937, and, by the mid-fifties, others in Chicago, Los Angeles, and San Francisco. Befitting an organization whose offshoots had sprouted from deeply planted WASP, New England, academically oriented roots, the headquarters remained throughout in Cambridge. By 1952, however, when the home office staff numbered 606 (an increase of 152 over the previous year), it was plain to Earl Stevenson and his fellow board members — senior among them the lawyer Alexander Whiteside, who had been a director for thirty-six years — that Dr. Little's research palace on Memorial Drive was getting overcrowded. So the company acquired a seven-acre tract — later expanded to forty acres — in North Cambridge, just off Route 2, Boston's main westward artery. Here it built a complex of offices and laboratories officially called Acorn Park and unofficially, by subsequent denizens, both the Mother Church and, perhaps inevitably, the Nut Park. A feature ever since of the main lobby has been an oil painting of Dr. Little standing in front of a Chinese vase. The artist, Margaret Fitzhugh Browne — among whose other notable subjects were Samuel F. B. Morse, Henry Ford, King Alfonso XIII of Spain, and Bobby Jones — had originally done Dr. Little's portrait for some Boston friends of his, who gave it to M.I.T.; a few years after his death, ADL commissioned her, for $600, to make a copy of it.

ADL has long stressed its egalitarianism. Chief Executive Officer Magee's secretary addresses him, both in and out of his earshot, as John. A laboratory technician has as much right to book a table in the company's reservation dining room as has a section chief. Most ADL employees get to work by car. Neither President Magee nor any of the vice-presidents — who numbered one in 1909 and sixty-six in 1985 — has a reserved slot in the company's parking lots. Whoever gets to Acorn Park first gets the choicest spot. (A visitor once cynically observed that in wintertime, when the weather in Cambridge is apt to turn nasty, there is a real incentive for arriving early and thus being able to park as close as possible to a building entrance.) To make Acorn Park seem more parklike, the management encourages its employees to tend little flower plots around their drab red brick facilities. The company tills and fertilizes the gardens and furnishes, on request, twenty dollars' worth of seeds or seedlings per garden per year. When the boss of one young secretary who thought she had been too long denied a promotion stopped by her garden in 1984 and inquired jovially what it was she was nurturing there, she was delighted to be able to reply, with thinly disguised asperity, "Impatiens." Another fringe benefit was the establishment in 1949 of an Employees' Benefit Fund, later renamed Leisure Fund, which obtained cut-rate tickets to plays, movies, and Boston Red Sox games at Fenway Park.

The cornerstone of the main building at Acorn Park — which

had two hundred thousand square feet of interior space, with 150 laboratories scattered around them — was laid, with grand-nephew Arthur Dehon Little's assistance, on November 17, 1953. As would be the case a generation later when the lead balloon contest reached its climax, employees who were invited to a cele-bratory lunch afterward at the M.I.T. Faculty Club were en-joined, "This ceremony does not justify any serious upset in your work plans." Ernest Crocker was allowed enough time off to go out to Logan Airport and pick up one of the guests of honor, Ed-ward Lane, whose cedar-chest company had by then been a client for thirty-one years and who came up from Virginia and gave a brief speech. Another guest of honor was the mayor of Cam-bridge.

In the cornerstone were entombed a 399-page survey on the impact of a switch from textiles to technology on the economy of New England, which, under the aegis of Cyril Herrmann, had recently been prepared for the Federal Reserve Bank of Boston; some algae that ADL was experimenting with as a food substi-tute; a jar of monosodium glutamate; a sample of glass fiber; a Joule-Thomson valve that was an integral part of the Collins cryostat; some fresh water from a Kleinschmidt still; a few pro-motional brochures; an acorn; and one small brick.

The brick and the place-card holders at the lunch (John Magee had not yet attained sufficient seniority to be invited to it) were fashioned from authentic Egyptian clay.* The year before, ADL had been invited by President Muhammad Naguib to help his government select the best available building material for inex-pensive rural housing, and ADL had concluded that this should be, as it had been for centuries, Nile River mud — though now mud mixed with petroleum products to make it water-repellent. Under the management of such veteran employees as Charles G.

---

* Another absentee was Alexander Whiteside, who had resigned from the Board of Directors two months previous. He was so senior a member of the ADL family that he had been an honorary pallbearer at Dr. Little's funeral while Earl Stevenson was a mere usher. But by 1953, Whiteside was eighty and had had a terrible falling-out with Steven-son, the attorney feeling aggrieved that the company was turning to younger men for legal advice. Whiteside's last known letter to Stevenson, with whom he had been corre-sponding on a "Dear Earl" basis for more than thirty years, was a "Dear Sir" communica-tion that went, "So far as I am concerned, over a period of several years you have been unkind and inhuman to me and I never wish to see you again or have anything to do with you." Stevenson's reaction was to state that he hoped never again to have a lawyer on the company's Board of Directors.

Harford, Earl Stafford, and Lawrence W. Bass, ADL had constructed a portable brick-making machine that could readily be moved from village to village. Bass, a Yale Ph.D., was in Egypt at the time of the cornerstone laying, and he shipped over ten pounds of genuine Nile clay to be suitably molded for the big day's events. Afterward, the *Chemical & Engineering News*, reporting on the occasion and on ADL's own foreign aid program in Egypt, said, "This is the kind of Point Four that will strike a responsive chord in the breast of the American taxpayer."

Also in 1953, ADL contrived to buy itself back from M.I.T., in a manner of speaking. Earl Stevenson became concerned in 1951 that two of ADL's chief rivals, the Battelle Memorial Institute and the Stanford Research Institute (later SRI), were tax-exempt; he thought that they should be required, like ADL, to pay taxes on commercial work they undertook; and he urged Royal Little to go to Washington and persuade Congress to make them do just that. Royal was knowledgeable enough about the ways of Washington to believe that such a proposal would win scant support, but he had an alternative suggestion: ADL could diminish its own taxes by setting up a profit-sharing trust for the benefit of its employees and allocate to it half of the company's pretax earnings. Thus came into being an entity called the Memorial Drive Trust. Royal Little was its first chairman, and he predicted back then — quite accurately, as it turned out — that one day not too far away the trust, if its funds were shrewdly enough invested, would have assets far greater than those of ADL itself.

That same year Royal, representing the new trust, arranged with the M.I.T. trust that owned some 55 percent of ADL — he was also the principal trustee of *that* trust — to sell its stock for $1.3 million to the Memorial Drive Trust. Eventually, the Memorial Drive Trust acquired the rest of the outstanding shares in ADL. Royal got the First National Bank of Boston to lend ADL the money to pay off M.I.T. and to accept as collateral for the loan the very stock the company was purchasing, an uncommon state of affairs. From then on, ADL put into its employees' trust about 15 percent of what each of them earned a year, and their nest eggs grew to heroic proportions: Quite a few ADLers became dazedly aware that, after being on the payroll for twenty-five or thirty years, they were destined on retirement to become millionaires.

In 1960, by which time the bank loan had been fully retired, Royal Little decided to hand over the reins of the Memorial Drive Trust to a full-time administrator. Playing court tennis at the Boston Tennis & Racquet Club, Royal had become acquainted with a young lawyer, Jean de Valpine, who was also an aficionado of that esoteric pastime. A native of Missouri, de Valpine had gone east to college and ended up in the Harvard class of 1943. (One classmate was Norman Mailer; they attended the same composition course, and it piqued de Valpine for years that their instructor almost always elected to read Mailer's themes aloud instead of his.) The Memorial Drive Trust was worth about $10 million when de Valpine took it over. Twenty-five years later, thumpingly fulfilling Royal Little's forecast, its assets were increasing at a rate of 30 percent annually and amounted to more than $300 million. De Valpine, blithely eschewing the caution characteristic of most trustees, had invested less than 10 percent of the money available to him in companies listed on the New York Stock Exchange. Instead, he had taken robust positions in many fledgling enterprises — cable television, robotics, artificial intelligence — that at the time much of the general public had never even heard of. He became a founder of the National Venture Capital Association and a man of so internationally recognized a golden touch that he received flattering inquiries about his modus operandi from such disparate sources as Hong Kong and the People's Republic of China. On his own, de Valpine prospered so handsomely that he was able to give more than $100,000 to a single Harvard fund-raising campaign, which was probably better than Mailer did.

In the late 1960s, ADL began hearing rumors that there were outsiders interested in buying the company from the Memorial Drive Trust. Royal Little knew a good deal about takeovers — his Textron Corporation had all but invented them — and it was his opinion that there might be a price offered at which, out of fiduciary responsibility, it might be imprudent *not* to sell out.* But he

* For three days in the winter of 1978, the *Wall Street Journal*'s business opportunities page carried a small advertisement: "Intl Management Consulting Co. for sale. Annual billing $100 million. Net profit $4 million. 10% annual growth, over 60% voting stock available. Reply in strict confidence. Box D-644." Inasmuch as ADL's gross the year before had been about $100 million and its net about $4 million, it was widely assumed that

didn't want to have to do that. Still, nobody knew for certain what ADL was actually worth. So to get a realistic value set for its stock, ADL decided to go public — or, at any rate, to put up 30 percent of its shares for sale. There was yet another reason: The Internal Revenue Service was muttering that unless some procedural changes were made, retiring ADL employees might be held liable for whopping taxes on their accumulated fortunes. Two hundred and fifty thousand shares were offered, at twenty-one dollars a share, on October 21, 1969. The stock went up and then down, and no outsider got rich buying it. (One former ADLer who has also worked for McKinsey and for Booz, Allen, both now privately held companies, has said, "It doesn't make much sense to invest in an organization where your inventory walks out the door every night.") To the Memorial Drive Trust, which retained ownership of 71 percent of the company, the fluctuations didn't matter much. For by the mid-1980s, even though by that time ADL's gross annual income had passed the $200 million mark, the trust's holdings in the company that had spawned it came to only 13 percent of the golden eggs in Jean de Valpine's brimming basket.

After the move to Acorn Park, the Memorial Drive building that had been the company's bastion for thirty-six years was converted into a site for its biological and biomedical research — known, from 1957 on, as its Life Sciences Division. ADL had been deeply involved in biochemistry since 1939, when Bristol-Myers had asked it to ascertain the physiological reactions of human skin to various chemicals embodied in its products. There had been many subsequent undertakings involving health care. A medical products specialist in the ADL ranks, John M. Ketteringham, devoted the better part of three years, for instance, to

---

it was the company up for grabs. The ad was traced to a professor of business administration at Northeastern University who taught a course on ethics and also ran a one-man consulting business out of his home. He apparently hoped somebody would come along and make an irresistible offer for ADL and that he would get a finder's fee. When eventually confronted and asked for an explanation, he denied that he had had any specific international management consulting company in mind. But he had slipped up; to some of the 150 people who replied to his ad, he had sent a xeroxed page of the ADL 1977 annual report, with all references to Arthur D. Little excised but with a footnote left intact that alluded to the Memorial Drive Trust. He was duly reprimanded by the Securities and Exchange Commission for making "materially false and misleading statements," and Northeastern replaced him with someone better qualified to teach ethics.

testing artificial lungs made of polymers for the National Heart and Lung Institute. The lungs were tried out on sheep, whose blood resembles humans'. The artificial lungs never worked out, but along with gaining some useful scientific insights, Ketteringham learned something about sheep: If their ears droop below the horizontal, they are not feeling up to snuff.

Much of ADL's work with animals has taken place in connection with commissions from the National Cancer Institute. A Ph.D. in biochemistry and microbiology, Andrew Sivak, busied himself growing tumors on rats and mice in the course of a study of carcinogenic chemicals. Also for that institute, ADL designed a bacteria-free isolation suit and tested the drug Laetrile on cancer-ridden rodents, finding it worthless. ADL spent more than $4 million in the early 1980s to modernize its animal facilities at Memorial Drive, and was pleased afterward to have them approved by the American Association for Accreditation of Laboratory Animal Care.

Among still other scientists quartered on Memorial Drive was Alan W. Burg, the director of ADL's Biosciences Unit. Burg was a Ph.D. in biochemistry from M.I.T. and a widely recognized expert on water quality criteria. On ADL's behalf he had conducted studies for the National Cancer Institute (on the physiological disposition of chemotherapeutic agents), the National Institute of Arthritis and Metabolic Diseases (on kidney dialysis), and the National Coffee Association. For the last, he determined that an average cup of coffee should be considered to contain 150 milliliters, or just over five ounces — the importance of which was that measurements had to be standardized for the dosing of rats and mice in studies of the metabolism of caffeine.

Other ADL scientists were no less busily engaged in tobacco research. Back in 1946, Liggett & Myers had hoped somehow to produce a cigarette harboring fewer bacteria than its own Chesterfields or any other brand. Not only could such a cigarette be promoted as "cleaner" than its rivals, but its enhanced sterility would conceivably endow it with a longer shelf life, a not insignificant factor when it came to shipping large quantities of cigarettes to the tropics. Liggett & Myers retained ADL — Stanley Cairncross and Johnny Sjöström were principally involved — to embark on one of the most arduous microbiological research tasks ever tackled. Cairncross and Sjöström wrestled with that problem for ten years, at one point testing a thousand cigarettes a day. (They were not obliged to smoke them all personally.)* They never did come up with a mass-produced cigarette that could be proclaimed sterile, but they were able to inform their client that Chesterfields appeared to have a less disagreeable aftertaste than many of its competitors. In 1953, when two university scientists issued a report to the effect that mice had got cancer from tobacco and the cigarette industry questioned the validity of the scientists' research, Liggett & Myers asked ADL to look into the situation from a presumably more detached viewpoint. ADL agreed, but only on condition that whatever it determined would be reported not merely to the cigarette company but also to members of the staff of the National Cancer Institute, the American Cancer Society, and Sloan-Kettering Cancer Center.

By then, that phase of ADL's operations was being run by Charles Kensler, a Ph.D. in pharmacology from Cornell University who had earlier worked at the Rockefeller Institute and was a professor at the Boston University School of Medicine. Kensler had consented to join ADL only if he could also go on teaching, which he continued to do until 1960. (A decade later, he was a visiting professor at M.I.T.) He was in certain respects the ideal person to deal with tobacco research; he was hardly ever seen in public without a cigar clamped between his teeth. Under Kensler's supervision, the Memorial Drive laboratories were soon swarming with mice whose backs had been coated with cigarette tar. Enough of them got cancer to substantiate the scientists' assertion. "Our client was disappointed," Kensler said afterward.†

ADL researchers also found that cigarette smoking seemed to inhibit the ability of cilia to sweep mucus out of lungs. One upshot of subsequent research was the development by ADL of the activated charcoal filters that were placed in Larks. Then the National Cancer Institute approached ADL with a radical proposition — radical, at any rate, emanating from that agency: It wondered if ADL could concoct a cigarette that had hardly any tar or

* Dr. Little had been a chain-smoker of Pall Malls. "His room, his clothes and everything, the whole damn Thirty Memorial Drive smelled of Pall Malls," Earl Stevenson once said.

† A much happier client had been the Ocean Spray cranberry people. In 1959, the government ordered them to halt production at a cranberry sauce plant because an alleged carcinogen had been found in some of their berries. This time, when ADL looked into the findings, it concluded that the berries were perfectly safe, and not only did Ocean Spray resume production, but the Department of Agriculture reimbursed it for lost sales.

nicotine in it but that smokers might nonetheless find tolerable. ADL had only begun trying to solve that problem when the institute judged on second thought that it would be inappropriate for it to sponsor any further research — it had already laid out $183,000 — in quest of the production of any sort of cigarette. Most of the funds that made ADL's lengthy research on cigarettes possible came from private industry, whose benefits from that support were at best moot.

IX *How Safe Is "Safe"?*

We live in an age in which new impressions so crowd upon
us that the miracle of yesterday is the commonplace of today.
— Dr. Arthur D. Little [n.d.]

By the mid-1950s, both Earl Stevenson and Ray Stevens, only two years apart in age, were getting on, and
it was clear that ADL would soon be needing a new chief executive. But who? There were a number of senior employees —
Leroy Marek, Howard Billings, Harry Wissmann among them —
who had been on the scene for quite a while and were esteemed
by their peers. But to the corporate board and especially to Royal
Little, on whose counsel the other directors still heavily leaned,
none had the public visibility nor the personal charisma that
might be helpful (if indeed not necessary) when it came to
charting the company's course in the foreseeable future.

Royal began looking around outside Acorn Park. He made
overtures, in vain, to the presidents of Purdue University and the
New York Stock Exchange. Then one day his secretary, Mary
Young, came up with a candidate whose credentials seemed impeccable. He was Lieutenant General James Maurice Gavin, one
of the nation's preeminent soldiers, whose most recent assignment — one almost tailor-made, it seemed, for service at ADL —
had been to supervise the army's research and development activities. And of course it pleased Royal, a veteran of one parachute
jump, to contemplate a close association with perhaps the most
glittering jumper of them all.

Gavin was available — so available, in fact, that not long before he had submitted his curriculum vitae to a professional head-hunting firm. He had worked with George Kimball in 1949, when both belonged to the Weapons Systems Evaluation Group at the Pentagon, and he had given a lecture at ADL on developments in military technology; but otherwise he knew practically nothing about the company.

Everybody knew about him. He had parachuted into Normandy on D Day. He had been the youngest commander of any army division — in his case, the famous 82nd Airborne — since the Civil War. He had been chief of operations research for the Joint Chiefs of Staff, and, while John F. Kennedy was a senator, his principal adviser on military affairs. (Kennedy wrote a favorable review in the *Reporter* magazine of Gavin's book *War and Peace in the Space Age*. It was widely believed that Gavin was instrumental in later getting Kennedy to start the Peace Corps.)

In 1958, Gavin was fifty-one. In both civilian and military circles there was talk of his soon getting a fourth star and, as a full general, becoming the army's chief of staff. But by then he had become disenchanted with President Dwight Eisenhower's position — largely influenced by Secretary of State John Foster Dulles — that the United States should rely for its defense mainly on massive nuclear deterrence. Gavin had been at Eniwetok when the H-bomb was exploded. At the Pentagon, it had horrified him to hear fellow officers airily discussing plans to retaliate against a hypothetical Soviet march into Europe by, say, obliterating Czechoslovakia. So Gavin had resigned, after thirty-three years' military service, and was looking for a job. "I had to find a place where I could be successful in business," he said years later. "If you leave the Pentagon on principle, and fail, you're in trouble. You have to make a go of it, and ADL gave me that opportunity."

Gavin had come a long way up from just about as unpromising a start as any native American of his time could have experienced. Born in Brooklyn on March 22, 1907, of Irish parents, he was orphaned at two. (Seventy-five years later, he was still trying to track down his real mother and father.) Through a Catholic agency, he was adopted by Martin and Mary Gavin, a coal-mining couple living in Mount Carmel, Pennsylvania. They, too, were Irish — poor, tough, and illiterate. The boy was selling newspapers at ten and watching the Allies' progress in the First World War on a map posted in a Mount Carmel shoe store. He quit school after the eighth grade and became an apprentice barber, then a shoe salesman. In April 1924, he convinced an army recruiter that he was a year older than he actually was and he was allowed to enlist. Stationed in Panama by June 1925, he had risen to corporal, and by prodigious off-hours studying had prepared himself to take and pass the examination for admission to the U.S. Military Academy at West Point, from which he was graduated in 1929. He made his first parachute jump in 1941.

On May 2, 1958, Gavin became a vice-president of ADL and a member of its board. Within less than a year, he was the company's first executive vice-president, and by early 1960 its president. Previously, his fellow directors had concluded that Leroy Marek, who was running the Management Services Division and was also in charge of central administrative functions, was being stretched too thin. So Marek had been relieved of Management Services, and Gavin had taken that over — a move that was calculated to expedite his becoming familiar with the bread-and-butter side of the company's business. Cyril Herrmann, who'd been Marek's deputy in Management Services, stayed on there, responsible for business development. Harry Wissmann moved over to Management Services, overseeing operations, from his leadership of the Operations Research Section. John Magee, climbing steadily up the corporate ladder, took over Operations Research.

When Gavin himself ascended to the presidency, he surprised some of his colleagues: Instead of installing someone like Wissmann as his successor in Management Services, he brought in an outsider — Bruce Henderson, a former Westinghouse executive who, like a diamond, was both brilliant and abrasive. Henderson made life so difficult for some of his associates — he was credited in ADL circles with once having broken a ruler in half by smashing it against the desk of the mild-mannered and horrified Ray Stevens — that John Magee, for one, begged Marek to find him some other position. To the relief of many of the old-timers around ADL, Henderson did not long stay on the premises. He departed, succeeded by Magee, and founded an exceedingly successful consulting firm of his own — the Boston Consulting Group.

Royal Little's initial enthusiasm for Gavin may have stemmed in part from Royal's anticipation that the general's high-level military connections would bring ADL lucrative government contracts and might also be helpful to Royal's fast-growing Textron Corporation. Not long afterward, when Royal was casting an acquisitive eye on Bell Aircraft's helicopter division, Gavin urged him to buy it; when he'd been at the Pentagon, he told Little, he'd been instrumental in getting the army to agree to equip all its divisions with helicopters. So Royal — though some observers of the business scene regarded the move as the height of foolishness — went ahead and bought Bell Helicopter. Then came the war in Vietnam, the first helicopter war. Bell Helicopter was not even a million-dollar enterprise when Textron took it over; Vietnam made it a billion-dollar one.

Gavin's arrival at Cambridge gave ADL a cachet it had not before enjoyed in that status-conscious community. He was soon tendered a reception, for instance, at the home of Michael Michaelis, an Englishman who had joined the company in 1951 and who would later run its Washington office. Michaelis and his wife, Diana, had many high-placed acquaintances. "We invited John Kenneth Galbraith and Arthur Schlesinger and a lot of other Harvard all-stars," Michaelis remembered later, "but within a few minutes of the general's arrival, all the women in the room were clustered around him, and all the other men were sore." Gavin, despite his glaring lack of conventional education, had no trouble competing in intellectual and literary circles. He wrote his own share of books. Given his choice of clubs in the vicinity of Boston, the first one he joined was the Athenaeum. Given his choice of members of the ADL staff to have lunch with, he exhibited, unlike any senior executive before him, a predilection for librarians.

When Gavin became president and chief executive officer of ADL in March 1960, Earl Stevenson became chairman of the board and Raymond Stevens chairman of the executive committee. There were some adjustments to be made in the exercise of the general's first civilian command: ADLers had never been indoctrinated in the concept of blind obedience to higher authority. (The annual report covering his first presidential year did, though, describe the company vis-à-vis its clients as "reserve staffs to management.") But ADLers quickly and gratefully perceived his usefulness in attracting new business. When a prospective client from, say, Tuscaloosa, Alabama, turned up in Cambridge, a fancy lunch would be laid on for him in the Oak Leaf Room, where he would sit goggle-eyed while Gavin went on chattily, "When Charles [de Gaulle] said to me. . . ." or "When Jack [Kennedy] telexed. . . ." Gavin could open doors that his associates sometimes found it hard even to get near. When one ADLer wondered how best to approach a NATO general in quest of some new business and Gavin learned of his quandary, Gavin simply picked up a phone, called Brussels, and had a meeting set up in a couple of minutes.

Pamela Fenrich, a young woman in the Washington office, accompanied a prospective client to a conference in Texas. The keynote speaker was General Paul Gorman, later the head of the army's Southern Command. Then stationed in Washington, Gorman went out of his way, when he learned of Fenrich's presence, to praise both Gavin and ADL. The client was impressed. So was Fenrich, and when she later thanked Gorman for the plug, he said that Gavin had always been a hero of his and that he would love to meet him sometime. There was the standard Washington line of "Let's have lunch." But Gorman actually pursued the matter, and one day when Gavin turned up in Washington, the three of them did have lunch at the Pentagon, in the dining room of the Joint Chiefs, whose chairman, General John Vessey, joined them for coffee. Fenrich, who, like everybody else at ADL, called most colleagues by first names, had always addressed Gavin as Sir, and she felt better about that when Generals Vessey and Gorman both called him that themselves. Gavin had by then become a true-blue civilian-oriented consultant. When, leaving the Pentagon in a taxi, Fenrich told him how delightful the lunch had been for her, he said, "I think it was mostly courtesy on their part. We didn't make a nickel out of it."

The soldiers Gavin always liked best were those who wore, or had worn, the shoulder patch of the 82nd Airborne. He would drop almost anything — even on occasion a client — to greet a former comrade in arms who turned up at Acorn Park.* Some ADLers vying for his time grumbled now and then that in retrospect it would have served them better to have enrolled in jump

* In 1976, the New England Chapter of the 82nd Airborne Division Association changed its name to the Lieutenant General James M. Gavin Chapter.

training at Fort Benning than the Harvard Business School. The war he had fought never seemed far from his mind. While he could be affable enough to former enemies when the occasion demanded — ADL once landed a nice contract from Siemens, the big German electronics company, after a vice-president who'd been a Nazi general swapped war stories with Gavin over an Oak Leaf Room lunch — he was never able to feel entirely comfortable with Germans. In West Germany one time, inspecting a factory of another client, Gavin remarked pleasantly, "You know, the last time I saw this place we were bombing the shit out of it."

Gavin continued to be much in the public eye. His wartime exploits were graphically depicted in *A Bridge Too Far*, the motion picture made from Cornelius Ryan's best-selling book that featured actor Robert Redford. Redford was the owner of a ski resort in Utah and hoped to operate it without fossil fuels, using energy from wind, sun, and waterfall. After approaching ADL for some advice, he was invited to Acorn Park. It was just about the only time that Gavin was upstaged on his own premises. The general had planned to take the actor on a tour of Acorn Park, but had to abandon that notion out of fear that one of his own female employees, hoping for a glimpse of the visitor, might fall out of a window. Gavin settled for a secluded lunch with half a dozen of his top energy people, during which several young distaff ADLers missed their own lunches while scuffling for a turn at a peephole in the dining room door.

Stevenson and Stevens, quite unlike Dr. Little before them, never traveled much overseas. Michael Michaelis, who carried out a number of ADL missions in Europe, once said, "For all either Earl or Ray knew, the Common Market might have been in Laos." When Gavin took over, it was apparent that the company, then still grossing no more than $12 million a year, stood the best chance of enlarging its business by moving in one of two directions: by increasing either its work for the government — especially the Department of Defense — or its work abroad. (By the 1980s, there were consulting firms in or around Washington, D.C., that had multimillion-dollar government contracts and did hardly any work for private industry; they were sometimes pejoratively called the Beltway Bandits.) ADL had enjoyed its fair share of government work. In the late 1960s, indeed, that work had generated just about 45 percent of all the firm's income from professional services. But Acorn Park was chary about getting any more deeply involved; the suspicion was well founded that whenever the government got to be too big a brother, it began meddling in the internal affairs of organizations it supported.

So ADL was quite content not to let its government contracts overwhelm it. Some of these had already been of considerable size and consequence. ADL engineers had played a prominent role, for instance, in the development of fueling systems for ICBMs, and ADL systems analysts had helped develop the navy's Trident program for submarine surveillance. When it appeared that ADL's engineering skills might be further put to good use in devising a cooling system for the proposed B-1 bomber, the company even set up a West Coast office in Santa Monica, California. There, Gavin and his colleagues reasoned, they would be happily situated to render whatever services the government might require at outposts like the Vandenberg Air Force Base, where many early missile tests were conducted. When the B-1 program fizzled, the Santa Monica office was shut down.

Gavin, of course, *had* traveled. He elected to follow the international path along which his predecessors had already taken exploratory steps — in, among other far-off places, Egypt and Nigeria. And by 1960, the Operations Research staff had for some time been doing work in London for clients there, chiefly on the initiative of Robert G. Brown, who had come to ADL in 1953 from the U.S. Navy's Operations Evaluation Group. In the fall of 1960, Brown, John Magee, and Martin L. Ernst, who had joined ADL the year before from the same navy group, gave a course on inventory control and production management for eighty European corporate executives at Oxford University's Balliol College. Two months later, at Versailles' Trianon Palace, they put on another splashy ADL operations research conference. Both of these events were of a sort that General Gavin's predecessors would scarcely have dreamed of sponsoring.

Ernst was new to ADL, but he was a veteran of seventeen years' worth of operations research enterprise for the U.S. Navy. ADL had been trying to lure him away since 1952, but he had resisted its advances, having had a generally low opinion of consultants until he became one himself. In due course, he also became Acorn Park's ranking futurologist: When, for instance, the strategic planning section of a large bank wanted to know what the world was going to be like fifteen years hence, Ernst would look into the crystal ball composed of his experience and his imagination and come up with at least a highly informed guess.

Gavin hoped that ADL, if it was not exactly to bestride the globe, would at least visibly scatter its footprints around it. By the 1970s, to cite just a few of hundreds of examples, ADL had drawn up a six-year plan for the Ministry of Development of Iraq; had prepared a study to identify future projects for a trade and industrial policy reform program in Bangladesh; had helped design a new, seventy-thousand-square-mile community for Peru; had organized an industrial park in Nogales, Mexico, just across the border from the United States, where U.S. companies could use comparatively cheap Mexican labor to assemble components for goods to be finished up north; had shown the National Bank of Greece how to simplify its operations by using computers; and had devised a milling method for a newly discovered lode of iron ore in India.

ADL operatives dispatched on such far-flung missions often had to contend with unpredictable situations. Stephen Moss, a chemical engineer with a degree from the Harvard Business School, belonged to the company's Operations and Technology Management Unit, and he was described in ADL literature, almost breathtakingly, as a specialist in position assessment, opportunity identification, strategy development, program planning, and implementation assistance. Moss was once sent to Brazil to try to cope with the difficulties of a rural steel company whose sewage system seemed to have broken down. Just about the only thing Moss was not was a sanitation expert. He did not have to call on any of his categories of expertise, however, to solve the problem. He ascertained that the company had three priorities — A, B, and C — for ordering supplies to be sent to its remote location. Toilet paper had been in category C, and it frequently ran out. When it did, the factory workers had to resort to rags, and these clogged up the toilets and caused havoc. Moss suggested that toilet paper be promoted to category A, and his overjoyed client, on learning further that it was his birthday, threw him a big party and gave him a gaucho knife.

ADL had had foreign assignments before Gavin materialized — the Egyptian mud brick project, for one, and another in

Honduras involving the stabilizing of soil with lime to facilitate the creation of all-weather roads — but the major part of its work outside North America had been only slightly offshore. Back in 1934, the year before Dr. Little died, he had told his Board of Directors that "there seemed to be an opportunity for the company to participate in the industrial development now under way in Puerto Rico and Mexico."

Nothing much had come of that until 1942, when, on M.I.T.'s recommendation, ADL was approached by Teodoro Moscoso, Jr., a Puerto Rican businessman who, ten years out of the University of Michigan, was running a family wholesale drug business. (In later years, Moscoso would be Puerto Rico's economic development administrator, U.S. ambassador to Venezuela, coordinator of the Latin American development project called the Alliance for Progress, and a director of Arthur D. Little, Inc.) Puerto Rico wanted to accelerate its progress in both industry and tourism. There didn't appear to be a good deal that could be done about that while the war was on, but Ray Stevens had come up with one fruitful idea. Puerto Rico had plenty of cement. Why not use it, he proposed, to make bicycle paths, and then Puerto Rico might profitably get into bicycle manufacture — all the more so if respected and prominent citizens like Moscoso would themselves ride around their island on two-wheelers. Next, in 1946, Puerto Rico launched a new economic uplift program called Operation Bootstrap. Moscoso was put in charge of it, and he invited ADL to help him implement it.

That same year of 1946 marked the arrival at ADL of D. Reid Weedon, Jr. On receiving a B.S. degree from M.I.T. in 1941, Weedon had gone into the navy and served with the Pacific Fleet Air Force. He had been a staff preservation officer; packaging things was his forte. After the war, he wanted to start a consulting firm in New York that would specialize in packaging advice. That didn't work out. But on a trip to Boston he met Ray Stevens, who offered him a job and assigned him to Benjamin Fogler, Sr., a mechanical engineer from Maine who had been at ADL since 1922 and among whose many responsibilities now was the Puerto Rico account. Fogler soon put Weedon on it, and Weedon persuaded the island's legislature to underwrite a promotional campaign to increase sales of Puerto Rican rum. During the war, the United States had been awash in it. Puerto Rico had a bottling plant and a carton-making plant, and there was plenty of cargo space on northbound ships that had brought food to the island. The ships were loaded with rum — raw, unaged, unpalatable. But there was a shortage up north of Scotch, and one result was that importers of hard liquor introduced tie-in sales; any distributor who wanted to buy a case of Scotch also had to buy a case of rum, and retail store customers, in turn, as often as not had to buy a bottle of all but undrinkable rum along with every bottle of Scotch they coveted.

That had not bothered Weedon personally. He was a non-drinker. But he was aware that rum's popularity could not be enhanced unless its quality was, too. He got the Puerto Rican legislature to decree that no more of it could be exported unless it had been aged in oak for at least three years. ADL engineers designed a pilot plant to distill, blend, age, and evaluate a new generation of rums. ADL hired an advertising agency and a public relations firm to sing rum's praises.* There was an all-expenses-paid junket to Puerto Rico for the officials of bartenders' union locals. There was a promotional lunch in New York at the University Club, for a somewhat more gentrified crowd, where every guest — ADL was then not averse to tie-in sales itself — not only had rum cocktails thrust upon him but also received as souvenirs a shaker of Ac'cent and a miniature Lane cedar chest.

There were so many advertisements that at one time Weedon was getting free subscriptions from twenty-five magazines that were hoping to be included in that budget.

A full-page ad was scheduled for *Life*, illustrated with a photograph of a mouth-watering Manhattan cocktail — one made, it goes without saying, with rum. Some whiskey importers saw an advance proof of the ad and demanded that it be canceled; they were outraged at the very notion that a proper Manhattan could be concocted from such an alien substance. *Life* was willing to drop the ad but not to refund the money — some $40,000 or $50,-000 — that had already been paid for it. Weedon's Scottish blood practically bubbled at that idea. "I decided to bite the bullet and run the ad," he said. "I decided to let the distillers know that we were going to promote rum and didn't care how they felt about

* The advertising account was to have gone to David Ogilvy. Moscoso came to New York to finalize the arrangements. While he and Weedon were talking in Ogilvy's office, the advertising man swiveled his chair around from his desk and began staring out of a window. He may have been seeking inspiration. Moscoso, though, thought he had been insulted. The account went to McCann-Erickson.

that." How some of the guests at his home felt concerned him
more. "For a while my friends used to hate to come to my house
because I pushed so much rum on them," he said. "There were
limits beyond which I could not prevail upon them to go. They
drew the line at rum martinis."

Reid Weedon would rise high in ADL ranks — also in
M.I.T.'s, becoming, like Dr. Little before him, both a member of
its governing corporation and president of its alumni association — and at the company he became celebrated for his upright-
ness and his frugality. On business trips, not infrequently to the
dismay of an accompanying colleague, he would whenever possible take public transport, instead of taxicabs or limousines, to and
from airports, and he would propose sharing a double hotel room
instead of taking two singles. Because of his concern for the interests of his clients — "Try this rum Alexander"; "How about a
refill on that rum and ginger ale?" — he was as time went on
more and more often given the not always welcome task of sooth-
ing disgruntled ones. (ADL once made a survey of 117 clients to
find out how they liked its efforts on their behalf; 70 percent pronounced themselves pleased, 17 percent displeased, and 13 percent neutral.)

Weedon was sometimes characterized by fellow ADLers as the
conscience of the company. "I've refunded a lot of money and
canceled a lot of bills, or both — unfortunately," he said. Once
General Gavin got a phone call from the president of a Texas
company who had paid ADL handsomely for a study of its operations. The client was not merely dissatisfied; he was well-nigh ap-
oplectic. Weedon looked into the matter and discovered that all
the client's money had been spent, and there was nothing in
ADL's files to show for it except one interoffice memorandum.
Weedon traveled to Texas, went to the company president's office, and said, "Before you start telling me what's wrong, I'd just
like to say that as far as I can see you've got absolutely nothing for
your money. So let me ask you a question. Do you still want the
information you requested at the start?" The president, tight-
lipped, nodded. "In that case," Weedon went on, "we'll start from
scratch. I'll put a new team on it, and we'll deliver the results
with no more payment." The work was accomplished without
further incident, except that the original case leader was transferred to Iran.

In the late 1960s, ADL had been engaged by Chad to help it try to develop its cattle industry. An American diplomat stationed there had been reassigned as ambassador to Zaire, and through his good offices ADL was invited to come to Kinshasa and discuss the formulation of a plan for developing Zaire's industrial potential. The job, had it materialized, would have amounted to $2 million — at that time one of the largest single commissions in the company's history. Weedon and a couple of colleagues went to Africa, met with the country's chef du cabinet and three ministers, and agreed to submit a proposal. Weedon did tell the American ambassador, however, that it was to be understood from the outset that ADL was not prepared to get involved in any "dash" — the under-the-table payments that were so often a concomitant of doing business in that part of the world.

Back in Cambridge, Weedon and others drew up a proposal, and Weedon hand-carried it to Kinshasa. The minister who was supposed to sign it on behalf of the Zairian government suggested, to the ADLer's surprise, that the formality be conducted at his home. The minister also professed not to be able to speak English. Weedon, whose French was minimal, brought along an interpreter. The minister said he wanted to speak to Weedon alone and told the interpreter to wait outside. Then, in perfect English, the minister said the proposal was eminently acceptable, but first. . . . He reached into a desk drawer, pulled out three slips of paper, and said that as ADL got paid in installments for its work, it would be expected to deposit 5 percent of its fees in each of three numbered Swiss bank accounts. It was late in the afternoon. There was a plane to Paris that evening. Weedon told the minister that there would not be one cent of dash, and that unless a contract was signed with no reservations by the time the plane left, he would be aboard it. He flew off that night. The minister did eventually get relieved of his job, but ADL never got *its* job, either.

When Gavin resolved to expand ADL's international operations, he turned first, naturally enough, toward Europe.* ADL al-

---

* For a brief spell, Gavin hoped to do some business with the Soviet Union. He was asked to chair a conference in Kiev, and while in the Ukraine he met a number of high-placed Russian bureaucrats who expressed interest in obtaining ADL's help in connection with, among other ventures, renovating their tunnels and bridges and developing a better

ready had a foothold there, but a tenuous one. During the Second World War, with German submarines devastatingly aprowl in the Atlantic, the British were eager to obtain food supplies from previously untapped sources. At Inveresk, on the bank of the River Esk, six miles from Edinburgh, they converted an old estate into the Institute of Seaweed Research. (The site had been a Roman military outpost and, much later, the residence of Admiral Sir Alexander Milne, G.C.B., K.C.B.) In 1956, Ray Stevens thought it might be useful to have a research affiliate in the United Kingdom, and the institute, which already had some laboratories and which was available for only $120,000 (the nutritional need for seaweed long since having been discounted), seemed a promising location. For seven years, accordingly, a staff, numbering at its peak thirty-seven, worked for ADL there on a variety of missions: investigating glucose polymers for the U.S. Department of Agriculture, for example, and the embrittlement of steel for the British Ministry of Aviation. But the Inveresk operation proved, all in all, to be unrewarding; too few prospective clients, even those based in London, seemed willing to take their problems up to Scotland to try to get them solved.

It would still be some time, indeed, before any of ADL's foreign installations turned a profit. The company's first real branch office in Europe — its purpose was to provide an outpost to conduct planning and acquisition studies and consumer-marketing studies for American companies of multinational bent — opened up for business at the end of 1957. The person selected to be in charge of it was Alexander Bogrow, a multilingual man of Russian origin who, when various sites were being considered, told his colleagues that the ideal spot would be in a small, neutral, centrally located country. Switzerland, he suggested. Zurich, Switzerland. What Bogrow neglected to add, though his associates ultimately forgave him for that lapse in candor, was that he had another compelling reason for picking Zurich: His girlfriend lived there.

That installation limped along for eight years, in the course of

toothpaste. ADL was well positioned to help in both respects. It had once analyzed the strengths and stresses of every bridge and tunnel in the state of California, and its taste and flavor experts had been working on toothpastes for years. But nothing came of it. "I thought I had made a convincing case," Gavin said afterward, "but I might as well have been talking to the moon. I got a lot of nice visits out of our conversations, but not five cents' worth of business. The Russians would pay for production, but not for advice."

which Bogrow had to quit because of illness and Harry Wissmann was sent over to replace him. Among the office's principal clients for a good part of its existence were the federal and regional ministries of trade and industry of Nigeria. Reimbursed in part by the U.S. Agency for International Development, ADL was supposed to help the Nigerians identify feasible projects and to help get these under way. When one foreign manufacturer asked Wissmann where in Nigeria he thought it might be most beneficial to set up shop, the ADLer gave the kind of advice for which consultants' clients are always grateful: If you're interested in a stable work force, he said, go north to Kano or Kaduna, because most northern Nigerians are Muslims, and Muslims don't drink.

Switzerland was neutral but nettlesome. For one thing, the authorities there made it so difficult for ADL to obtain necessary work permits for Americans it wanted to send over that in 1965 the company moved part of that office to the more hospitable environs of Brussels, a city that has been crucial to its continental operations ever since. Twenty years after it began functioning, the Belgian outpost was so firmly entrenched that it seemed a logical enough host for a cocktail party — King Baudouin was among the guests — to celebrate the twenty-fifth anniversary of the local Harvard Club.

When the Brussels operation was getting under way, ADL's presence in Europe was chiefly for the purpose of representing American companies seeking to expand their export trade. The ADLers abroad could fulfill their obligations if they had a reasonable acquaintance with the French or German language. But after a generation or so, the picture changed. European firms wanted to expand *their* export business, and because there were then few French or German or British consulting companies, they turned to ADL for advice. It soon became clear that prospective European clients, the major source of ADL business on that continent from then on, would not deign even to look at a proposal unless it was couched in their own tongue. By then, Nicholas Steinthal, who had joined ADL in 1960 and spoke five languages himself, had on his staff representatives of ten nationalities who could conduct business, as the occasion might arise, in Dutch, Swedish, Danish, Norwegian, and Arabic.

Meanwhile, a small project office had been opened in the Knightsbridge section of London by the Operations Research

Section. A decade later, as business there gradually increased, there was a full-fledged branch office, and it had moved to much plushier quarters on Berkeley Square. Visiting indigenes would sometimes raise their eyebrows on perceiving that, as at Acorn Park, file clerks and secretaries were encouraged to call their bosses by their first names.

By 1985, the London managing director, J. Michael Younger, a graduate of Switzerland's Centre d'Études Industrielles and other institutions, presided over a Management Consulting staff some seventy strong. Complementing them, under Phillip W. Hawley, were eighteen professionals chiefly engaged in energy-related projects. One was a $1 million commission to study all the conceivable hazards — earthquakes, corrosion, airplane crashes, heart attacks, environmental pollution — that might interfere with the orderly operations of two multinational firms planning to bring natural gas from the North Sea to the coast of Scotland. According to J. Gordon Sellers, a technical risk assessment specialist based in London, "My job is to look at things that might blow up and try to determine, 'How safe is "safe"?' Ever since the nineteen-seventies, there's been mounting interest in risk calculations. It's our job to try to calculate the probability that something unexpected will occur, and to further calculate what the consequences would be if it did. It's been interesting to learn that although the public thinks, understandably, largely in terms of big disasters, historically, most people who die in industrial accidents die in those that kill just one or two of them."

Another energy specialist in London, David J. Barker, came to ADL in 1974 with gilt-edged credentials: He had spent fifteen months in Abu Dhabi working for a national oil company and then had done a stint with Mobil. "In March nineteen-eighty-two, when nearly everybody thought the oil market was in a state of collapse," Barker said, "we did an analysis and concluded that, to the contrary, it was going to firm up; and as a result, a couple of our clients — I would rather not disclose their names — made a few hundred million dollars, though, unfortunately, not on a profit-sharing basis with us. Similarly, after the nineteen-seventy-three petroleum crunch, we strongly advised one client who was bent on building a huge new refinery not to, but he was stupid — perhaps he should remain nameless, too — and he spent fifty million on it before we could get him to stop. Still, as it was, we saved him yet another fifty or a hundred million."

Simon Lister of the London staff once saved a containership client a somewhat smaller but no less welcome sum of money. It seemed that some Saudi Arabians, on receiving containerized shipments, didn't realize that the containers were reusable; in fact, they were worth five or six dollars apiece a day to their owners. The Arabs would truck filled containers out to desert outposts, empty them, and leave them there to rust — though some ingenious locals did build structures out of them, including at least one mosque. Lister's job was to organize search parties to retrieve the containers, and before he was through he had managed to return nearly four thousand of them to their grateful dispatchers.

Yet another Londoner, Adrian R. D. Norman, once undertook a computerized survey of such containers delivered to the Republic of South Africa and was surprised to discover that quite a few of those were being used for homes in the hinterlands. The holder of degrees both from Cambridge University and, in the United States, the Columbia University Business School, Norman got into computers very early in their existence, and by the 1980s he was regarded as one of the world's leading experts in the esoteric field of computer crime. He became a prominent member of the Computer Crime Club, and was much in demand as a lecturer on computer crimes and how to get away with them. "Today, using computers," he would tell his audiences, "it is at least theoretically possible to commit a crime in one country while in a second, pick up the proceeds in a third, and hide them in a fourth. Location is no longer a determinant in what you can do."

It has been said by associates of Norman's that his long-standing ambition is to perpetrate a £1 million fraud against the Bank of England with computers and then, of course, to return the money. Norman has denied harboring any such mischievous notion, but in one of his books, titled *Computer Insecurity*, he did devote some space to an Operation GOLDFISH (an acronym for Global Online Data Files and Information System Haven), a data haven being a place granting its users "the freedom to seek, receive, and impart information . . . of all kinds, regardless of frontiers . . . through any . . . media." National governments aspiring to pry into the secrets of data havens, Norman went on, would be foiled by something called Goldfish User Program Purveyors by

International Electronic Systems — a name he conjured up, of course, so that he could conveniently shorten it to GUPPIES.

In the preface to Norman's *Computer Insecurity*, published in 1983, the author wrote, with respect to the career he had been pursuing for more than a decade,

> Consultants remain in business because their clients know that collecting all the information and learning all the skills that might be useful, and then extracting the few that are relevant, is much more expensive than buying the particular skill or information or hiring someone to identify it. Or, as one . . . client put it, "At least by hiring you we expect to make original mistakes, not repeat other people's."

The London office has no laboratories. ADL's technological research in the United Kingdom has been handled, since it forsook Inveresk in 1963, by an up-country outpost called Cambridge Consultants Ltd., or CCL for short. CCL is situated in that university city's equivalent of Silicon Valley: an eighty-three-acre enclave called the Cambridge Science Park, which since 1960 has been home to more than two hundred high-tech companies. (During the Second World War, the land, owned by Trinity College, had served as a marshaling base and repair station for American tanks earmarked for the invasion of Europe.) CCL was founded, also in 1960, by a few young Cambridge graduates, principal among them Timothy N. B. Eiloart, a Trinity man who had earlier attained the questionable academic distinction of having attended ten different schools by the time he was ten years old. Always restless, in later years Eiloart once tried valiantly and vainly, though without vanishing, to cross the Atlantic by balloon. He is remembered in consulting circles as the author of the apothegm "Consultants are people who can tell you how to blow your nose better." Conceivably in part owing to Eiloart's irreverence, his fledgling company went into receivership, and ADL was able in 1961 to acquire 80 percent of its stock for only $250,000.

Now valued at more than $10 million, CCL has 175 employees housed in a spanking modern building, at whose dedication ceremonies, on August 1, 1979, the Prince of Wales, another Trinity grad, was pleased to officiate. The prince made a tape at Buckingham Palace, and the doors of the new structure were rigged electronically to unfold when they heard his voice intone, "I declare this building open." Prince Charles, who was then thirty, was surrounded by contemporaries that day. The average age of the CCL staff was only thirty, and the young men and women there sometimes refer to their parent company, over at the American Cambridge, as Uncle Arthur. They call their own establishment, because it happens to be on a thoroughfare called Milton Road, the Milton Hilton.

When ADLers from the home office are in England, they like to drop in at CCL and observe their youthful colleagues brooding over problems involving electron microscopes, laser beams, and all sorts of up-to-date contrivances. ADL's nephews and nieces play with expensive toys. In the winter of 1983 alone, CCL — assisted by a grant from the British government's Microelectronic Industry Support Program — acquired £400,000 worth of new computer-aided design and computer-aided manufacturing equipment.

A CCL geophysical and instrumentation group has busied itself measuring, on behalf of an oil exploration client, the thickness of Arctic ice; and a CCL optics group, on behalf of the British government, has measured highway pavement irregularities with laser beams hooked up to a computer in a trailer towed along at speeds of up to fifty miles an hour. Also at the bidding of the government, CCL scientists designed and built for the Milk Marketing Board an automated machine to test milk samples for brucellosis. The CCLers like to give their projects gag names, many of them unprintable. A study of cracks on the bridges over motorways became "Fallen Arches"; a computer-integrated manufacturing study for Sweden "Abba"; and the adaptation of lasers to blast furnaces "Hell Hole."

One CCL group spent several high-precision years perfecting a method of nonimpact printing in which ink is broken into tiny dots by ultrasonic vibration, forced through arrays of pinpoint nozzles charged by electrodes, and then deflected rapidly and electronically onto almost any imaginable substance: paper, glass, metal, rubber, human skin, whatever. To demonstrate their nonimpact-printing prowess, CCL scientists have even aimed their jets at bunches of grapes and have ended up with the words "Printed in England" — they have not yet got around to bothering with edible inks — on every visible grape.

X   *Places Where We Hadn't Much Been Before*

We have, as a nation, acquired the habit of being vastly
satisfied with what we have accomplished. ... *What we do,*
we do on a great scale, but we often do it very badly. It is
time for us to pause in our self-congratulation long enough
to inquire whether the things we are doing cannot be better
done.

— Dr. Arthur D. Little, 1909

*W*hen John F. Kennedy was elected president in
1960, he asked General Gavin, for whom France
and Charles de Gaulle had entertained cordial feelings ever since
D Day, to be his ambassador in Paris. Gavin had only that year
ascended to his own presidency at ADL, but he felt that the
honor was one he wanted to accept and could hardly refuse. The
ADL Board of Directors thereupon gave him a leave of absence
for eighteen months, starting on February 17, 1961, and also gave
him $50,000. In his absence, Ray Stevens was to resume the com-
pany's presidency, with Earl Stevenson staying on as chairman.

None of that was accomplished without friction. It was then
the practice to put senior staff men on the board for a year at a
time. Warren Lothrop, the head of Research and Development
and a protégé of Stevenson's, was the incumbent. Howard
McMahon was Stevens's protégé. Lothrop wanted to be the in-
terim president himself. McMahon let it be known that if that
came to pass he would leave. When Stevens's name was put before the board, Lothrop cast the only negative vote, and soon afterward *he* departed.

Gavin retained his seat, and while he was in Paris he got a
monthly report on ADL's fortunes, good and bad, from Howard
F. Hamacher, its assistant treasurer. Whenever Gavin could manage it, he came home for board meetings. During one visit in the

spring of 1962, he made a date for lunch at the Harvard Faculty Club with Henry Kissinger, whom ADL had now and then retained as an outside consultant while Kissinger was on the Harvard faculty and at whose instigation Gavin had become associated with the university's Center for International Affairs. Then Gavin learned that there was a conflicting company lunch the same day. His priorities were clear to him. "The luncheon that you planned for Thursday with ADL people," he wrote to a colleague at Acorn Park, "is far more important to me than any lunch with Henry Kissinger."

While Gavin was ambassador, some of his ADL executives thought the time was ripe for ADL to set up shop in Paris. Gavin himself demurred. He was willing enough to talk informally with the Hires root beer people about their going into the French market (Coke and Pepsi were struggling there, and Johnny Sjöström was studying the impact of various American soft drinks on Gallic taste buds), but the general felt that if ADL actually opened an office, people might infer that he was using his temporary diplomatic post to feather his more or less permanent nest.

It was not until May 1968, when Paris happened to be largely paralyzed by a general strike, that ADL began operations there. As its own legate, it engaged Michel d'Halluin, an urbane, forty-year-old thermodynamics graduate of the Swiss Institute of Technology. D'Halluin had been the fourth-generation proprietor of a family textile company until he sold it off and joined a French consulting firm. John Magee had been introduced to d'Halluin by Dean John McArthur of the Harvard Business School, who had formed a high opinion of d'Halluin's acumen while engaged in research on the structure of French businesses.

Gavin returned to Europe for the opening of the ADL Paris office, and de Gaulle invited him to the Élysée Palace for lunch. When he arrived, de Gaulle asked him where he had come from. He'd flown in from Cologne, Gavin said; he'd had a meeting there with some Bayer aspirin people. De Gaulle, thinking that all his airports were closed, was astonished. He did not know that d'Halluin, a former pilot, had arranged with a pilot friend to ferry Gavin out of Paris and back in a small private plane. "They never tell me the truth!" de Gaulle complained at lunch. "It is not a general strike after all!" When he calmed down, he asked Gavin where the new ADL office was located, and on being told it was on the Champs Élysées, de Gaulle said, "*Oh, Monsieur, très cher!*"

ADL had only a three-room office there at the start, and it was hard-pressed to find enough work to keep its staff of six occupied. Even by 1985, the Paris staff, by then housed on the rue du Faubourg St. Honoré, was merely thirty-six strong; but d'Halluin, still in charge, had the capacity of investing a platoon with the grandeur of an airborne division. One of his most difficult and delicate tasks was to persuade the socialist government of François Mitterrand that the only sensible way of keeping Boussac Saint-Frères, a giant textile concern, from going bankrupt was to lay off four thousand of its eighteen thousand employees. When the Renault and International Harvester operations in France were both imperiled and seemed fated to founder, it was d'Halluin and his staff in Paris who suggested that they merge and were instrumental in preliminary negotiations.

Not long after the Paris office got under way, d'Halluin asked his superiors back in Cambridge if they had to keep on using as the company symbol the flying acorn that ADL had been getting along with comfortably enough for more than fifty years. A flying acorn was to many Frenchmen, he thought his *confrères transatlantiques* ought to be aware, a rather low-class sex symbol. After due deliberation, the company switched to a symbol it felt reasonably confident could not be misconstrued anywhere on earth — a variation of a capitalized Greek delta, into the triangular configurations of which the letters *A*, *D*, and *L* could all be more or less squeezed.

Gavin's high-level associations in France — along with work ADL had done for OPEC — helped smooth the way for the company's entry into Algeria when that former French colony attained independence in 1962. Once there, ADL's presence was much enhanced by the efforts of a petroleum economist on its staff, F. Cort Turner, who established and maintained a good working relationship with the appropriate Algerian authorities. For several years after that, ADL had as many as twenty people in Algeria at a time, advising the new government in particular on how to make good use of its reserves of oil and natural gas. Algeria needed help; the French civil service had all but disappeared, and in any event the new nation wanted to reduce its reliance on French expertise. ADL did a good many feasibility studies on processing, distributing, and marketing Algerian resources. In due course, however, these efforts incurred the irritation of some French owners of assets there who thought that ADL seemed to be siding with its new African acquaintances at the expense of its good old friends back in Europe in the negotiations for the deliverance of those assets into Algerian hands. (The left-wing Algerian government had besought such assistance from Russian and Chinese advisers with whom it felt more ideologically at ease, but it had found them wanting in know-how.) Back in Paris, the satirical journal *Canard Enchaîne* — Chained Duck — went so far as to call General Gavin a traitor to France. Gavin asked his public relations advisers what, if anything, he should do to counter the allegation. "Gather as many journalists as you can at the foot of the Eiffel Tower and parachute off the top of it" was one suggestion. Counselors of a less sportive bent advocated doing nothing, and the minor furor, much to the relief of Michel d'Halluin and his staff, soon abated.

For a company with an unreservedly capitalistic outlook, ADL often found itself much involved — as Reid Weedon had been in Zaire — in the economic affairs of the predominantly noncapitalistic Third World. ADL, in the sixties, helped Togo to develop a long-range agricultural plan, and it advised Ghana on the feasibility of setting up a free trade zone. For Cyprus, there was an evaluation of oil-refining operations, and for Liberia, an analysis of its iron ore industry. Tanzania, Senegal, Zambia, and Ethiopia all called on ADL, in more halcyon days, to set up national tourism programs. Winslow Martin, who came to the company in 1960 and for a while ran its London office, spent a lot of time flying at low altitudes over Ethiopian beaches, looking for potential sites for seaside resorts. Ethiopia's minister of planning at the time particularly wanted a tourist haven on the Red Sea; Martin felt constrained to discourage his client from pursuing that hope because his aerial reconnaissance had revealed that nowhere along the desolate stretch of coast to which the minister hoped tourists would swarm was there any greenery more than eighteen inches in height.*

* ADL did research on tourism in its home world, too. The state of Maine once asked it to assess different categories of visitors to its domain on the basis of how much money they spent and how little damage they did to the environment. It may have been with mixed feelings that the state so traditionally hospitable to outdoorsmen received ADL's findings that delegates to business conventions came out best on both counts and campers worst.

In ADL's dealings with Third World nations, ideology often seemed of little consequence, though that had not always been the case. Before Fidel Castro assumed power, the company had had an amicable relationship with the National Bank of Cuba, advising it on the suitability of establishing new industries there, ranging from steel to catsup; but then Che Guevara had taken over the bank, and its officers turned cool. Castro himself, though, seemed disinclined to break things off. He had at least one meeting — again to discuss Cuba's industrial outlook — with an ADL team. Its members concluded afterward that American interests, political as well as economic, would be better served by cooperating with him than by alienating him; but nobody in a position to do anything about that ever saw fit to consult them on the matter.

Angola, on the other hand, was happy to invite ADL to help it reconstitute some of its government ministries and to help it try to revive a once-flourishing coffee industry that had all but collapsed after the onetime colony became independent in 1975 and its Portuguese plantation owners and managers decamped. Libya's petroleum officials, too, were glad to avail themselves in turn of ADL expertise. It was not always easy, however, for representatives of an American consulting firm to work there. When Roberto Batres, the head of ADL's Mexico City office, arrived at the Tripoli airport one day, he saw his luggage move along on a conveyor belt and then disappear. He found out that the Libyan authorities routinely took fifteen or so suitcases from each arriving flight and stashed them in a warehouse. He managed to get inside the warehouse, where he saw thousands of pieces of luggage, some mildewed, with markings on them indicating they'd come from Japan, Holland, Peru, and all over the world. Batres spotted his own bags, but guards prevented him from retrieving them. Eventually he was told that the Libyans had adopted this annoying practice as a means of reminding foreign visitors that while they had to be admitted to allow Libyans the advantage of their skills, their status was that of a necessary evil.*

* Batres joined the Mexico City office in 1965, quite by mistake. Just out of the University of Texas with an M.B.A. degree, he had been hired by Arthur Andersen & Company, the accounting firm, to work in its Mexico City branch. He was walking along the Paseo de la Reforma to report for duty, but he entered the wrong building, saw the word "Arthur" on a lobby bulletin board, and took an elevator up to the ADL premises. He seemed confused when he arrived — he had never heard of Arthur D. Little, Inc. — and when a receptionist asked him what he wanted, he explained that he was the M.B.A. who had just

Merely losing one's luggage was an inconvenience to which ADLers who had to travel frequently became stoically inured. Some of them, as they moved around the globe, also became inured to physical danger. Michael Younger, in Bolivia one time for a presentation to a prospective client, found himself obliged to make it during a revolution, crouched under an office table while dive-bombers zoomed overhead; inasmuch as Younger was well over six feet tall and the table was a fairly low one, his companions were impressed equally by his agility and his sangfroid. When Donald Sparrow, a forest products specialist (also, along with Jean de Valpine and Norman Mailer, a member of the Harvard class of 1943), submitted a proposal for the exploitation of wood resources to a Philippine government minister which contrasted sharply with that minister's own view of the situation, there was such a furor that at one point Sparrow was afraid he was going to be lynched. Similarly, there was apprehension back in Cambridge about the safety of Benjamin Fogler, Jr., in the Philippines after a report of his to the Philippine government dwelt more harshly than any officials in Manila would have liked on corruption in the financing of rice production.

Between 1961 and 1971, one of the main ADL preoccupations in Africa was the organization and operation of the Nigerian Industrial Development Managerial Training Program, one object of which was to prepare young Nigerians to run both government agencies and private industries. The Nigerian government wanted its future managers to be trained in situ, and for a while ADL, under the auspices of the U.S. Agency for International Development, sent instructors over there from the United States, recruiting them mostly at Tufts and Syracuse universities. But there seemed to be too many distractions at home for the students, so it was decided in 1961 to teach them at Cambridge, using ADL staff members for a faculty, at the Management Education Institute, whose curriculum included business planning and policy, international finance and banking, and strategies of economic development.

---

been engaged but perhaps he was at the wrong place. The receptionist knew that ADL had been looking for a Mexican with an M.B.A. and told him to sit down. She ran inside and reported her discovery to Richard L. Bolin, who'd been transferred from Puerto Rico to Mexico City as an offshoot of Operation Bootstrap, and within an hour Batres had switched employers without ever laying eyes on the one he'd set out for.

From the outset, it was ADL's determination that the institute focus on the Third World. (The company, which was not after all in the education business, had hoped that some American university or college would run the program, and for a couple of years it did get Syracuse to collaborate on it.) By the early 1980s the MEI had attracted students from seventy-six countries, their tuitions paid by such sponsors as the Tanzania Rural Development Bank, the Ecuador State Oil Company, the Management Institute of Indonesia, and the Korean Trade Association. ADL recruiters, like college athletic coaches, roamed the backwaters in search of promising students and advertised for them in journals like the *Far Eastern Economic Review* and *Malaysia Business*.

In 1973, the Massachusetts Board of Higher Education authorized the MEI to grant the degree of master of science in administration, retroactive to the graduating class of 1972. The MEI thereupon became the only degree-granting institution in Massachusetts wholly owned by a private, profit-making organization. (Two comparable academies, those of the Wang Institute and the Massachusetts General Hospital's Institute of Health Professions, are nonprofit entities.) In 1976, the MEI cleared another hurdle, becoming a fully accredited graduate school; the degree it could now award was a master of science in management. Accreditation requires a full-time dean. Between 1980 and 1985, that post was occupied by Arnold K. Weinstein, a Columbia M.B.A. and Ph.D. who had taught in Canada, Australia, and Switzerland and, when ADL recruited him, was a tenured professor of marketing and international business at Boston College. Weinstein moved on to become dean of the University of Massachusetts Business School in 1985.*

The MEI, like most business schools, adopted the case study method of instruction. (There were field trips to the New York Stock Exchange and World Bank headquarters in Washington.) Most of its cases were constructed around ADL experiences in the entrepreneurial world, and that was fitting, inasmuch as almost all its instructors were ADLers. Robert C. Terry, Jr., for example, who taught public administration, organization, and en-

---

* Weinstein, who was happy to have under him a totally untenured faculty, fired one teacher who told him, just an hour before he was scheduled to meet with a class, that he couldn't make it because he had to confer with a client. "You have ninety-five clients waiting for you," Weinstein said, and told the consultant not to bother to come around anymore.

vironmental management, had by 1985 twenty-five years of far-flung experience — including teaching stints in Egypt and Kenya — at posts in India, Pakistan, Bangladesh, the Philippines, Iraq, Syria, Jordan, and New Hampshire.

Most of Weinstein's students came from areas where social issues (environmental concerns, for instance) were traditionally of little consequence, and to make the students aware of some of the ethical conflicts they might be called on to resolve in future years, in 1980 the dean added one outsider to his teaching roster — Verne Henderson, a Congregationalist minister well versed in non-American cultures. An African student who on graduation was slated to run a bank branch in a rural community once asked Henderson what he should do if he were approached for a loan by the chief of the dominant tribe there, a man notorious far and wide as a bad credit risk. Give him the loan by all means, was Henderson's reply; without the support of the chief in that kind of community, a bank would be doomed.

One of the MEI's star teachers, and its president for eleven years, was Joseph Voci, who came to ADL in 1951 after graduating from Northeastern in chemical engineering and then spending two years in Iowa designing a plant to make starch derivatives from corn. "When I got my job at ADL it was the biggest day of my life," he said more than thirty years later, "and I told my wife, 'I'll never want to go anywhere else,' and I didn't." Much of Voci's long career at the company was spent abroad — four years in Brazil, for instance, in the course of which he set up an ADL branch in Rio de Janeiro, and long enough in Tanganyika, when it was getting ready to become independent Tanzania, to set up a cashew-processing industry and to earn the sobriquet Mr. Cashew Nut. Voci had such good rapport with Africans that sometimes in his freewheeling lectures he got away with statements that other teachers might hesitate to express. In a classroom discussion one day about a factory in Kaduna, Nigeria, he said that he could pick up a telephone in Concord, Massachusetts, and have a bulldozer delivered to him in five minutes. "If I pick up a phone in Kaduna," Voci went on, "I can't even get an operator." None of the several Nigerians in his class seemed offended.

The base tuition at the MEI for the Master of Science in Management Program is $12,000 a year. For matriculants in the Petroleum Management Program, the cost is $7,900 a year. (Those students take field trips to Louisiana and California.) By 1985, the MEI had 1,343 graduates scattered around the globe and holding such jobs, when they last reported in, as deputy minister for information and tourism in Venezuela, vice-president for credit and marketing of the National Housing and Savings Bank of Liberia, planning director for the Ministry of Petroleum in Angola, managing director of the General Petroleum and Minerals Organization of Saudi Arabia, acting director of the Management Development and Productivity Institute of Ghana, manager of the Management Services Department of the Korea Development Bank, and director of information and computers for the Ministry of Oil in Kuwait. Musing on where his former students were located and on the influence they were bringing to bear on the affairs of their nations, Voci exclaimed in 1984, "Christ! That's the future of ADL in the world market!"

One of the first ADLers involved with the Nigerian training program was Harland Riker, who after joining the company initially had left it and spent nearly five years in Iran, where he set up a management-training program sponsored by the oil companies then in good standing there. Riker's comings and goings were not especially exceptional. Andrew Sivak, for instance, a life sciences expert, worked at the company from 1961 to 1963, departed to spend eleven years teaching at the New York University Medical School, and then came back. Brian Layng, a marketing specialist, defected for five years to Levi Strauss. On the other hand, when Elliott Wilbur, eventually ADL's vice-president in charge of Resource Consulting, arrived at age thirty-five in 1965, he had decided before he began working that he was going to use his stay at ADL simply as a stepping-stone to something better. "I came here to be from here," he said in 1984 — never having gone away at all.

When Riker became president of Arthur D. Little International in 1984, he was on his third tour of duty. A Bostonian, Riker had a bachelor of science degree from Tufts and an M.B.A. from Harvard.* During his second go-around at ADL, he was much im-

---

* Riker's ancestors came to the New World from Amsterdam, and eventually owned part of New York's Bowery, part of the acreage that became La Guardia Airport, and, of course, Rikers Island. They sold everything in the middle of the nineteenth century. "When I think of how I could have helped to handle that transaction!" Harland said one day at Acorn Park.

mersed in the company's activities in Saudi Arabia. (Until ADLers became familiar there, they sometimes had to remind Arabs they encountered that they were not connected with another organization that used the same initials — the resolutely Jewish Anti-Defamation League.) The company found all sorts of ways to be useful to the Saudis. The minister of Industry and Electricity, for example, was so overwhelmed by visitors whom he felt out of politeness he had to receive that he couldn't get any work done. ADL solved his problem by having a film produced; the minister could greet strangers audiovisually without actually having to meet them in person.

In 1968, Riker had a proposal to make to the Saudi government for a far larger undertaking, and he thought his chances of getting it approved would be enhanced if General Gavin — by then the chairman of ADL's Board of Directors — would come over and talk to the government officials involved. Gavin did not, as a rule, like to deal with anybody's subordinates. So when Riker urged him to make the trip, he said he'd be glad to — but only, of course, if a meeting could be arranged for him and King Faisal. "I work best at the head-of-state level," he told Riker.* "When the general invited you to do something," Riker remarked later, "there wasn't much debate. Where he'd come from, you didn't debate with your superiors."

An audience with the king was not easy to set up. But the year before, because of his opposition to the war in Vietnam, Gavin had publicly resigned from something called the Massachusetts Democratic Advisory Council, whereupon a Citizens to Draft Gavin movement had started in that state. As a dark horse presidential candidate, he had been featured on the cover of *Business Week*. Riker hadn't been able to make much headway with the king's chief of protocol, and he was trying to figure out what to do next when a copy of the magazine arrived in Riyadh. Riker rushed over to the protocol office, brandishing the publication, and said, "I'm going to save your career." His Majesty's man looked puzzled. "When word gets out that you prevented your king from having a private meeting with our next president even

* ADLers who knew Gavin well treated him with a mixture of respect and amusement. "Gavin likes to meet with heads of state, or better," one of them once said at lunch. "Better?" a companion asked. Did the speaker mean with God? "I've often wondered" was the response.

before he's elected," Riker went on, "and thus giving His Majesty a chance to influence future American policies, you'll be finished." By the time Riker got back to his office, he had a message that the appointment he'd sought had been made.

By 1985, ADL had so many activities going on in that part of the world that back at Acorn Park it had — much in the manner of the Department of State — a Saudi Arabian desk. However, in 1966 its work there was just getting under way, and nobody was disposed to volunteer to oversee it on a year-round basis. So a quadrumviral presence was established — each of four men staying in residence for three months at a stretch. (The system had its minor advantages: Whenever the landlord of the villa ADL had leased for the men wanted to raise the rent, the occupant of the moment would say that the matter would have to be discussed with his successor.) Riker, with his Iranian background, was a logical choice for the foursome. So was Kamal N. Saad, a Lebanese Quaker trained in chemical engineering at the American University of Beirut who joined ADL that year and whose fluency in Arabic and familiarity with the Islamic world would prove invaluable to the company on many a scene thereafter.

Still another member of the group was John H. Reedy, a veteran of months of ADL service in Nigeria, where his mettle had been sorely tested. ADL was working for the government — being paid through the U.S. Agency for International Development — in Lagos, and when the company was asked whether Nigeria should buy some machinery that American firms were eager to sell it, Reedy had advised against it. A couple of the rejected firms (ADL clients themselves, as it happened) were furious. They complained to the U.S. ambassador that while they were paying taxes and Congress was giving their tax money to AID, here was ADL being reimbursed by AID and blocking the efforts of would-be investors. Reedy came under considerable pressure to turn over his negative reports to the disgruntled firms, but he had stubbornly refused; the documents, he said, belonged to his client, the government of Nigeria, and anybody who wanted access to them would have to ask the appropriate ministries. The interests of the client, ADLers have long been indoctrinated to believe, are paramount.

The fourth member of the team in Saudi Arabia was another ADLer fluent in Arabic, Polyvios Vintiades. Born in Egypt, where his Greek father was working for the Suez Canal Company, Vintiades had also attended Beirut's American University and had then obtained a master's degree in civil engineering at M.I.T. He got his start at ADL in Operations Research, under John Magee. Vintiades left ADL in 1981, after a twenty-year association, to join an investment management company in New York, but while he was around he was dispatched on all sorts of overseas missions.

In 1967, on behalf of AID, he traveled to South Vietnam to help try to determine what were that country's real needs in corrugated steel, cement, and pharmaceuticals. The United States had been subsidizing South Vietnam's imports of all those commodities, and it had occurred to someone in Washington that the huge amounts being shipped over exceeded the apparent requirements of the civilian economy. What was the civilian economy, anyway? What was the population? It seemed to be twice as large in the daytime as at night. Where were all the goods going? To the Vietcong or what? Vintiades and his colleagues spent six weeks in Saigon and Da Nang, ferreting out whatever information they could in that stressful environment, and they concluded that much of the material was being exported from Vietnam, at vast profits to the exporters, to Thailand. Here was an instance of ADL's submitting a report that the client, all things considered, would just as soon not have wished to receive.

ADL decided to open a Middle East office in 1976, and after briefly considering Beirut (too much fighting) and Cairo (too poor a telephone system), settled on Athens and put Vintiades in charge, which was agreeable to him because by then his mother was living there. When he quit the company, that office was closed, and Middle East operations have been conducted subsequently out of London by a British economist, L. Ray Kelly. Vintiades had met Kelly in Saudi Arabia and enticed him away from a rival, SRI, for whom Kelly had been supervising a project for the Ministry of Planning. After switching companies, Kelly helped organize yet another consulting concern — a joint venture with ADL called the Saudi Consulting House. "Trying to teach people consulting is not the easiest task in the world," Kelly said afterward. "It's sort of like trying to teach people to breathe."

In 1984, ADL spent $6 million on employee travel. (The company is the third-largest user of telephones in Cambridge, out-long-distanced only by Harvard and M.I.T.) *The Little Paper* routinely carries notes on visa processing, and another in-house journal gives information on hotel discounts in St. Louis and Bangkok. ADL's clients are customarily billed for 10 percent more than actual travel expenses. Among oft-repeated ADL apocrypha is the yarn about one peripatetic consultant who got into trouble with his section leader because he stayed in a forty-dollar-a-night motel in Arizona; his superior said that surely somewhere in that state there was at least an eighty-dollar room, which would have netted the section an extra four dollars per night on that particular trip. The superior was subsequently relieved.

When airlines began giving bonuses of one kind or another to frequent fliers, including half-fare tickets that some employees found it agreeable to pass along to their spouses, one cost-conscious executive decreed that thenceforth any such benefits acquired in the course of business properly belonged to the company. ADLers tend to be individualistic and resentful of what they deem to be excessive authority. One of them promptly drew up and issued a supposedly supplementary memorandum to the staff instructing all hands to be sure to turn in any paper napkins, swizzle sticks, macadamia nuts, magazines, emergency evacuation instructions, and vomit bags that they might have accumulated while in flight.

Men and women operating in the international field often spent nearly 50 percent of their time away from home. "Nobody here knows where anybody else is much of the time unless they need to know," Chairman of the Board Robert Mueller has remarked. "You're sort of not supposed to tell people where you're going because it might turn out to be a place that somebody else regards as his territory." (One of Mueller's biggest shocks, on moving to Acorn Park after years as a high-level executive at Monsanto, with all the perquisites that entailed, came when he flew to Toronto one day on behalf of ADL and nobody met him at the airport.) It was fortunate for the company that one member of the staff, Charles R. Hadlock, once did make his movements known, though out of a sense of responsibility less to his employer than to the parents of thirty-three Boy Scouts he was leading on a hiking trip through the Pyrenees. The Junta de Energia Nuclear, Spain's atomic agency, needed some quick advice on disposing of nuclear wastes. That was the scoutmaster's specialty. Acorn Park tracked him down and persuaded him to leave his troop long enough to meet with some of the junta's officials. Hadlock had no clothes with him other than his scoutmaster's outfit, but that proved to be no hindrance; his uniform resembled that of a Spanish army officer, and he received respectful salutes all the way along his path to the consultation.

A mathematician, Hadlock was one of several ADLers who developed a computer software system called WAPPA — Waste Package Performance Assessment — for improving the disposal of all sorts of trash. Sometimes he collaborated with an ADL geologist, Peter D. Mattison, who was color-blind and, needing something other than hue as a means of identifying minerals and soils, had hit upon taste as a substitute. Out in the field, Mattison would startle a companion, after thoughtfully rolling an object around in his mouth, by saying, "Here, sample this piece of granite; it's really quite different from gneiss."

ADL's first office in the Far East was opened in Japan in 1978. Six years after that, another was established in Singapore. It was inaugurated with a reception at the Raffles Hotel — suitably enough inasmuch as the hotel and ADL both dated back to 1886. John Magee flew over for the unveiling; stopping off in Tokyo on the way, he was a guest speaker at a symposium on "New Waves of Technology in the United States" put on by the *Nihon Keizai Shimbun*, the Japanese counterpart of the *Wall Street Journal*. The auditorium in which Magee spoke would seat only 650; so avid were local businessmen to hear what he had to say that 2,000 of them applied for admittance.

Most of the work that the thirty-person ADL staff in Tokyo engages in is technological, and most of the professionals are engineers. Yoshimichi Yamashita, who presides over that branch and who in 1984 directed a multiclient study titled "The Japanese Optoelectronics Industry: 1982–1992," is himself a mechanical engineer. The Tokyo office had a hand in a feasibility study for Toyota on a manufacturing venture in the United States; and when agents of the People's Republic of China wanted sound advice on how to go about purchasing Japanese steel, Japanese refrigerators, and other such amenities, it was to ADL that they turned. Even so, the majority of ADL's clients in Tokyo are representatives of American companies, and it presumably makes their hearts beat faster upon visiting Yamashita's domain to hear, whenever a phone rings, some chimes playing "Home on the Range."

The company had long been acquainted with that part of the world. For instance, under the direction of William A. W. Krebs, Jr., a onetime professor of legal studies at M.I.T., an ADL team had spent two years conducting a Southeast Asia regional transport study.* That project had got under way in the fall of 1969 when eight states — Indonesia, Singapore, Laos, the Philippines, South Vietnam, Thailand, Brunei, and Malaysia — convened at Kuala Lumpur, Malaysia, and resolved to have a study made of what sort of transportation facilities they had and would need by 1990. Brunei later dropped out; the seven remaining countries then had a total population of 230 million and an average per capita income of $130. The Asian Development Bank was the titular client for the survey, which cost $2.9 million; the actual money came mainly from AID and the United Nations Development Program. By the end of the project, fifty-six ADLers had worked on the study, and its final report, printed in Singapore, filled five fat hardcover volumes. One of its forecasts was that while there were 181,200 automobiles in the region in 1960, by 1990 there would be 10,766,000.

It was just about the first time that those nations, most of them remnants of colonialism, had got together on any large regional undertaking. "Of course, it would probably have happened, sooner or later, without us," Krebs said later. "But it did kill off a lot of pork-barrel, politically oriented projects that made no economic sense locally or regionally — ports or airports located with no rational justification for their being there, for instance. That was of immense importance to the countries involved. And what was important to ADL was that it put us solidly in places where we hadn't much been before."

* Krebs, among whose classmates at the Yale Law School were Supreme Court Justice Potter Stewart and President Gerald Ford, was general counsel for the National Science Foundation in the early 1950s and as such got to know Earl Stevenson. Soon after Stevenson's falling-out with ADL's longtime lawyer Alexander Whiteside, in 1953, he asked Krebs to become the company's legal adviser. Krebs came over full-time in 1956, and in the ensuing twenty-nine years represented ADL in forty countries, most of them in the Third World.

XI *The Excitement of Foresight*

> *. . . in the early days of science, chemists patrolled the shores*
> *of the great ocean of the unknown, and seizing upon such*
> *fragments of truth as drifted in within their reach, turned*
> *them to the enrichment of the intellectual and material life of*
> *the community. Later they ventured timidly to launch the*
> *frail and often leaky canoe of hypothesis and returned with*
> *richer treasures. Today, confident and resourceful as the*
> *result of many argosies, and having learned to read the stars,*
> *organized, equipped, they set sail boldly on a charted sea in*
> *staunch ships with tiering canvas bound for new El Dorados.*
> — Dr. Arthur D. Little, 1913

*A*DL is a little like a university," Polyvios Vintiades
once said. "You don't leave. You graduate." (Indeed,
in the fashion of an alumnus, Vintiades didn't sever all connections when he moved on; he remained a director of Arthur D.
Little International.) In the late 1960s and early 1970s, there was
much of the same ferment and turbulence at Acorn Park as on
many a strictly academic campus. Business was down in 1971,
and Howard McMahon, then in the seventh year of his presidency, felt obliged to cut the staff by 10 percent.* He also established a social responsibility unit, one of whose initial functions
was to inquire into the feelings of ADL wives whose husbands
had to travel a good deal. The responses to a questionnaire circu-
lated among the spouses revealed considerable discontent. One
woman with three small children said that her husband traveled
half the time and that even when he was at home he worked every
night and all weekend long. "No father for Boy Scout banquet,"
she complained. Her reply was later tersely annotated "This couple separated a few months after interview."

The social responsibility committee eventually issued a report
that said, *inter* many *alia,*

---

* McMahon, to his relief, stepped aside as president the following November and returned to research, which he much preferred to administration.

Three presidents — of the United States, France, and Arthur D. Little. Above: The James Gavins, on leave from ADL, are the guests of honor at a lunch for the John F. Kennedys at the ambassador's residence in Paris in May 1961. Below: The Gavins at the Élysée Palace in September 1962, for a farewell lunch given by the Charles de Gaulles before the ambassador's return to the United States and to Acorn Park.

ADL's Management Education Institute is unique: a degree-granting academic entity (since 1973) belonging to a profit-making organization. Above, in second row, Chief Executive Officer John Magee chats with Governor Michael Dukakis of Massachusetts during the academic procession before the 1983 commencement exercises. (*Photo by Richard Hosterman*) Below, students in a mid-1960s management training program being escorted by, at left, Harland A. Riker, now senior vice-president of Arthur D. Little, Inc. (*Photo by Ted Polumbaum*)

Over the years, Acorn Park has attracted many visitors from abroad, among them, above, a delegation of visitors from the People's Republic of China, who were greeted by (right to left) veteran ADL executives William Reinfeld and Bruce S. Old. His Royal Highness Prince Henri of Luxembourg, then heir apparent to his country's throne, led a group of his compatriots in 1978, when their steel industries were being modernized and, with a large number of workers facing unemployment as a result, ADL was asked to encourage new industries to locate there. Shown below (right to left), Prince Henri; Michel d'Halluin, head of ADL's Paris office; Prime Minister of Luxembourg Gaston Thorn; Emmanuel Tesch, head of the Luxembourg steel company Arbed; and ADL Vice-President Harry G. Foden.

ADL in the United Kingdom: Above, Sir Geoffrey Howe, secretary for Foreign and Commonwealth Affairs, attends a London lunch in October 1984 to celebrate the twenty-first anniversary of the establishment of the company's office there. Pictured, from left to right: Sir Geoffrey, J. Michael Younger, Robert Kirk Mueller, and Harland Riker. (*Photo by Strat Mastoris*) Upcountry, distinguished visitors to the ADL research center Cambridge Consultants Ltd. have included (bottom left) the Prince of Wales, here watching a demonstration of a wave weaver, an adaptation of electronics designed for the textile industry; and (bottom right) Tian Jiyun, vice-premier of the State Council of the People's Republic of China, shown examining some samples of nonimpact printing. (*Photo by Michael Manni*)

Arthur D. Little at work in Asia: Vonna Deulen, head of ADL's projects office for Bangkok, signing a contract for a $330,000 study of the restructuring of Thailand's transportation and communications services. At left, Dr. Snoh Unakul, secretary general of Thailand's National Economic and Social Development Board. At right, U.S. Ambassador John Gunther Dean. (*Photo courtesy of the National Economic and Social Development Board of Thailand*)

Members of the ADL family travel extensively, so it was perhaps only meet that they developed, for American Airlines, the first computerized reservations system. (*Photo courtesy of American Airlines*)

ADL in space: Left, Peter E. Glaser and an early model of his mind-boggling satellite solar power station. (*Photo by David A. Marlin*) Right, a heat flow probe — part of an advanced lunar scientific experiments package — designed and built by ADL, in collaboration with the Lamont-Doherty Geological Observatory of Columbia University, for an astronaut to drill a nine-foot-deep hole on the moon to measure its subsurface heat flow and thermal conductivity. (*Photo courtesy of the National Aeronautics and Space Administration*)

Chief Executive Officer John Magee chats with chemist Carol Porg in a modern-day chemical analysis laboratory.

The company cannot undertake to alter or to improve the personalities and problems of its employee wives. Perhaps the most that it can do is to show that it cares about the tensions created by its style of business and to do those peripheral things it can do to reduce tensions. . . . In all of our discussions we have overlooked the feelings and problems of the husband torn between family and job and suffering the inevitable guilt of loving both. It is possible that this can be better done in a group than in a bedroom at two in the morning.

Some disgruntled employees sent out another questionnaire that July, this one to the Board of Directors relating to their grievances; the minutes of the next board meeting recorded that "There does seem to be some significant misunderstanding and failure of communication." That did not jibe at all with Gavin's conception of handling complaints through an orderly hierarchical chain of command. He turned up in the employees' cafeteria a few days later, removed his suit coat, rolled up his sleeves, stood up straight, called for attention, and said, "From now on if you want to deal with the company, you deal with *me*."

Other employees started working on an in-house newspaper in which they had hoped further to vent their spleen. They planned to spend $1,200 a year to put it out. Just two hours before the publication was scheduled to go to press, Chief Executive Officer Gavin announced that he was allocating $25,000 to his chief personnel officer, James Jagger, so that a much more ambitious journal could be published — one, of course, over which management would have control. Harking back to his martial career, Gavin commanded further that it was time to close ranks, and to that end he inaugurated a series of employees' meetings; these would not get under way, however, until after the close of the regular work day. One upshot of *that* was a study of ADL's corporate responsibility. The company's primary allegiance, the inquiry concluded, was to its clients, and after them, in descending order of importance, to its employees, its survival and growth, its shareholders, and, lastly, the public at large.

The chairman of the group that conducted the study was a member of the board, Eli Goldston, Jr. Goldston was, among other things, chief executive officer of Eastern Gas & Fuel Associates, the holder of no less than four Harvard degrees (in economics, law, and business management), and the person responsible for one of Boston and the nation's most visible works of art: the

172 / THE PROBLEM SOLVERS

huge gas tanks just off the Southeast Expressway that had been so strikingly striped by then-nun Sister Corita. Goldston was a colorful executive. Once his company bought a firm that serviced oil-drilling rigs in the Gulf of Mexico. Curious to know more than his associates had told him about the new acquisition, he betook himself to the scene and — accompanied by a son of the previous owner — boarded a small boat that was ferrying supplies out to one of the big rigs. Goldston noticed a rack of candy bars, among them Tootsie Rolls bearing a five-cent price tag. He asked his young companion how anybody could possibly hope to make any profit selling them there for a nickel. "Mr. Goldston," the son replied, "why do you think we sold you the company?"

By early 1972, ADL was once again concerned about its managerial future, with Royal Little more or less in charge of developments. Gavin was getting on. Magee had succeeded McMahon as president, but Royal didn't believe that Magee was yet ready to become chief executive officer. "In those days I didn't think John could make it," Royal said in 1984. "I've since had to apologize. I made a mistake." As had been the case when Gavin was recruited, Royal thought someone not already on the staff should take the helm. This time, among those he approached in vain was George Shultz, then President Richard Nixon's secretary of the treasury.

Soon Goldston emerged as the leading candidate. The rest of the board decided in December 1973 that he would become the company's chairman and chief executive officer as of April 1974, with Magee staying on as president and Gavin shifting to chairman of the executive committee. But the very next month, Goldston suffered a fatal heart attack. A board committee trying to sort out the question of managerial succession recommended in June 1974 that Magee step up to chief executive officer and that Gavin continue to be chairman until his retirement. The recommendation was carried out.

Meanwhile, as in the rest of the nation, ADL had to come to grips not merely with the laments of its male employees' wives but with its corporate attitude toward women on its staff. Thirty-one percent of its professionals were female by 1985, but a decade earlier the percentage was only 24. There have been those (among them one woman who once put together a case study of ADL for a business school) who have contended that women have the wrong psyche for the intense demands of the consulting business.

ADL's own female employees, though, did not at all concur. They resented the fact, or so it seemed to them, that not infrequently the company would hire female college graduates as secretaries, apparently in the belief that this would give the organization a certain cachet. The dimensions of a position offered to one woman with an M.B.A. degree, for instance, consisted of half-time as a research assistant and the other half as a secretary. She took a job at a bank instead. Another young woman, who did sign up, not long afterward invented a new and highly marketable medicine. When the company applied for the patent on it, that was done in the name of her male superior, and shortly thereafter she was transferred to a job as a librarian, though as it happened she knew next to nothing about libraries.

One college graduate who was hired as a secretary, Ellen I. Metcalf, moved up the corporate ladder — in due course she had charge of much of the strategic-planning work that ADL did for the major automobile companies — but mainly because some sympathetic men let her help them with their professional chores during the daytime; she attended to her secretarial functions evenings and weekends. Ellen T. Curtiss, who in 1975 became the first woman ever sent by ADL to the advanced management program of the Harvard Business School, had been employed for thirteen years before she was thus honored. "It wasn't that they were exactly prejudiced, mind you," she said much later. "They're just slower than most. They do have to take care of the men first."

In 1976, Curtiss became a vice-president of an in-house subsidiary called, since 1980, Decision Resources, which evolved from a succession of specialized industry information services and became a substantial profit center. Today it brings in $4 million or $5 million a year by, among other services, providing computerized data about two hundred manufacturers in sixty-two countries. Decision Resources, which is careful to say at the same time it touts those services that it does "not assume any liability for the accuracy or comprehensiveness of the information presented," used to give away an annual appraisal of the automotive industry. Now this is sold, for $2,000 a copy.

Along with putting out such specialized tracts as "Outlook in

Iran," "Strategies to Compete for Chinese Business Opportunities" (both 1980), and "Youth and Aging in the '80s" (1982), Decision Resources runs some programs and publications that command very stiff yearly subscription fees — $5,000 to $15,000 for *Telescope*, $15,000 for *InfoTran*, $15,000 for *Impact*. In a preface to one 1984 quarterly issue of the last, Curtiss, who is also the co-editor of the book *Corporate Responsibilities and Opportunities to 1990*, declared, pretty much reflecting some of the major concerns of ADL at the moment,

> Our preliminary plans for the fall include further studies and seminars addressing the chemical, electronic, telecommunications, biotechnology, and health care business arenas. Research letters and executive briefs we have added to our work in process since January include leveraged buyouts, boardroom questions about environmental assurance, an update on the coal industry, a summary of developments in office automation in Japan, [and] the independent telephone companies after restructuring.

The same issue also announced that there would be a series of meetings for *Impact* folk on "Home Health Care: Exploiting Corporate Resources in an Emerging Market" on five successive days in five cities where ADL believed its own impact had been solid: Cambridge, New York, Chicago, Los Angeles, and Houston. The agenda called for three ADL experts in fields related to health care to

> analyze the home health care industry — including product/service distinctions and likely developments, opportunities for a variety of business participants, and critical strategic issues. In particular, competitive strategies for utilizing existing corporate strengths will be examined — e.g., getting existing products onto the market, designing new products to fit the market, and innovative ways of doing business. A comprehensive examination of major participants in various segments of the industry and future prospects for both present and future participants will be included.

Impact subscribers were further advised that in the near future they could expect to be made privy to such ADL studies as "Applied Artificial Intelligence Technology — Promises and Realities," "Biotechnology: Opportunities in the Biomedical, Chemical, Agricultural, and Food Industries," "Impact of Lower Crude Oil Prices on Middle East Competitiveness in Petrochemicals," "Worldwide Outlook for the Desalination Industry Through 1990," "World Markets for Information Processing Products to 1993," and "Conduct Becoming a Corporation" — this last by Robert Mueller, ADL's own board chairman, one of whose contributions to corporate terminology has been *board-worthiness*.

A relative bargain among Decision Resources offerings is a publication titled *Futurescope*, which was launched in 1984 and costs only $975 a year. Subscribers to *Impact* get it free. *Futurescope* subscribers receive a fat plastic folder at the start of each year and a short report every month to tuck inside it. "Executives won't read a fifty-page treatise on artificial intelligence," Curtiss says, "but they want to know something about it, so we try to give them one page on it, and a carefully constructed page. If we tell them to spend several minutes looking at a piece of paper, it'd better be good."

Futurescope sometimes brings ADL new business by its horoscopic ratings. If, say, it rates in order the prospects of eighteen companies in an industry, the company that finished eighteenth is as likely as not to come around and ask to be studied and analyzed in the hope of moving up a peg or two from the bottom.

The foreword to an early *Futurescope* said,

> To blame problems on solutions is an easy trap to fall into, and the proposition that technological growth is the source of many of society's problems is enticing. Then again, the wheel was undoubtedly a threat to some, and the use of fire. Probably even the violin. . . . Where should we make our technological bets? Even though our vision is necessarily faulty, who can resist the urge to try to foresee the future? *Futurescope* is designed to help all who read it join in the excitement of foresight.

Somewhat excitedly, *Futurescope* proceeded to furnish one scenario:

> The rocking chair by the wood/coal stove is not empty: Grandma (or Grandpa, if he defies the odds and outlives her), now 85 years old, sits there recently retired from her 3-day-a-week job. Two children (5 and 7 years old) play on the floor; she has a game of computer cards with them before supper. Father works in the kitchen; it's his turn to cook tonight before he works the night shift as a process engineer in a chemical plant. Mother, home from her day at the medical center training department, is in the study doing the family financial

accounts and taxes on the computer. The year? 1990. . . . A teenager studies her lessons on another terminal in her bedroom. . . . She studies Spanish because by 1995 one fourth of the population entering advanced education in the United States will speak Spanish as a primary language and English as a secondary language. . . . She will finish college at age 18 and plans . . . to work to age 85.

Early in the 1970s, yet another committee was formed, this one to address itself specifically to the question of whether ADL was doing enough for its female employees. It was the sort of philosophical problem in the anticipated solution of which another company might have consulted ADL. In this instance, one of the first steps ADL took was to engage an outside consulting firm — one whose principals, fittingly, were all women. ADL's own women were soon apprised that if they wanted to make as much headway in the company as men did, they would have to start going to lunches and cocktail parties, play softball (Joan B. Berkowitz, a hazardous wastes expert, organized her own softball team and later became a vice-president), and remember to ask Charlie Kensler about his wife's horses and not to open windows to get rid of his cigar smoke until he had left the room. A few women even took up golf.

Sensitivity groups were also the order of that troubled day — for men as well as for women. Employees would be packed off to Woods Hole or other contemplative oases for let-it-all-hang-out weekends. Sometimes clients were invited to join the fray. Lying on their backs on the floor of an indoor tennis court at a secluded estate one winter day, some ADLers and a couple of client representatives got to musing about the common cold, and out of their communal, sniffling meditations there eventually evolved Nyquil, which contained aspirin to handle pain, enough alcohol to induce numbness, and a taste designedly disagreeable enough so that nobody would be tempted to ingest too much of it.

Back in Cambridge, there were evening lectures with such speakers — many of them relatively unfamiliar in the business community — as Noam Chomsky, Father Robert Drinan, and Charles Evers, the mayor of Fayette, Mississippi. At one point, General Gavin asked Evers what Fayette needed most. A garbage truck, Evers replied. ADL looked around, found a secondhand one, and various members of the staff, filled with a new sense of moral uplift, chipped in to buy it and have it renovated. But they had a rude awakening; Evers said he didn't want any white men's used garbage truck. Gavin was somewhat baffled by it all — people running around his corridors in beards and beads, and women complaining that while men were listed in company directories just by their names, they were qualified by a Miss or a Mrs. He had five daughters, after all, he said, and ought to know something about the problems of women. So he switched to Ms. and got criticized for that.

Soon there were female vice-presidents. Joan Berkowitz made the grade, but not until 1980, when she had been around for twenty-three years. (By this time ADL, like an advertising or insurance agency, had sixty-two vice-presidents in all.) So did the Washington office's Pamela Fenrich, who'd had that memorable lunch at the Pentagon with Gavin and his admiring generals. She once complained to John Magee about the company's sexist practice of prefacing proposals to government agencies with "Dear Sirs" or "Gentlemen." Magee countered, quite accurately, by reminding her that Katharine Graham, the publisher of the *Washington Post*, referred to herself as chair*man* of its board. Vice-President Fenrich was fond of recounting an incident that had taken place when, in connection with a long-running ADL government assignment, she hobnobbed with rural sheriffs in Mississippi. They had been leery of her at the outset, because she was both a woman and a northerner, but when she was ready to leave one of them escorted her to the airport and, putting his arm around her, said, "Hey, for a Yankee broad you ain't so bad."

ADL's first woman vice-president, who arrived on the scene in 1975, was Alma Triner, who was hired to take charge of the company's public relations after serving in that capacity for a decade at the Macmillan Publishing Company. At the book-publishing house, she had made her mark by fostering the publication of a children's edition of an annual corporate report — with comic strip illustrations.* In 1972, moreover, ADL for the first time elected a woman to its Board of Directors — Mary I. Bunting, the

---

* Consultants are no less prone than other business people to tell, with relish, stories about their competitors. Triner was fond of recalling how an efficiency expert from McKinsey & Company had once come around to Macmillan and, to save storage space, had recommended that the publishers throw out some musty old correspondence that in his view was cluttering up its filing cabinets: letters from a poet, initials W. B., whose surname the McKinsey man pronounced "Yeets," and postcards from a crochety dramatist who'd been bombarding his editors with messages signed "George B. S."

president of Radcliffe College. When she retired in 1983, she was succeeded on the board by the president of Smith College, Jill Ker Conway. Out of all the turmoil of the era emerged also a black vice-president, Lewis M. Rambo, in charge of personnel; and for a six-year stretch from 1974 to 1980, a black board member — John H. Johnson, the publisher of *Ebony* and *Jet*.

By 1974, too, ADL thought it should have a resident ombudsman, and Rambo assigned that task to a woman, Diana B. Fahey, who had been around since the mid-sixties, except for a four-year spell when she left to be a consultant to a Catholic seminary. Asked by a couple of women at one group meeting how they could move upward at ADL, Fahey answered with an analogy to sports: Be big and scary, she counseled, or be really good, or have charisma, or be a friend of the coach. "All the good work in the world will not get women to the top," she concluded, "unless they have the *personal* trust and confidence of John Magee or Charlie Kensler."

Reflecting on some of the changes that had taken place at ADL over the years, Richard F. Messing, a chemical engineer who joined the company in 1945 and stayed for thirty-nine years,* said on the eve of his retirement, "One of the big differences between the old days and the present is in the marketplace. If I were going to, say, Kansas City to meet a client, my arrival there would be a big event, with maybe even a reception in my honor. Now you travel to some such place and, like as not, they've talked to people from two other consulting firms in the last two days, and if you're lucky you can join somebody else's lunch date. Once, in the late nineteen-forties, Roy Marek and I were on our way to Oklahoma to make a presentation to Continental Oil. We got stuck in a blizzard in Chicago and sent a telegram saying we were going to take a night train out, and somewhere in Kansas the next morning the conductor paged us, and the train stopped, and a Continental plane landed in a pasture alongside the tracks and picked us up. Oh, people cared about you then!"

ADLers often counsel their corporate clients to think hard about changing their cultures; and ADLers — at least those fairly

---

* One of Messing's proudest possessions was the very same couch, he believed, that Dr. Little had used in his office and that Messing had inherited by way of Earl Stevenson. When Messing retired, in June 1984, the venerable couch was passed along to a conference room.

high on their own ladder — are no less concerned about changing their own. Chairman of the Board Mueller, the subtitle of whose study "Conduct Becoming a Corporation" was "A Value-calibrated Board Culture," once told an interviewer, "ADL is a blend of cultures. First, you have the 'tribal' culture. The tribal culture is embedded into the 'section' formed around an industry, a discipline, or a region. You have the chief of the tribe, the section manager, who is respected by his people. He can never be someone parachuted as manager. He is promoted from the tribe. Then you have the 'task' culture, centered around the case with its own network of relationships, alliances, and allegiances. The 'Apollonian' culture also is present, but to a lesser degree. The Gods from Olympus, the management, organize, shape, and define the rules. You have the president, the senior vice-presidents, and the vice-presidents. . . . The art of management at ADL is to make all these cultures coexist and [be] compatible without top down direction. It is a challenge to stay away from bureaucracy, keep the organic nature of the organization, and, at the same time, to maintain control and accountability. It is a real art, you can believe me."

When Richard S. Cresse, who began marketing government jobs for ADL in 1971 (earlier he had been in the jai alai business and written a book about dog racing), started working for the company, he was sometimes confused by the attitude of some of his colleagues. "For a while," he says, "it seemed to me that I was seeking money and they were seeking truth." Seeking remunerative business for ADL, Cresse once called on the head of a large shipping company and brought along an ADL colleague with professional expertise in that field. "My colleague took off his jacket, hung it on the back of a chair, rolled up his sleeves, put his hands behind his head, leaned back, and said to the shipping company executive, 'Well, tell me what's on your mind.' The prospective client started to explain his problem, and suddenly my companion said, 'Well, I don't think I'm professionally interested in working on that.' I almost fell out of my chair. So did the shipping man. But then our guy went on to explain that there was nothing his particular expertise could do to improve the other guy's situation. It was cold-blooded honesty, though from my point of view extremely confounding." Richard Stone, the swimming pool and Chappaquiddick man, once said, "There are only two requirements for working at ADL: Contribute to the reputation of the company, and tell the truth. We never tell our clients that we work like that, because they'd never be able to run their own businesses that way."

Turning down potentially lucrative assignments does not normally rate high on the agenda of any profit-making institution, but every so often ADL has done so — once, for instance, declining to undertake a study of transportation to Las Vegas because the prospective client was a casino there of suspect ownership. When, on the other hand, the company did accept a commission from a couple of racetrack characters already under indictment, some ADLers were deeply offended and made no secret of their distaste. "I don't think we should be working for people like that," one lawyer on the ADL staff said. "I'm not aware that the Constitution and the Bill of Rights guarantee you access to a management consultant." ADLers who for one reason or another — the Vietnam War, say — choose not to get involved with Defense Department projects are excused without prejudice, provided, that is, that they can find some other remunerative use for their time.

As a congregation of individualists, ADLers tend to go about their business pretty much on their own, although over the many years the company has tried valiantly to restructure itself into new groups or divisions or sections (at one point even engaging John McArthur, dean of the Harvard Business School, as a consultant to advise them on that). Every other Monday there would be a 4:00 P.M. meeting, in the MEI auditorium, of the company's senior executives and whichever corporate staff members and section leaders happened to be in Cambridge at the moment. A tray of cold cuts was at every place. At a minute or two before five, Magee and Kensler, until he retired in 1985, would edge toward closed cabinets flanking the chamber and, precisely on the dot of five, open them up to reveal two bars, accessible to all present. Part of these sessions was devoted to a report to the assemblage from Alfred Wechsler, who in 1980 acquired the title of senior vice-president and general manager of Professional Operations, on how much new business had been negotiated since the previous get-together. Then there was usually a presentation, from one section or another, of what it had been doing lately. One time Elliott Wilbur perked up the proceedings by putting on a live demonstration of a singing commercial some of his people had created for a barbed wire client — a performance that, since it didn't take place until after the bar opened, was received with far greater acclamation than might have been the case an hour or so earlier.

Every working day, at 8:30 A.M., about ten members of the staff convene — they get good parking places for their pains — for what is called a lead management committee meeting. Coffee is served. The committee, whose composition is changed quarterly, is composed of five members and five alternates; they are joined by any senior management people who choose to sit in. The presiding personage at these cockcrow sessions is Karl H. Klaussen, who joined ADL in 1949 and in 1953 became its contracting officer.

Here prospective jobs are discussed, sometimes a dozen of them in as many minutes. On a typical day the committee might review a potential assignment, price unspecified, for an oil-refining company in Abu Dhabi (it would not conflict, those present are reassured, with work already under way in Angola); a $100,-000 job in Paris having to do with a nonimpact-printing outfit's use of magnetophotography; a $40,000 job to study the effect on flavors of food- and beverage-can liners (Anheuser-Busch had recommended to the potential client that ADL be approached on that); a $30,000 job for a Korean chemical firm contemplating diversification into electronics; a job of approximately $50,000 for American Telephone & Telegraph, which wanted to know more about how customers perceived one of its private line services; and a job — cost again as yet undetermined — to draw up a strategic plan for a multinational corporation's operations in Austria. Of still another prospective undertaking, for a client reluctant to be identified even to that elite gathering, Klaussen remarked offhandedly, "This job entails going to Thailand for two or three weeks, which shouldn't be a problem for anybody."

The committee considers five thousand or six thousand leads a year. In about three thousand instances, ADL proposals are forthcoming, and some fifteen hundred of these eventually turn into actual work.*

---

* One waggish ADL house organ, some years back, published what purported to be extracts from the minutes of a lead management committee: "Study of equal employment opportunities for women — D. Juan; Study of the spending habits of British tourists in New England — George III; Study of Spanish maritime insurance practices — Francis Drake; The investigation of fireproof materials for musical instruments — Nero; Feasibility study of the Hovercraft for sea crossings — Moses."

Once ADL has decided to make a bid on a case, Klaussen usually gets together with a few other managerial executives and designates someone to handle negotiations with the prospective client. After a bid has been accepted, the chances are that the chief negotiator will become the case leader in charge of the project. Case leaders have considerable autonomy in selecting the people they want to collaborate with them. A very junior employee may, if he or she so chooses, invite the chairman of the board to join the team. Naturally, the leaders lean toward specialists in whatever field or fields the work is to be done, but they also tend to invite cronies to collaborate.

It is thus imperative for anyone new to the company to establish, as quickly as possible, a network of relationships, and to nurture these as tenderly as house plants; and it can be awkward for an ADLer who, for example, has been stationed in Saudi Arabia for two or three years to find on returning to Cambridge that there is no network to slip back into. People get miffed when they are not asked to join case teams they believe they belong on. One time David L. Fishman, the holder of advanced degrees in both business and law, was peeved when he was passed over for service on a study for a proposed shrimp-farming industry in Texas — not because of the appropriateness of his surname, but because while he was in business school, fish farming had been his hobby, and he regarded himself as something of an expert on the subject. The lead management committee was leery about even applying for a job advising *Playboy* about going into motion picture production. Once, though, the committee had given that notion its blessing, and *Playboy* had designated ADL to pursue the matter, practically every male at ADL begged to get in on the case. Fishman didn't have to fret; he was in charge of it.

A saying not infrequently voiced in ADL circles goes, "Honor thy commitment, and thy commitment is to thy client." Another proverbial phrase is "The value of our time is how it is perceived by the client." Every ADLer, from the chief executive officer on down, is supposed to fill out a time card every week indicating what he or she has done every day, hour by hour. Woe betide the staff member whose billability — the number of hours, that is, that can properly be charged to a client — falls below 60 percent of forty hours a week. When Robert Mueller arrived in 1968 from Monsanto (his last salary there had been higher than anybody's at ADL), it came as something of a shock to him that he, like everybody else, was supposed to achieve acceptable billability. Howard McMahon was president of ADL, and he gave Mueller a break; the newcomer could have a few months' period of grace, he was informed, before he had to shape up. Mueller wasn't worried at first; he figured he could sell his — and ADL's — services to various corporate executives he'd been giving advice to on one subject or another for three decades. But he had a rude awakening; his old friends were all delighted to take him to lunch, but they apparently saw no reason to pay him for the sort of counsel they'd previously been getting from him for nothing.

There are exceptions to the billability rule, as there are to most corporate shibboleths: If a proposal for a government job estimated to be worth millions of dollars takes four hundred unbillable man-hours to prepare, that is a calculated risk worth taking. "Billability can be a shield around here," one ADL old-timer says. "If you're highly billable, bullets bounce off you, and you can toss lighted cigarettes onto your rug." (Not that many people have rugs. It has been suggested that General Gavin felt at home at ADL because the place resembled an enlisted men's barracks in the Panama Canal Zone.) Billability is not universally admired by those subjected to it. To show his distaste for the concept, one professional kept a taxi meter on his desk, and every time a client walked in he would drop the flag.

Inevitably, there have been some clients — like the one Reid Weedon went to Texas to assuage — who have taken such a dim view of ADL's performance, or alleged lack thereof, that they've declined to pay when billed for it.* (It may say something about the mores of big business that one of the very few large jobs ADL had difficulty getting reimbursed for involved a client with whom a staff member had first struck up an acquaintance on a golf course.) When a client appears to have good cause for dissatisfaction, adjustments are usually deemed to be in order. The responsibility for dunning recalcitrant debtors eventually devolves — much to the relief of others — on the company's in-

---

* ADLers' remuneration has since 1963 been tied to something called a performance factor. Every quarter of the year, a certain percentage of everybody's salary — in some instances, as much as 25 percent — is withheld. At the end of the quarter, what the company took in is measured against what it had hoped to take in. The withheld pay is multiplied by that factor. If the factor should be 1.8, the rewards are ample. If it should fall below 1.0, a lot of belts may have to be tightened.

house attorneys, chief among whom since 1961 has been Richard T. Murphy, Jr., who came to ADL in 1957 straight from Harvard Law School. Murphy sometimes says despairingly that his free-wheeling associates "wander all around the world making commitments and saying things with potentially unbelievable implications." When Murphy joined the company, nobody there worried much about lawsuits, but Arthur D. Little has not been immune from the litigiousness that has more and more become a concomitant of doing any kind of business in the United States.

"Our business is giving a client, for a consideration, advice which he may either accept or reject," Murphy likes to say. Clients have not always viewed the relationship in such simple terms. In 1954, for instance, ADL embarked on a long-range economic survey of the Canadian province of Manitoba, which was rich in gold, zinc, copper, and timber. Principal among the company's recommendations was the construction of a huge pulp and paper mill. A 1957 article in the *Little Acorn* said that "the enthusiasm and help offered demonstrated very clearly that the people of Northern Manitoba are thoughtful and resourceful and can be relied upon to carry forward well-conceived development plans."

But the people had second thoughts. A Canadian commission looking into the matter concluded that ADL had been taken in by a promoter, and it applied to the American firm such hurtful words as *negligent* and, worse yet, *incompetent*. And next the province of Manitoba filed a lawsuit against ADL, contending that the company had somehow not fulfilled an obligation, one that, ADL insisted, had never been contractually assumed in the first place. The legal proceedings dragged on and on, somewhat frighteningly; in its annual report for 1973, ADL felt constrained to note that "The amounts which might be claimed could exceed the total assets of the company, and the costs of defending the litigation may become material in relation to earnings." By 1985, the case was still unsettled, the costs had been heavy, and at Acorn Park nearly an entire storeroom had been turned over to filing cabinets devoted to the bothersome proceedings. But by then the company's auditors had become relaxed enough about the whole pesky business to let it be omitted from the annual report.

Over the years, however, ADL had benefited quite handsomely from its involvement in litigation. Expert testimony, after all, had kept Dr. Little fairly solvent back when chemical analyses were hard to come by. And nearly a century later some of the company's fattest fees resulted from the appearance at some tribunal or another of one of its latter-day specialists. One of these was Irving H. Plotkin, a Ph.D. in mathematical economics from M.I.T. who came to ADL in 1967 when, at the age of twenty-six, he published a widely acclaimed report on casualty insurance finance. Plotkin has allocated much of his time ever since, in return for what he describes as "not insignificant" fees, to expert testimony. He has often worked with David M. Boodman, a management technology specialist who preceded him on the ADL scene by seven years, on what they call forensic economics — that is, resolving adversarial issues in such public policy areas as antitrust regulations and tax law.

Plotkin has spent almost as much time in courtrooms as in his own Acorn Park office. (He keeps an open copy of the *Rubaiyat* of Omar Khayyam on a table there and is fond of likening ADL to a tent full of wise men.)* "I charge my clients the top dollar," Plotkin says, "and they have the right to expect efficient utilization of their funds." Plotkin, who equates the right to expert testimony with the right to counsel, is unusual among expert witnesses in that he is equally comfortable working for small plaintiffs or large corporations, for government or industry. He was once so efficient a witness for the Internal Revenue Service when the Mobil Corporation sued it for a tax refund that soon afterward, in another lawsuit, Mobil asked him whether ADL would appear on its behalf.

Other knowledgeable ADLers have achieved high rates of billability in product liability cases. They testified, for example, on the side of a company whose synthetic fiber stuffing was part of a quilt that had been in a station wagon along with some matches when, it was alleged, the quilt caught on fire and badly burned two children left alone in the car. In that instance, ADL procured a similar vehicle, set various fires inside it, and established that among all its contents that kind of quilt could not have been a

---

* While still a student at M.I.T., Plotkin, working as a consultant for ADL, wrote an analysis of automobile insurance rates. When it was published, his name wasn't on it, and somebody asked if that didn't bother him. Alluding to the *Rubaiyat*, he replied, "I'll take the cash and let the credit go."

major contributor to the blaze. Roger Doggett took part in that experiment. Among his many accomplishments in nearly a half-century's faithful service to ADL was his work with Edward S. Shanley — also a longtime ADLer — on an automatic toilet bowl cleaner for which a patent was granted. The cleaner ultimately was added to the client's Ty-D-Bol product line. "We don't really go after that kind of work," Doggett said later. "We don't refuse it, either."

One senior member of Information Systems, Frederic G. Withington, a computer expert who came to the firm in 1960 from the National Security Agency, once found himself in the unusual position of being the target of a lawsuit levied against him by no less than a federal judge, David N. Edelstein. (Withington, the author of, among other works, "The Organization of the Data Processing Function" and "The Real Computer — Its Influences, Uses, and Effects," solved a vexing problem for the National Bank of Greece, which was disturbed because its key-punch operators, who were paid by the card, had a low productivity rate. Withington ascertained that the trouble was that nobody had ever explained to the employees why they were doing what they were doing; once they were enlightened, their productivity went up by 30 percent.) In 1975 the Department of Justice charged IBM with illegal monopoly practices. ADL's Decision Resources auxiliary had been putting out reports on computer companies since 1960, and Withington had been in charge of that work from 1964 on. Because Decision Resources had said in one of its reports that IBM had more than 70 percent of the computer market, the Justice Department thought Withington would make an estimable witness for its side. But he begged off; government witnesses weren't as a rule paid much for their pains, and besides, ADL didn't want to risk offending IBM, a longtime, faithful client.

Withington was then subpoenaed to appear but declined to, contending that "the government is seeking the very core of my expertise, which I do not wish to provide and which I consider to be a proprietary asset available solely to my employer or to those for whom I wish to work." Judge Edelstein retorted with the argument that Withington wasn't being summoned as an expert but as "a member of the public" in a case that "greatly affects the commonweal." A court of appeals ruled in favor of the jurist. Before IBM's attorneys interrogated Withington, they requested —

and ADL turned over, to avoid further squabbling — almost every piece of paper in the company's possession that contained the word *computer*. The documents were duly furnished, a breathtaking 180,000 of them.

Before the whole drama came to an end (Justice eventually dropped the suit after a decade of costly wrangling), Withington came out of it all perhaps the only winner. He spent twenty-one days on the stand in the summer of 1978 and, by further decree of the court of appeals, was reimbursed at his regular billing rate for testifying — $700 a day.

In recent years, ADL and its resident experts have often found it beneficial to advise other big companies — Royal Little's burgeoning Textron among them — on making acquisitions. ADL rarely works on a basis of what are called success fees, but once, for assisting an industrial products company in a $14,000,000 acquisition, it received a robust 1 percent contingency fee for its pains, and the ADLer most instrumental in the negotiations, Richard Messing, got a juicy 10 percent of *that* for himself.

When the Coca-Cola Company asked ADL to help it further diversify in 1980, a case team under J. Stewart Ward spent several months screening sectors of U.S. industry to help Coca-Cola identify areas for a suitable acquisition. The team proposed eight industries for detailed study, one of which was the entertainment industry. As a result of ADL's research, the soft-drink company acquired Columbia Pictures for $750 million. ADL was delighted that its efforts had borne fruit, even though the initial reaction of the financial community was skeptical. The consultants recognized the match between soft drinks and the entertainment business and knew that Coca-Cola executives, by virtue of their involvement in mass advertising and promotion, would be comfortable with the management of a creative enterprise.

Coincidentally, David Fishman, the ADL expert who'd headed the entertainment sector study in the Coca-Cola case, turned out a report titled "Trends in the Motion Picture Business," the import of which was misconstrued in the press to mean that he didn't think there would be any market for motion pictures. Actually, what he had foreseen was the erosion of theater attendance by the growing market for movies shown at home, which he projected for the mid-eighties.

Starting way back with Dr. Little's Cellulose Products Company and his Petroleum Chemical Corporation, ADL has acquired, and not infrequently later discarded, subsidiary enterprises of its own. Some have fared better than others. In 1954, after M.I.T. decided to stop performing some metallurgical research for the Atomic Energy Commission, ADL teamed up with the Allegheny Ludlum Steel Corporation and formed a new entity called Nuclear Metals, Inc., to take over the work. ADL — the Memorial Drive Trust, technically — had a two-thirds interest in Nuclear Metals. Bruce Old became its president. After five years, the ADL holdings were sold (to Textron, as it happened) at a profit of more than $1.5 million. When ADL went public in 1969, it bought Lester Gorsline Associates, which specialized in setting up programs and facilities for hospitals and medical schools. That seemed like a good idea just then, inasmuch as the government was underwriting the costs of much of that work. But soon after ADL took over, the government stepped out. Another investment that didn't flourish was ADL Systems, a 1971 entity established to develop and market software that would facilitate other companies' billings and collections. Much more successful was the acquisition in 1975, for just over $2 million, of the Opinion Research Corporation, the well-known Princeton, New Jersey, polling organization.

Among others to be sheltered for various lengths of time under the ADL umbrella were The S. M. Stoller Corporation, consultants for the nuclear power industry; and Delphi Associates, a developer of information systems relating to health and human services. ADL Enterprises was created in 1984 to market and manage inventions and also — comparable to but quite separate from the Memorial Drive Trust — to make venture capital investments. It was ultimately put under the direction of Walter J. Cairns, who'd been handling inventions for the parent company since 1955. Thirty years afterward Cairns and a staff of eight were examining about a thousand inventions a year, only a tenth of them emanating from within ADL's own ranks. Merely a few of the projects with which ADL Enterprises soon found itself concerned were a process for recovering precious metals from scrap, a system whereby two television pictures could be simultaneously transmitted over a single channel, and a biodegradable pellet that could release predetermined dosages of drugs over more than a year's duration.

By 1985, ADL Enterprises alone was making new investments at an annual rate of more than $5 million, a sum greater than the firm's gross income in any year over its first half-century of existence; and it was doing so through a subsidiary of a subsidiary — a limited partnership called ADL Ventures in which ADL Enterprises had, as did Harvard University and a Pittsburgh investment firm, a one-third interest.

XII It's Hard to Introduce New Things

Today our civilization has developed such complexity that we cannot hope to maintain our position except through the assistance which only science can afford.
— Dr. Arthur D. Little, 1928

Roughly 20 percent of ADL's work, as it approached its second century of operations, continued to be for federal government clients. For the Department of Transportation, it was investigating the extent and frequency of unrepaired automobile crash damages. For the Department of Energy, it was examining the potential of electric vehicles. For Health and Human Services, it was looking into catastrophe insurance. For the Bureau of Mines, it was assessing the detectability, at ground level, of signals transmitted by miners trapped deep below. For the Federal Aviation Administration, it was lending a hand in the preparation, to use ADL's own lofty jargon, of "master system development milestone schedules." For the Federal Railroad Administration, it was conducting a three-year study of tracks, which would conclude that, with better maintenance, American railroads could save $500 million every year.

For the navy, ADL was perfecting underwater acoustic command link systems. For the Internal Revenue Service, it was — with a boost from its own Opinion Research people — ascertaining how burdensome that agency's paperwork was to both corporations and individuals. (Congress made it mandatory for the IRS to measure that onus by passing something called a Paperwork Burden Act.) For the Treasury Department, it was developing a private digital communications network. For the Postal Service, it was in the midst of an $18 million assignment, under the terms of which ADL was expected to provide that institution with continuing support in planning and managing new technologies. Fifty ADLers were assigned full-time to that one project. Among many other things, they advised the Postal Service on its plan to buy no fewer than one hundred thousand small aluminum and plastic delivery vans that, breathtakingly, were supposed to last for twenty-four years.

ADL had by then had numerous dealings with the Postal Service. In 1967, ADL helped it restructure its delivery system for Chicago, after that city had been smitten by a postal version of gridlock. Earlier in that decade, when a commission headed by Frederick Kappel, the chairman of AT&T, was drawing up recommendations that resulted in the sweeping reorganization of the service, ADL did most of the staff work for the commission, assembling on its behalf a large team of organization, engineering, finance, and marketing specialists. At one point, to illustrate dramatically the options available to the members of the commission, ADLers staged a debate with staff members passionately arguing against one another about various alternative courses of action.

In 1974, Congress passed a Juvenile Justice and Delinquency Prevention Act, and to implement it appropriated $70 million. Two years later, the Department of Justice engaged ADL — at $1 million a year for six straight years — to give it a hand. At that time, 70 percent of the girls in state institutions were status offenders — that is, individuals charged with offenses (running away, truancy, incorrigibility) for which adults would not normally be held accountable. Parents had the right to have such offenders locked up, even though the girls in question might have fled their homes because they'd been sexually abused there. One accomplishment attributable to ADL was the deinstitutionalism of status offenders in many states.

Another was to propose an acceptable alternative to institutionalism in the form of emergency shelter and rehabilitation programs. The case was managed by ADL's Washington office, with Pamela Fenrich — who, fittingly, had degrees in both public administration and philosophy — in charge. When boat people were flowing into the United States from Haiti and Cuba and there were hundreds of parentless children in Florida detention camps, nobody knew quite what to do with them. By then, Fenrich and her staff (sixteen full-time assistants abetted by 150 consultants in twenty-six states and the Virgin Islands) had a network of acquaintances all across the country; and in a few hours she was able to provide her client, the Department of Justice, with a list of fifty places where the hapless children could be sheltered.

Consultants like to put things in writing, often hedged with caveats. A single proposal that the Fenrich group made to Justice on "Studies of technical innovations that can be used in drug law enforcement" ran to eighty-six single-spaced typed pages, not counting appendices. A whole shelf full of publications stemmed from proposals that were accepted, among them "Confidentiality of Juvenile Offense Histories," "Selected Readings on Child Abuse Prosecution," "Programs for Young Women in Trouble," "Publicity Strategies" (which embodied the injunction "Be considerate of the press"), and "Youth Gangs: The Problem and the Response."

In 1964, the National Broadcasting Company was preparing a television special called "Congress Needs Help" about the functioning of the legislative branch of the federal government; and NBC, apparently feeling it needed help itself to do the job right, called on ADL to provide it. That investigation lasted a whole year and resulted in a whole book, with the same title. Its co-authors were Philip Donham and Robert J. Fahey; David Brinkley, who was featured on the television program, wrote an introduction in which he described ADL as "an estimable assembly of talent ... devoted to the clear and professional examination and analysis of large enterprises, identifying their flaws and weaknesses, and then suggesting remedies."*

ADL's objectives, Donham and Fahey wrote, were to help

---

* Between 1953 and 1978, Fahey, a specialist in institutional change and improvement, had three separate tours of duty with ADL, in the course of which he worked on behalf of Yale University (which wanted advice on investing its endowment), General Motors (which wanted advice on the competition of small Japanese cars), the Jesuit Order (advice on adapting to Vatican II), American Airlines (advice on the centralization of flight crew training), the government of Spain (advice on reorganizing its railroads), the National Football League Players' Association (advice on bargaining strategy), and the Penn Central Railroad, which was so pleased with Fahey's advice on how to restructure itself after bankruptcy — the trustees untangling the affairs of the smitten line had requested an ADL team headed by John Magee and Jeffrey W. Traenkle to help them out — that it hired him away.

Congress "make efficient use of the modern techniques of information, communication, and management" and to "define Congress's purposes, methods, resources, and practices; to identify its operating problems; to suggest ways in which it might apply management techniques in its operations." Among the consultants' conclusions were that Congress should stay in session longer than had been its wont, that its committee chairmen tended to be too old, and that it needed a better code of ethics. "Congress should conscientiously set about improving its public image," the authors declared. Although once ADL has finished its research on a case and submitted a report on its findings, it is often difficult to ascertain what if anything the client has done, in this instance there was at least some evidence of implementation of ADL's suggestions. The same year the book came out, Congress established a new committee: a Joint Committee on the Organization of the Congress.

Both for governmental and private clients, ADL has been much preoccupied, almost constantly since Roger Griffin's dreadful death, with the risks and hazards attendant to the human environment. As calamities have intensified in their scope (many large businesses now have staff officers called corporate risk managers), so have the company's efforts to prevent them. Once, ADL made a comprehensive study of firemen's gloves and concluded that one reason many of those in use were impractical was that in some American cities firemen were given a cash allowance to buy their uniforms, and that often the money was distributed just before Christmas, with the result that the recipients, with other kinds of shopping on their minds, sometimes bought the cheapest and least protective gloves. Following a 1980 hotel fire in suburban New York that took twenty-six lives, ADL was commissioned by the state government to make a study of combustion toxicity, smokes, and gases; after six hundred tests it came up with a set of recommendations for suitable tests and a regulatory scheme that could be implemented if the state determined a need to regulate existed.

And the New York City administration paid ADL $100,000 for a study of possible ways of moving nuclear wastes from the Brookhaven National Laboratory on Long Island to a depository in Idaho without their having to pass through any portion of

Mayor Edward Koch's domain. ADL evaluated shipping the touchy trash across Long Island Sound to Connecticut and trucking it through, among other locations, the city of Hartford — pointing out that the population density of that state capital was far smaller than that of either of the New York City boroughs through which the wastes would otherwise have to pass. New York appreciated ADL's findings, but Connecticut (such is life in an era of environmental concerns) was much less enthusiastic.

Environmentalists, with their understandable apprehensions and demands, have in recent years radically altered the consulting business. ADL has devoted what some members of its staff consider an inordinate amount of the company's time grappling with environmental issues. "We take tremendous risks, tackling jobs no sane person would undertake," one senior scientist at Acorn Park says. "But when we succeed we're sometimes very poor at exploiting our victories. One reason for that is that we're a mass of petit entrepreneurs, interested in advancement and change, and our people simply don't want to do the same job four times in a row no matter how well or how profitably it may have been done before."

The jobs, moreover, have become more complicated. ADL was invited in 1984 to make a feasibility study for a World's Fair tentatively scheduled for Chicago in 1992. Because the impact of the event on the city's environment was naturally a matter of high priority, ADL saw fit before it was through to call in six other firms to assist it: one to develop capital cost estimates, a second to analyze transportation, a third to evaluate cultural and social impacts, a fourth to evaluate residual benefits, a fifth to obtain the views of foreign governments that might consider exhibiting, and a sixth to make an overall market analysis.

The sixth was easy to come by; it was ADL's own subsidiary, the Opinion Research Corporation, which conducted a nationwide telephone survey to ascertain projected attendance figures. ("Are you planning to travel from Kennebunkport to Chicago in 1992 to take in a World's Fair, if there is one? Well. . . .") The leader on that case was Harry G. Foden, a veteran ADLer specializing in development planning and institutional management, especially for communities — Fall River, Massachusetts, for instance, and the Sultanate of Oman. (Fall River wanted a change in its image, which has suffered ever since Lizzie Borden picked up an axe; Oman's Ministry of Commerce underwrote a study made in anticipation of creating a new industrial site.)* From all their sources of information, Foden and his cohorts felt confident enough to predict in 1985 that the 1992 fair "could generate about $8.357 billion in economic activity and $286 million in increased tax revenues," and that an attendance figure of forty-five million was "most likely." Their accuracy never reached the point of being tested; the fair was canceled.

Charles M. Apt, a Ph.D. in physical chemistry who joined ADL in 1954 (he had studied philosophy, too, at Oxford, under Sir Isaiah Berlin), was assigned soon after arriving to carry out a mission for the American Gas Association. Natural gas has no odor, and the association wanted a smell put into it so that leaks would be more readily detectable. Since 1968, when ADL had played a leading role in the analysis of the odorous elements of exhaust fumes on behalf of the Automotive Management Association and the Environmental Protection Agency, the company has been universally recognized as an authority on the emissions of diesel engines. For the EPA, also, ADL developed a method of assessing the risks associated with waterborne toxic pollutants. In 1977, working yet again for the EPA, which wanted to know more than it then did about pollutants exuding from sewer systems, ADL dispatched sixteen operatives to St. Louis, where they spent many vigilant hours perched inquiringly alongside open manholes. Consultancy cannot be exclusively characterized as white-collar work.

In 1980, the army wanted to declare as excess, and make available for other uses, a dumping ground at its Rocky Mountain arsenal, near Denver. The burial area covered half a square mile and was twenty-five feet deep, with innumerable nasty chemicals entombed in it. The army's idea had been to dig up all the contaminated soil and put it in a giant incinerator until it was sufficiently burned to become sterile. ADL was asked to appraise that scheme. Its risk and hazards people made some calculations and concluded that to do what the military proposed would require the construction of the world's largest rotary kiln incinerator; to

---

* Back in 1967, when Foden was running a case on strategies for shaping model cities, he had both James Gavin and John Magee working under him, along with nine outside consultants — among them five from Harvard, one from M.I.T., and one from the Harvard-M.I.T. Joint Center for Urban Studies, which an outsider might have thought could handle such a study all by itself.

get it to the site and assemble it and put it to use would take fifteen years and astronomical amounts of money. Even then, they pointed out, there was no certainty that it would work. John T. Funkhouser, still another ADLer with a Ph.D. in chemistry from M.I.T., who arrived at Acorn Park in 1963 and eventually became director of the firm's Center for Environmental Assurance (in 1985 he moved to Los Angeles to run the branch office there), once declared that the trouble with dealing with risks was that they fell into three not altogether manageable categories — known, unknowable, and unknown.

Joan Berkowitz has worked on many hazardous wastes problems. A 1975 handbook that she co-edited with Funkhouser, on alternatives to landfill disposal, has been much used ever since by the EPA.* By 1984, Berkowitz had become somewhat fatalistic about dealing with dangerous materials. "I can't tell you how many yards of asbestos I've wrapped around things or how much benzene I've had on my hands," she told a visitor to her office. "Once, about nine years ago, my daughter wanted to see what mercury looked like, so I took some home in a vial and then brought it back to Acorn Park and put in on a bookshelf. Reaching for a book later, I knocked it over, and it broke and spilled. In the old days, somebody would have sprinkled sulfur dust on the mercury and gathered it up and thrown it away. I had to go to a meeting and asked someone to clean it up, and when I got back my office had been quarantined and there were men in funny suits and masks all over the place, and I was afraid they were going to incinerate my rug. Today, they might feel they had to demolish the whole building."

In the late 1970s, the EPA put a novel challenge before ADL. The agency wanted advice on how best to dispose of radioactive material with a half-life of about ten thousand years — longer than recorded history. What would be the best sites? On earth? In water? In space? One assumption was that if the stuff was going to be buried underground, it should be at a spot where no one lived. But how could anybody be assured — even if the climate didn't change — that there would be any such place a thou-

---

* Once the EPA had put it out, it was in the public domain, and the authors were surprised, in 1978, to learn that a photocopy of their work had been issued, priced at forty-two dollars, by a commercial outfit in New Jersey, but with no attribution to ADL or to them.

sand decades hence? ADL conferred with astronomers and archaeologists and climatologists and geneticists, and it got involved in fascinating speculations: If the material were to be buried, it had to be in a secure location, but what kind of structure would last for ten thousand years? And how could it be marked to warn future generations of its threat? No language had yet lasted ten thousand years. And what would future generations be like, anyway? Might they have a higher tolerance to radiation or even have become immune to it? Would they still be living in the open air, or would the ozone layer have become so thin that people would have to stay inside protective housing? Might there be a change by then in the orbit of the earth around the sun? And when it came to that, would there be any United States of America? After all, no other nation had ever lasted that long. Ellen Metcalf was one of the ADLers assigned to the case. "We never did come up with a solution," she said afterward, "but it was fun, and it was probably the only problem I'll ever work on where nobody would have been able to prove, whatever we might have come up with, whether we were right or wrong."

One scientist who took part in much of ADL's risks and hazards work was Philip L. Levins, who died in a skin-diving accident in the summer of 1983. In mid-October, when ADL installed a new thirteen-hundred-square-foot laboratory, which Levins had helped to design, at Acorn Park, it was named after him. An ADL press release trumpeted that it was "a facility which breaks new ground in safety standards for the handling and analysis of hazardous chemicals." In a corridor outside the Levins Laboratory, there were lifesaving fire blankets and a sign reading "In case of fire do not enter." Inside, there were safety showers and more admonitions: "Safety glasses required beyond this point," "Danger: hazardous materials," "Authorized personnel only." The laboratory was fitted out with redundant air- and water-treatment systems, with two-foot-thick charcoal filters a part of them. The personnel authorized to enter were required first to be trained in toxicology, first aid, and fire fighting; to pass psychological and physiological tests; and to go through an indoctrination process called a Chemical Personnel Reliability Program. ADL even paid two rival consulting firms to inspect the premises; they pronounced them as safe as safe could be.

Then began what some ADLers soon were referring to as The

Trouble. The first job handed over to the spanking new lab was, by latter-day ADL criteria, a trifling one: a $250,000 commission from the Department of Defense to study the detoxification of three nerve agents and two blister agents. Even before the Levins Laboratory was finished, Magee had told his Board of Directors that "these projects would be limited under present policy to the detection or destruction of such agents and under no circumstances to their development." ADL was certainly a logical place for such work to be carried out; after the Second World War, it had tested all sorts of filters to detect and destroy aerosols and gases; and it had once devised, for the Atomic Energy Commission, filters that would block all but one of twenty thousand particles of radioactive dust in a cubic inch of ordinary atmosphere — filters more inhibiting than anyone had previously dreamed of.

The nerve and blister agents were mean ones. One scientist estimated that one liter — about one quart — of the most toxic nerve agent contains about three million times the theoretical lethal dose for an adult. But there was no way they could be scattered outside the awesomely secure Levins Laboratory (a fire would have incinerated them harmlessly) and, in any event, ADL never had on hand at one time more than one hundred milliliters' worth — about a third of a cup — of all nerve agents combined. Moreover, the new facility had been inspected and approved, before any of the stuff arrived, by the Department of Defense, the Massachusetts Department of Public Health, the two consulting firms already mentioned, and Cambridge safety officials.

But what was going on was still largely unknown to the politicians of that city and to the general public. In late October 1983, the Cambridge City Council got concerned; one of the loudest voices raised was that of Alfred E. Vellucci, a longtime anti-establishment councilman from East Cambridge who for many years had vented his impressive wrath mainly against Harvard University. Once he had suggested that the Harvard Yard be turned into a bus and taxi terminal, and he had summarized his philosophy by declaring, "When Harvard is for something, I'm against it, just because Harvard is for it."

Now — conceivably much to Harvard's relief — Vellucci and his cohorts had a new neighborhood dragon to try to slay. Various ADL executives betook themselves to city council meetings to try to explain that they were not developing nerve gases but, rather, trying to figure out ways of neutralizing them. John Magee, pointing out that his office was in the same complex as the Levins Laboratory, said, "I have no interest in either bankrupting Arthur D. Little or leaving my wife a widow. When you hear the fright talk about nerve gas, please keep these practical considerations in mind. I have no intention either of betting my life or betting the company's future on unsafe work."

The council did not appear to be impressed. It instructed its public health commissioner to ban all such nerve gas testing. Thereupon ADL got a superior court injunction lifting the ban until the matter could be thoroughly investigated and adjudicated. The company suggested that it might get into trouble with much loftier tribunals if it reneged on a contract with the federal government.

Meanwhile, the local press leapt into the fray. A *Boston* magazine article was chillingly illustrated with a page-and-a-half-wide drawing of dead and dying citizens; the text contained an admonition from Alfred Vellucci to John Magee: "You tonight get the blue ribbon for being the biggest con man that ever appeared before this council." (R. Scott Stricoff, an ADLer who'd had much to do with the Levins Laboratory, was identified in the article as Strickoff, which made him sound more sinister.) The *Arlington Advocate* ran an anonymous letter purportedly from an ADL employee who said that the company wasn't competent to judge whether the work in question was safe or not, and who added, "We must not stand idle and allow ADL or the Pentagon to open this laboratory without the proper community examination of its facilities and their purported use." Magee remarked at the next Monday afternoon get-together of the ADL brass that he doubted the letter's authenticity because it was too well written to have been an inside job. "Far from posing any type of threat to our community," Magee himself wrote to the *Advocate*, "we regard this work as socially beneficial. In fact, I submit that it would be irresponsible of our company to refuse work, which our scientists are eminently qualified to perform, and which society needs done."

ADL's attempts on several fronts, however, to defuse the explosive atmosphere were unavailing. Magee kept trying. So did his public relations people. ("I have both Clorox and ammonia in the trunk of my car," Vice-President Alma Triner told an inquiring journalist, "and if I got into an accident and they interacted, the results could be worse than any mishap here.") So did Reid Weedon, who wrote in *Massachusetts High Tech* in November, "The work we're doing is not designed to create or enhance delivery systems used to kill people. The company would not accept such a contract. Our work is directed toward the issues of protection, detection, and destruction of nerve agents. The problem has already been created; we're part of the process of helping to manage it."

In December 1984, a superior court judge lifted the injunction against the ban on further testing, but declared that whether or not such work could be considered reasonable would have to await a further decision. By then ADL, which had thought more than a year before that the whole contretemps would soon blow over, was viewing it with such seriousness that in January 1985 Magee took the unprecedented step of sending a "Dear Neighbor" letter more than a thousand words long (plus a fact sheet) to every resident of the area. The letter said, in small part:

> We are doing the work here in Cambridge because this kind of chemical analysis cannot be performed in isolation. It is a key link in a chain of activities. Many other activities are required to support the work of the Levins Laboratory and, in turn, draw on the laboratory for analytic work. For all practical purposes, moving the laboratory to a remote location, would mean moving much of our technical work out of Cambridge. This we do not want to do. We have been a part of Cambridge since the beginning of this century. We have a record as good citizens of the community and a major investment here.

Magee did not add, as he might have, that when ADL was contemplating enlarging its facilities at Acorn Park, he had gone out of his way to assure one of his staff environmentalists that pains would be taken not to disturb the nesting grounds of resident woodcocks.

But all that proved to be in vain. The matter was removed from the jurisdiction of the superior court by Massachusetts' loftiest tribunal, the supreme judicial court. On August 1, 1985, by a four-to-one vote, that court's members upheld the right of the city of Cambridge to prohibit the work, and decreed that local health considerations preempted any contractual obligation ADL might have to the federal government. ADL accepted the verdict as graciously as it could, and the offending agents were soon removed, inside a steel cylinder sealed within another steel cylinder, to the Aberdeen Proving Ground in Maryland, a neighborhood apparently less fearful of toxicity.

The Levins Laboratory was to be used thenceforth for chemical research of a nature not likely to put the enclosure's costly security features to a severe test. John Magee could not, however, resist reminding the chairman of the Massachusetts House of Representatives' Committee on Health Care that the ruling against five specific toxic agents left moot the question of what, if anything, the commonwealth meant to do about the hundreds of other such chemicals deployed within its borders. Magee sent a copy of his letter to the chairman to Governor Michael S. Dukakis of Massachusetts, who may or may not have been given pause by the sentence "Other states solicit us and other companies to relocate where we can have what the governor of one such state characterized as 'corporate peace of mind.'"

It is a source of much comfort, and much cash, to consulting companies that there always seems to be some government agency or other that needs to have its work done for it. Once, ADL was asked by the U.S. National Highway Safety Administration to ascertain the prospects of the average American motorist's car being stolen in his or her lifetime. ADL came up with the gloomy news — or opinion — that there was a 30 percent chance, and that Massachusetts car owners were the most vulnerable of all. Not long afterward, the company initiated regular patrols of its own parking lots. ADL has done work for just about every major automobile company, foreign and domestic; one of its studies, made in the early 1970s even before the oil crunch, predicted that Americans would soon become disenchanted with the gas-guzzlers of the past and would welcome smaller, more compact vehicles.

ADL's own principal corporate car since 1978 has been a boxy Checker limousine, which was acquired only after considerable in-house research. Would a stretch Cadillac be consonant with the company's hoped-for image? Too pretentious. What about a Buick? No — people might infer that the company couldn't afford a Cadillac. Some executives who were consulted thought that a London taxicab might be just right, but to obtain one of those appeared to be more trouble than it was worth. Then John Magee, who had long legs, happened to be given a blissfully uncramped ride in a Checker while calling on a client. That settled the matter.

One time Elliott Wilbur was supposed to make a presentation to the chairman, the president, and the executive vice-president of a big French conglomerate. They traveled in style — by Concorde to New York, by private jet to the Hanscom Air Force Base, in Bedford, Massachusetts, the landing field closest to Acorn Park. Wilbur was waiting with the Checker to take them on their last lap. Halfway to ADL, the car ran out of gas. ("You don't buy gas around here for the Checker," one ADL cynic said afterward, "until you've got somebody billable to pay for it.") Wilbur was not especially perturbed. "The Checker, like our buildings, is an understatement, and that is part of our style," he said. "I always teach my people to skew their necktie or have a spot on their clothes somewhere, but there may be times, especially with three impatient Frenchmen in tow, when I think we overdo this grunginess."

ADL has frequently given advice on rapid transit. The Metropolitan Transportation Authority of New York, which hoped to install an electronic fare-collecting system to replace tokens on subways and buses, gave ADL $1.6 million to study, with its customary exhaustiveness, the methods of big cities other than New York. Before he was through, Douglas W. Palmer, an ADL specialist in transportation technology, was credited by somebody who took the trouble to keep track with having spent more hours on New York City buses in two weeks than the average New Yorker spends in three years. Peter J. Metz, the case leader, felt obliged — subway riding can have attractive side effects — to conduct research in Tokyo, Osaka, Hong Kong, and Paris. Prior to recommending a new device (it would probably involve a magnetic fare card and ultimately cost the MTA about $150 million to install), ADL technicians also studied the rapid transit systems of Paris, Stockholm, London, San Francisco, Atlanta, and Washington, D.C. Back at Acorn Park, they tested various machines with kicks and hammer blows and stuffed them with, among other impediments to smooth functioning, chewing gum and french fries.

For a proposed but subsequently aborted bullet train to cover the 110 miles between Los Angeles and San Diego — a two-and-a-half-hour journey by automobile — in fifty-nine minutes, at 160 miles an hour, ADL transportation experts were invited to make all sorts of forecasts: how many people would use it, how much income it would generate, how it would affect the communities it passed through, and so on. David Boodman, who spent ten years at M.I.T. on operations research work for the military before moving over to ADL in 1960, says, "It's a real challenge to be asked to make forecasts about what's going to happen to something that doesn't exist and will have to interact with so many other things; but it's just that sort of challenge that produces psychic rewards and keeps so many people like me at ADL when they could probably be making much more money somewhere else — that challenge and a kind of curiosity about the workings of the world and a recognition that this is one of the few places where, if you have that itch, you can scratch it."

Along with its delvings and probings into travel on earth, ADL has been much involved in space travel, too. (One early astronaut, Philip K. Chapman, a scientist who earlier spent two years at the South Pole, came aboard the staff in 1977.) There was at least one piece of ADL-engineered equipment on every flight of the Apollo program: meteor bumpers for spaceships, for instance; lubricants to enable telescopes on satellites to function efficiently for ten thousand hours; and insulation for space suits and mannequins for evaluating them. After the Apollo 13 spacecraft exploded on its launchpad, ADL compiled data for designing launching sites that could withstand explosions during lift-off. One ADLer who contributed to some of the earlier space projects was Bernard Vonnegut (a brother of the novelist), another Ph.D. from M.I.T., who arrived in 1952 and left in 1967 to become a distinguished professor at the State University of New York in Albany.

Vonnegut's field of expertise was atmospheric studies — lightning, tornadoes, seeding clouds with dry ice to create artificial snowstorms. He was interested in the use of rockets for meteorological research and, by the time he left the firm, had got some of his colleagues so enthused about meteorology that ADL embarked on one venture which, in retrospect, it would just as soon never have heard of. This was a ten-thousand-acre artillery range on the Vermont-Quebec border operated by the Space Research Corporation, a business set up by a Canadian physicist, Gerald V. Bull. A few years later, by which time ADL had turned over its interest in the company to the Memorial Drive Trust and Jean de Valpine had given up his chairmanship of the Space Research board, it turned out, embarrassingly, that Bull was violating an American embargo on armaments traffic with South Africa by selling technology, ballistics-testing equipment, and more than fifty thousand shells to that grateful country.

Meanwhile, a longtime corporate client had asked Karl Klaussen to have ADL take on the job of grading the performances of American companies operating in South Africa that had subscribed to the principles drawn up by Leon H. Sullivan, the Philadelphia clergyman and director of General Motors. Klaussen and John Magee were reluctant to oblige. Making judgments — conceivably adverse ones — about American corporate actions in South Africa might well offend many old clients, and ADL was not likely to get much compensating new business from black Baptist churches. But the client who'd broached the matter persisted. Magee and Klaussen thereupon decided that they'd better give the assignment to someone they reckoned could withstand pressure either from corporate board rooms or from anti-apartheid activists. They picked Reid Weedon. It was, all things considered, far from Weedon's happiest task. At one point, while he was visiting South Africa, he got into a shouting match with the head of the American Chamber of Commerce there, in the course of which, according to an account in *Fortune* — which not inaccurately described the ADLer as "an idealistic management consultant with the manner of a prep school headmaster" — the two men almost came to blows.

At a joint meeting in New York of the British and American Chemical Societies in September 1921, Dr. Little had made a speech in which he talked about the potential of solar energy. A *New York Times* report on the occasion said, "The world, he adds, awaits the genius who will convert that radiant energy (sun hitting Sahara daily with energy equalling that produced by 6 billion tons of coal) into electric current." Of all latter-day ADL explorers of outer space, the most adventurous and imaginative has indisputably been Peter E. Glaser, who, when *he* is addressing scientific convocations, sometimes reminds his audiences that Archimedes was able to temporarily protect Syracuse from the Romans during the Second Punic War by using mirrors to deflect the sun's rays onto their ships and setting the fleet afire.

Born in Zatec, Czechoslovakia (the site, he was much later informed by a brewmaster at a Columbia University alumni dinner, of the world's best hops), Glaser escaped the Nazis and got to England three months before the outbreak of the Second World War. After graduating from the Leeds College of Technology in 1943, he joined the Free Czech Army as a tank driver and eventually rolled into Prague with General George Patton's liberating army. Czechoslovakia gradually came under Soviet domination, and a factory belonging to Glaser's father had been nationalized, but Peter remained in his native land long enough to get a bachelor's degree in mechanical engineering. In 1948, he immigrated to the United States, and while employed by a textile firm took night courses at Columbia, getting a master's degree in 1951 and a Ph.D. in 1955. Working in a laboratory, he had seen and been impressed by a Collins helium cryostat, and as a result he applied for a job at ADL.

The subject of Glaser's doctoral thesis had been the thermal properties of evacuated materials, and his first ADL chore, appropriately, was to improve the insulation of Whirlpool refrigerators. Glaser's efforts led to a commission from the air force to investigate what took place when airborne materials were exposed to extremely high temperatures, and that in turn led to his building one of the first solar furnaces in the country. To his subsequent surprise, ADL sold thirty of his models for $30,000 apiece. Then came Sputnik. Glaser was soon part of a group at the Hanscom air base, measuring the properties of powders that it was believed might simulate the moon's surface. (In a then-ongoing debate as to whether anybody who stepped on the moon might sink out of sight, Glaser was an outspoken advocate of the moon's capacity to sustain the weight of a human body.) That got Glaser into the space program, and his first contribution to it was the fabrication of a quartz thermometer that could measure lunar temperature to within a thousandth of a degree Fahrenheit.

In 1968, Glaser unveiled what was surely the most ambitious and expensive space project ever conceived: a satellite solar power station. The most modest estimate yet made of its cost is $720 billion. Glaser proposed transmitting sunlight back to earth by microwaves. The idea was to have astronauts in low earth orbit — perhaps four hundred of them to a work crew — assemble photovoltaic cells into an array twenty square miles or so in dimension, roughly the size of Manhattan Island. Then the arrays would be nudged into geosynchronous orbit 22,300 miles above the equator. He envisioned, ultimately, fifty or one hundred of these floating monsters, each weighing fifty thousand or one hundred thousand tons. Their receiving stations would be equally impressive — each one an ellipse between five and ten miles in diameter. However, Glaser was quick to point out, the land on which these stations were to be placed wouldn't have to be removed from mortal use; they could be made of openwork, and farmers could till their fields beneath them.

People at ADL were worried when Glaser first launched his scheme; it sounded to them a bit too much like science fiction, and they feared that clients who got wind of it might be scared away. But Gavin supported Glaser and went to bat for him with NASA, which in the ensuing years — along with the Department of Energy and the National Academy of Sciences — took the notion seriously enough to spend between $15 million and $20 million just thinking about it.

ADL has taken it seriously, too; its Life Sciences people, under the leadership of Sam P. Battista, constructed a microwave irradiation facility so they could study the effects, if any, of Glaser's harnessed sunbeams on birds that might fly through them — using, on the one hand, house finches, blue jays, white-throated sparrows, dark-eyed juncos, zebra finches, and budgerigars; and, on the other, ethnologists, behavioral and physiological ecologists, pathologists, physicists, ornithological biophysicists, a veterinarian pathologist specializing in bird diseases, and a specialist in the migratory orientation of birds. Their preliminary findings were that birds could navigate microwaves all right unless these were of such intensity (far greater than any Glaser had in mind) as practically to cook them.*

---

* In 1984, the company's San Francisco office, with David Hurley in charge, was asked by Chevron and Texaco (which were jointly contemplating a $3 billion project to run pipelines from drilling platforms off Santa Barbara to the mainland) to conduct a similar inquiry — to ascertain what effect the pipelines would have on whales, fish, and fifty-two species of marine birds.

Glaser's lofty concepts have not been unrewarded. He became the editor-in-chief of the *Journal of Solar Energy* and the leader of a 120-client ADL study on the entire future of the solar energy industry. Between 1964 and 1984, in no small measure because of his presence on the scene, the company did $34 million worth of business in space research and development. Glaser was not entirely satisfied. "Space is an especially difficult place to do business in," he says. Back in 1973, he had remarked, "I don't know what reaction the oil companies would have to solar energy. I also don't know what reaction the buggy whip companies had to the first Ford autos."

He was still hopeful that his solar power satellite station would get under way before the start of the twenty-first century, though its timetable was not keeping pace with a fictitious *New York Times* article, dated February 16, 1988, that had been printed in ADL's annual report for the year 1976. According to the story, a U.N. Committee on the Peaceful Uses of Outer Space, which had a thousand members, had been set up in 1986. (That tied in nicely with ADL's forthcoming hundredth anniversary.) Now, in 1988, the president of the United States, who was not named, was announcing on the eve of the New Hampshire primary that a solar satellite system, strictly nonpolitical, would be in operation within three or four years. Before the end of 1989, the president was happy to be able to say, both the United States and the Soviet Union were expected to ratify a code drafted in 1986 by the International Institute of Space Law. And there would be commercial solar power available in 1996.

While waiting for all that to come to pass, Glaser was able to shift his sights easily from the theoretical to the practical. He was working with one group of ADLers who had developed the protocol and the hardware for a blood storage study in space. Blood has a limited shelf life on earth; whether the changes in its cells that eventually render it unacceptable for transfusions are attributable to the containers it is preserved in is not known. It has long been suspected that perhaps the earth's gravity somehow alters the cells, and that led logically enough to the idea of studying cells in space. Meanwhile, along with representatives of ADL's food and flavor sections, Glaser had been helping NASA solve the problem of catering in space, and worrying about such specifics as how astronauts could more tidily than ever before put together, in orbit, peanut butter and jelly sandwiches. The consultants were also exploring the psychobiological mystery of why there seem in space to be changes in the perceptions of odors and flavors. Ernest Crocker would have been fascinated.

By 1984, a year in which ADL's revenues came to $213,363,-000, the whole consulting industry was getting bigger. ADL had 125 significant competitors, and these included not only the old-time firms like Booz, Allen and McKinsey, but accountants and banks and universities, all competing vigorously for a chance to advise people, for robust fees, on how better — or, at any rate, not worse — to conduct their affairs.* "Listen carefully," the chief executive officer of one ADL client told his management executives one day when Elliott Wilbur appeared before them to make a presentation, "because he's costing us a dollar a word."

To attract promising young men and women, high-pressure recruiting had become the order of the day, with newly minted M.B.A.s from the Harvard Business School able to demand, and receive, starting salaries of $55,000 a year and perhaps a $10,000 bonus for signing on. ADL, which has traditionally had a pay scale lower than those of its chief rivals, used to recruit more assid-uously than it has in recent years — there would be cocktail parties at Boston hotels with General Gavin circulating magneti-cally among the guests — but it still does have a summer intern program for business school students. On their last day at Acorn Park the interns are treated to a meal in the directors' room (with portraits of Gavin, Earl Stevenson, and Ray Stevens looking down patriarchally from the walls), which it is hoped they will fondly remember: steak, mushrooms, asparagus, ice cream with strawberries — even sherry. Some contemporary ADLers rue-fully concede that their company can probably never hope to compete with its big rivals because of different standards and ob-jectives. "I'm never quite sure what McKinsey people are out

---

* Harry Wissmann liked to cite an incident that in his view exemplified the difference be-tween ADL and at least one of its rivals. The Grocery Manufacturers Association of America, an ADL client, was having a meeting in Greenbriar, West Virginia. The presi-dent of General Foods offered Wissmann a ride down in his private plane. Another pas-senger was a McKinsey man who was working on a General Foods account. Wissmann noticed with awe that when they were getting under way the McKinsey man addressed the General Foods executive by his first name and then — this was even more im-pressive — kissed the president's wife. "It was the McKinsey style to develop that sort of intimate relationship with clients," Wissmann said. "Some ADLers found that hard to do."

for," one senior Acorn Park person says, "but we are in search of excellence."

Modern technology has, naturally, altered both the activities and the modus operandi of large consulting firms. ADL has been working with computers almost since they came into being. Its first big computer job was a 1956 analysis, for Blaw-Knox, of the stresses in pipe systems used in oil refineries and power plants. Not long after that, Frank L. Allen, an information systems specialist who plays host at the summer intern lunches and who by 1984 had twenty-nine years' worth of ADL experiences to chat about, was a key person in helping the Michigan Bell system to convert a whole series of its operations to computers. (Once ADL bravely persuaded the Chase Manhattan Bank — often called the Rockefeller bank — to discontinue a computer project, which meant abandoning a system that another Rockefeller-dominated company had gone to considerable trouble designing for it.) As the ADL London office has in Adrian Norman a resident computer security expert, so does the home office boast John Wilkinson-Heap, who achieved a measure of notoriety one time when, asked what he thought would make a foolproof password for computer users, replied, "The name of your mistress's dog. If that's the sort of thing you bring up in casual conversation, you probably shouldn't be allowed access to the company computer."

Computers, it goes without saying, have infiltrated almost every phase of ADL's activities, though the company still highly values the functioning of the human brain. According to Martin Ernst, "Mostly we use computers to evaluate problems we have solved already." Ernst and others in the firm have been working since 1972 in the still somewhat arcane field that has become known as artificial intelligence. ("We won't know what artificial intelligence really is till we know what intelligence is," Ernst has said.) Most of their efforts have been directed toward designing KBSs (knowledge-based systems) for such occult institutions as DARPA (Defense Advanced Research Projects Agency). By 1985, ADL had fifteen staff members — with advanced degrees in management sciences, business administration, medicine, biology, political science, mathematics, psychology, and engineering — probing the elusive mysteries of artificial intelligence, which is, basically, a computer program that draws inferences from a large body of knowledge and not only arrives at conclusions, advice, and additional questions, but also can explain why it arrived there. If computers can be fed all the processes by which experts make decisions, then the computer can presumably make them itself. So optimistic are some of the individuals in the field that they predict a market of more than $100 billion for artificial intelligence by the year 2000. By 1984, Jean de Valpine had already committed some of his Memorial Drive Trust resources to it.

Artificial intelligence may be widely employed in, for instance, diagnosing diseases, locating mineral deposits, deciding where to drill for oil, and maybe even for dowsing by the turn of the century. Notable among the practitioners in the area at ADL has been Karl M. Wiig, who got interested in 1959 while attending a lecture on the then still arcane subject by the Nobel laureate Herbert A. Simon. Wiig, who sometimes refers to the machines he communes with as animals or beasts, was born and raised in Norway. He immigrated to the United States in 1957 to study mechanical engineering at the Case Institute of Technology because, he says, his grades weren't good enough for advanced study in Norway. Wiig got a master's degree at Case in instrumentation engineering — computer control of very complex systems. He went back to Norway for a few years and returned to the United States in 1964 as a research physicist on the dynamics of the arterial systems of hibernating hedgehogs. After further work, mainly on the automation of steel mills and cement plants, he joined ADL in 1970. He keeps a gilded abacus on his desk, a memento of a short-lived computer company he formed in 1981 called Abacus Alpha. Wiig is held in awe by ADLers familiar with his work habits because — he, coming from the Land of the Midnight Sun, does not consider himself unusual — he often turns up at Acorn Park at 5:00 in the morning and holds conferences, whenever he can get anyone to confer at that hour, at 11:00 at night. He nonetheless describes himself as lazy.

Akin to the company's interest in artificial intelligence has been an involvement in machine vision: the use of computers, in lieu of human beings, to examine merchandise for flaws by means of translating such anathemas as bones in fish products, burn marks on cookies, and unevenness in bacon slices into numerical values and then ascribing to these acceptability and rejectability. Computers endowed with machine vision can pass judgment on eighteen hundred slices of bacon a minute and can transmit signals to have the bacon sliced thicker or thinner, whatever the goal may be. George Gagliardi, who, not surprisingly, has also worked with robots since he came to ADL in 1980, has busied himself since then applying machine vision techniques to pizzas (monitoring, for one thing, the precise quantity of mozzarella per wheel), and to paper money (spotting imperfections at the Bureau of Engraving and Printing). In an image processing laboratory at Acorn Park where Gagliardi holds forth, he has one machine known as an international robomatic intelligence image buffer, by means of which he can determine, for example, how tightly packed the weaves are and should be in blue denim cloth. Like most other ADLers, Gagliardi is constantly concerned about his billability, and he usually keeps his laboratory door ajar, hoping that some colleague strolling by will wander in and ask to use his buffer or some other handy device in connection with a case he's been assigned to. Off duty, Gagliardi has sought to draw attention to the applicability of machine vision to the food industry by writing articles for publications like *Cereal Foods Journal.* "You have to market your own skills around here," he says.

A visitor to ADL's London office, waiting in the reception area for Michael Younger, once bemusedly looked on while a young woman, facing a corridor beyond the observer's line of vision, was apparently training a dog. "Hold it, Toby," she was saying. "Stop, boy. Right. Hold it." When the object of her instructions came into view, it was not a dog but a robot. A few weeks later, the same visitor rounded a corner at Acorn Park and came upon another young woman, clutching a bunch of inflated balloons. Not wishing to be fooled again — after all, this was the birthplace of the lead balloon — the visitor asked her what kind of case the balloons related to. "They're a surprise for my friend's birthday," she said.

ADL has been in robotics almost from the beginning of that industry, and one of its principal robot operatives has been, since he joined the firm in 1979, Gerald J. Michael, a Cornell Ph.D. in electrical engineering. Once, Michael earned the gratitude of a client by purveying some thumpingly negative counsel. A machine tool company had spent three years and $3 million on developing a robot. The company besought advice from ADL on marketing the product. "We felt obliged to recommend a fairly bitter pill,"

Michael said. "Our analysis convinced us that they should terminate all their activities in robotics and divest themselves of the whole operation, and I had to stand in front of their CEO and express that opinion. I felt quite uncomfortable. But not only did they accept our recommendation but a month later they came back to us with a new assignment — to find a buyer for their technology. By preventing them from going on, we probably saved them twelve or fifteen million dollars. Of course, if they'd come to us before they got started, we could have saved them even more."

"It's hard to introduce new things," Peter Glaser once remarked wistfully when somebody asked him how soon he thought his near-trillion-dollar satellite solar power station might come into being. Innovativeness, an area in which Glaser unarguably excels, is much on contemporary ADLers' minds, and in 1984, as an indication of how their thoughts were running, Chairman of the Board Mueller compiled a list of fifty-nine innovations attributable to ADL and considered memorable enough to be chronicled. Among them were, for a small retail products company, "New set of books created which revealed company was budgeting less than 1% on new concepts and not spending what was budgeted." For a pharmaceutical manufacturer, "Unique approach to market definition for over-the-counter home diagnostic products of the future with respective product lines, advertising strategies, etc. Examples: anxious mothers, confidentiality seekers; and the 'worried well.' " For a major multinational financial services corporation, "Characterization of U.S. federal bureaucracy and its connections with private and public sectors." For ADL Business Development, "Development of a background theory to link various ADL activities, including qualities needed for information to have substantial value, a spectrum of pragmatic information, the role of planning and other corporate guidelines in establishing context with implications for management and to ADL in the areas of office automation, artificial intelligence, and core development group programs." For a U.S. manufacturing company, "Served CEO by assessing the extent to which senior managers understood, accepted, and gave high priority to implementing a newly authorized corporate strategy. Helped adjust roles and job descriptions of senior line managers and corporate staff officers whose functions were discovered to be inconsistent with the new strategy. . . ."

"We used to do technical audits for our clients," Derek Till said that same year. "Now we talk to them about strategic management of technology. That word *strategic* gets them every time."

When it comes to strategic management of technology, nowhere on earth has ADL had a greater impact than in Saudi Arabia. The company's quadrumviral presence there came to a halt in 1969, but five years afterward it started up again when that kingdom decided to modernize its telecommunications. There had been fewer than two hundred thousand telephones in all of Saudi Arabia. An ADL telecommunications team undertook to revamp the system, and a decade later there were more than a million phones in use. (ADL has also carried out large-scale telecommunications missions for Egypt, Mexico, the Philippines, Thailand, and Uruguay.) Saudi Arabian shopkeepers who formerly sent their cousins or nephews out to purchase caftans or coffeepots for their souks now place orders by phone and spend hours talking to one another across narrow alleys, over which in the past they'd had no recourse other than to shout. Much of the more recent telecommunications work there has been supervised by Alan B. Kamman, who came to ADL in 1974 after sixteen years with the Bell system, and who in a decade made more than seventy trips to Saudi Arabia. By 1984, ADL was working on a satellite telecommunications system designed to link up thirteen Arab nations. On the doorknob of Kamman's Acorn Park office he has hung a Do Not Disturb sign in Arabic — a keepsake from one of the many Middle East hotel rooms he has occupied. ADL has had permanent office space in the Saudi Ministry of Post, Telegraph, and Telephone since 1975.

When Egypt decided in 1981 to update its telecommunications, a $5 billion undertaking, it obtained much of the funding it needed from the U.S. Agency for International Development. AID wanted to be assured that its money was being properly expended, and it called upon ADL to look into that. Eventually, the responsibility for developing programs and control methods, among other things, for the Egyptian telephone network was turned over to a fairly new ADL subsidiary, the Program Systems Management Company, or PSMC, which had been set up in 1977 for the specific purpose of helping clients embarking on large-scale projects.

In the course of carrying out the Egyptian mission, the PSMC found a new trade for women there — running a computer center, an occupation that most Egyptian men deemed insufficiently macho to warrant their participation. ADL also discovered a way to get around one aspect of Middle Eastern culture that had long frustrated foreigners trying to conduct business in that region. It was generally considered infra dig to criticize anybody face to face for dereliction of duty. To chastise an employee for, say, being late was not acceptable; but there could be no objection to a project manager saying to a delinquent, "I'm sorry to have to inform you that the computer says you're late."

From its inception, PSMC has been commanded by a retired navy captain, Albert J. Kelley (his brother Paul simultaneously had his own far-reaching command: the U.S. Marine Corps), who while dean of the business school of Boston College had done consulting work for ADL. When barely out of the naval academy in 1945, Kelley joined Admiral William Halsey's carrier group and was one of the first Americans into Tokyo after V-J Day. He had almost been an astronaut, at the start of the space program, but had been turned down because he stood an inch over six feet and the Mercury capsule wouldn't comfortably hold anyone over five nine and a half. So he had become a project manager for the navy at NASA. "People often ask me what PSMC is," Kelley told a visitor to his Acorn Park office (which has on its wall a hoary bit of naval advice to a crew: "If everything seems to be going well, you have obviously overlooked something."). "I can tell you what I think it does, but I'm not sure I can make it understandable. We work with people who work on projects — big projects, like a weapons system or a new oil city, or a movie. We support a client by providing him with project managers, systems engineers, and the like. And we can call on the rest of ADL for specific technical skills, when and as needed. We go out and live with the people who've hired us, but it's always understood that we won't become lifetime members of whatever the institution is."

PSMC has been gratifyingly approached by the so-called military industrial complex, of which Kelley is emphatically a member. (So is his chief representative in Washington, Milton E. Key, a retired army major general who, starting as an infantry private first class in the Second World War, had risen swiftly in the ranks — command of a Pershing missile brigade in Germany, chief nuclear planner at Supreme Headquarters Allied Powers in Europe, assistant to the secretary of defense for nuclear energy.) PSMC at one point had thirty people deployed on a tactical communications system for one of the Defense Department's highest-priority projects, a joint tactical information distribution system. And Kelley's own tactical forces were simultaneously engaged in helping to devise technology, again on behalf of the Pentagon, for the Strategic Defense Initiative — "Star Wars" — Program (lasers were a part of it), on which the government contemplated lavishing $32.5 billion between 1985 and 1989.

Early in 1985, when Kelley declared that the time had come "to use Arthur D. Little's unique strengths to leverage the opportunities created by today's realities," his confidence was emphatically rewarded: PSMC was asked to take charge of program management and technical support work for, among other government entities, NASA, the Department of Energy, the Central Intelligence Agency, the Department of Transportation, the National Security Agency, the Defense Intelligence Agency, and the Department of Defense. When the PSMC got under way, it was pretty much a one-man operation. By 1985, Kelley's crew was more than a hundred strong, and John Magee was saying to him one day, not at all unhappily, "When are you going to be bigger than ADL?"

Magee himself, as the company was rounding out its first century, was giving much thought to its future, and indeed he had set up a committee to ponder the subject: himself, Alfred Wechsler, and Samuel Fleming, a Harvard Business School M.B.A. whose forte was solving management problems in the chemical industry. (Some ADL scientists were still doing the kind of innovative research that had characterized the firm's earlier days — the mechanical engineer David Lee had not long before achieved a breakthrough in kitchen appliances by devising an eye-level broiler for gas stoves — but as Martin Ernst put it one day, "You don't get big fees anymore by doing chemical analyses. You get them by giving advice to a CEO.") The committee was inclined to the belief that in at least the foreseeable days ahead ADL's emphasis would be on telecommunications, electronics, financial industries, and biotechnology. Magee himself was voicing concern that the world's political, social, and economic systems weren't accelerating quickly enough to keep up with technological changes. "We live in an interesting time," he declared in one public speech. "Whether that proves to be a curse — as the ancient Chinese saying would have it — or a blessing, as I believe, depends on our ability to face up to and manage the interaction of technology and society." Long before that, in a reflective 1981 paper titled "Our Management Values and Systems," he had tersely indicated in what direction he expected the company to move. "We go where the client's needs are," he said.

On Tuesday, October 1, 1985, one year before the observance of ADL's hundredth anniversary, Board Chairman Robert Mueller, among a dozen or so other undertakings, had a long phone call, in his capacity as chairman also of the National Association of Corporate Directors, about that group's forthcoming annual meeting; chaired a meeting in Boston of the audit committee of Colby-Sawyer College and finished the preparation of an invocation for the college's president to deliver at his next trustees' session; drafted a proposal for a multinational oil company aspiring to set up an advisory council to deal with technological, economic, political, and cultural forces worldwide; and worked with an ADL psychologist on the development of an executive screening methodology for the human resource office of a prospective client. Once again, Mueller was too tired after all that, and more, to practice on his bass fiddle.

Stephen Ritterbush, airborne to Southeast Asia after a busy week divided between Acorn Park and England, arrived in Hong Kong early in the morning and was soon back at work helping a company there assess the ability of the People's Republic of China to produce precision metal castings as subcontractors for American manufacturers. Next, Ritterbush met with the head of the largest venture capital fund in Hong Kong, who wanted to learn in what ways ADL could help him appraise new technologies and possible investment opportunities. That evening, Ritterbush headed wearily back to the airport and homeward to Singapore, where by now, although the ADL office there was less than two years old, he already had six professionals on his staff.

Stanley Werlin, still concerned about defense against chemical and biological warfare, was in Cambridge revising a proposal to the Toxic and Hazardous Materials Agency of the U.S. Army to work at military installations on developing decontamination methods for buildings and equipment. He took time off to celebrate, with Arthur Schwope of ADL's Product Technology Section, the signing the day before of a multimillion-dollar contract with the EPA, which wanted ADL to develop improved protective equipment for workers exposed to hazardous materials.

Alma Triner put in a not unusual ten-hour day at Acorn Park, in the course of which she finished a memorandum to Chief Executive Officer Magee on recommended strategies for avoiding community relations problems like those arising from the Levins Laboratory contretemps; had two meetings with David Benjamin, one of her public relations assistants, who was just back from a mission in Tokyo; and edited some press releases, including one about new ADL senior vice-presidents, before going home to spray her dog, which, lamentably, had fleas.

Michael Younger had traveled from his London base to Edinburgh to discuss the implementation of the study on the recovery of Scottish engineering ADL had made over the preceding twelve months for the Scottish Development Agency. That was the good news. The bad news was that a valued colleague had been lured away from the ADL London office to become the head of a new venture capital company. "I guess that's the price," Younger told another associate ruefully, "of success."

Alfred Wechsler spent a good part of the day — and eventually dined — with Ray Kelly, ADL's Middle East manager, who'd come over to Cambridge from London to discuss his activities and his budget. There were other meetings with members of the staff and with a prospective client who wanted to be reassured about professional availability and competence; and there were several talks about the agenda of a forthcoming gathering of the American Institute of Chemical Engineers, over which Wechsler had flatteringly been invited to preside.

Phillip Hawley was getting ready for the next — and, he hoped, conceivably final — round of negotiations on the huge contract ADL was helping the Angolan government and Sonangol draw up with Gulf and Chevron for offshore exploration and production. Hawley spent a couple of hours on the phone from London to Luanda and London to San Francisco, and he felt afterward that he might have cleared up some nuances of meaning in the proposed agreement.

George Gagliardi, having allocated much of the previous

twelve months to advising clients interested in the application of computer-aided visual inspection (CAVI) systems in such industries as robotics and aerospace, traveled from Orlando, Florida — where he called on several companies involved in electronic test automation and completed, for a French client, an overview of 3-D machine vision measurement technology — to New York City, to confer with a potential client interested in the application of CAVI to various aspects of semiconductor (integrated circuit) manufacturing.

In London, Bruce Williams, after a daylong series of meetings with the top executives of a British telecommunications company, who wanted his opinion of the prospects of a manufacturing facility of theirs, hopped across the English Channel for a date early the next morning with Nicholas Steinthal, who would be flying back from Germany to share ideas with Williams about the links between telematics and computer-integrated manufacturing.

Richard de Filippi was at Acorn Park reviewing with Robert Mueller and others the possibility of the sale of a controlling interest in de Filippi's Critical Fluids Systems to an outside venture capital group. De Filippi had to dine at home alone again because his peripatetic son was by now in Pittsburgh, studying architecture at Carnegie-Mellon University.

John Ketteringham, who the month before had been invested with the new title of senior vice-president for Health Care and Chemical Product and Process Development, attended a meeting of ADL's Biomedical Research and Technology Section at the Memorial Drive building, and also got together with David Wheat and other biotechnologists to discuss marketing strategies for ADL's novel spin filter technology for growing cells.

Harland Riker, still glowing with satisfaction that his meeting with a Swiss aluminum company the year before had resulted in an important strategic planning job for ADL, was in Toronto conferring with Paul White, the president of Arthur D. Little of Canada, Ltd., about the growth and development of ADL's operations in Canada in 1986 and the years beyond.

Santhanam Shekar went from his base at Wiesbaden to Vienna to compare notes with Minister of Transportation and Industry Ferdinand Lacina about the status of an ongoing ADL project with Austrian Railways on the planning of a high-performance rail network for that country.

Ray Kelly, in his conversations at Acorn Park with Al Wechsler *et alii* about ADL's Middle East activities, was especially anxious for his colleagues to hear his views on the significance of an expansion of ADL business in Africa and on the Indian subcontinent.

William Reinfeld had what for him was becoming a fairly routine sort of day: talking on the phone to Bangkok about the implementation of the contract ADL had been bidding on the year before and had been granted; talking to Panama about widening the canal; and reading, with elation, a telex to the effect that Tunisia had authorized ADL to proceed with the next phase of its export strategy study. Reinfeld was in no hurry to get home; Hurricane Gloria had knocked out his power.

Christopher Ross played host at dinner in Houston to Shuhe Mitome, over from the Tokyo office. It was the first time they'd got together since, nearly two years earlier, they worked on a case for an American natural gas producer. Now they were contemplating another joint effort, this one involving the collaboration of Houston- and Tokyo-based companies on behalf of an ADL client in Japan.

Ladd Greeno, befitting the new title he was about to acquire — manager of the Environmental Management Section — was putting the finishing touches on a long-range plan for the development and implementation of an environmental, health, and safety auditing program for a large chemical company.

Roberto Batres, whose Mexico City office had come through the big earthquake unscathed, spent much of the day conferring with Nacobre, the largest brass products manufacturer in Mexico, which wanted his advice on what effect the quake and its aftermath would have on the company's operations.

David Lee, following his by now customary early morning single-sculls workout, spent most of his working hours at Acorn Park with the other members of his Engineering Sciences Section. They reviewed the status of cases they were working on and discussed prospective new ones — including yet another from the U.S. Air Force.

Michel d'Halluin, who liked nothing better than to think big, was engaged in Paris in a highly gratifying colloquy with the French minister of finance about an ADL contract to advise the government on the feasibility of not just one but two tunnels beneath the English Channel.

Samuel Fleming, principally concerned as always with the strategic management of chemical companies, spent a gadabout day with the president of the American subsidiary of a major British concern in his field: breakfast flight from Boston to Chicago, full working day there, dinner flight from Chicago to Allentown, Pennsylvania. Fleming did not mind; ADL had had a happy and rewarding five-year association with that client.

Robert Tomasko devoted most of the day, from his Washington office, to a series of phone calls to executives of, for instance, Xerox, Masonite, and IBM, all of them active in South Africa and signatories to the Sullivan Principles. It was the time of year when ADL was supposed to evaluate signatories' performances in the increasingly turbulent South African environment, and one of the things Tomasko wanted to find out was to what extent they had tried to put pressure on the Botha government to eliminate apartheid. Tomasko also sandwiched in a call to Richard Stephan, who was about to go from Cambridge to Bangkok about a multiyear contract with petroleum officials in Thailand.

Stephan, a vice-president of Arthur D. Little International and an oil company specialist, bade Tomasko farewell and headed for Logan Airport en route to Bangkok via Singapore, where he was going to pick up Ian Moncrieff of ADL Singapore so they could confer before their scheduled meeting with the top management of Thailand's national oil company. The session was of particular importance in Stephan's view because, as he put it on returning to Acorn Park, "it represents an extension, or expansion, of our oil company work into Asia. This means that organizational techniques used successfully in other parts of the world had to be adapted to suit the requirements of a very different and sophisticated culture."

Anne Neilson, during a Cambridge meeting of food and flavor people about their 1986 marketing plans for pharmaceutical, tobacco, beverage, and other companies, was pleased to be reminded that the spiritous product she'd gone to the United Kingdom to work on the year before had finally gone on sale and had been favorably received by what its progenitors called their target population.

David Wheat got to his Acorn Park office at 6:30 A.M., which may have explained why his first computer input went "Modified autoexec.bat file for PC." His second was "Wrote memos requesting computer enhancements and new software." Once he had pulled himself together, Wheat consulted Juliet Zavon as to who should represent ADL at corn and soybean research meetings in Chicago of the American Seed Trade Association; persuaded the Contracting Department to expedite the release of a proposal to a major agricultural products company; wrote a report on some of the aspects of using biotechnology in corn breeding; discussed, over a noontime sandwich, ADL's biotechnology industry data base; had a long afternoon meeting about the possibility of developing ADL's spin filter technology for monoclonal antibody production and mammalian cell culture applications; got the agricultural proposal and sent it off; and at 6:30 P.M., after twelve nonatypical hours, put one last entry into his now fathomable computer: "Left for home."

In Tokyo, Yoshimichi Yamashita, while waiting to hear from Shuhe Mitome about his trip to Texas, assembled most of the rest of his ADL staff for a no-holds-barred brainstorming session on how they could best expand their activities in the area of artificial intelligence.

Richard Heitman betook himself to upper New York State to review the status of a case involving the development, with ADL assistance, of some artificial intelligence software.

Jeffery Lapham traveled from Los Angeles into the depths of California's Silicon Valley to confer with the senior executives of a large aerospace company on strategies to be presented to their board of directors for improving the company's performance and, it was to be hoped as a concomitant, its profitability.

Jerry Wasserman was also in California, having gone to San Diego from Cambridge to explore, for and with electronics people of General Dynamics, opportunities for them to diversify into aerospace industries.

Andrew Sivak had to set aside much of the day for his regular weekly meetings with unit managers in his Biomedical Research and Technology Section and his regular monthly meeting of his core staff; but he saved time to get together with Ketteringham, Wheat, and others and bring himself up to date on ADL's spin filter project.

Gerald Michael was en route to Florida, where he'd been invited by a robot manufacturer to counsel that client on obtaining a decent share of the burgeoning and tumultuous U.S. robotics market.

Lois Dreiman was at the Burlington, Massachusetts, outpost, preparing a final report for the Republic of China. The Taiwanese had asked ADL to draw up a comparison of their information industry with other nations', hoping thereby to more than quadruple the $1 billion a year it was spending on products and services.

It was an eventful day for Nicholas Steinthal. Exactly one year after his trip to Germany to discuss a strategic plan development with a pharmaceutical company, he was back there for an important briefing from that multinational's senior vice-president. What the executive had to report was that after twelve intensive months, recommendations jointly formulated by ADL and a team of high-level company officials had been accepted and were going to be presented for adoption by the board of directors the very next day.

John Clancy, who earlier in 1985 had managed to authenticate three ancient Peruvian bonds, was in Lausanne, Switzerland, conferring on behalf of the Bureau of Engraving and Printing with Dr. Fausto Giori, research director of De La Rue Giori S.A., the world's preeminent firm in manufacturing equipment for the production of paper currency. Clancy's mission was part of a technology assessment study ADL was making for the bureau, which wanted a report on what the options for its engraving needs would probably be at least through the early years of the twenty-first century.

Paul Littlefield, who had theoretically retired in July as senior vice-president and chief financial officer, was still at Acorn Park, by now holding the title of consultant on financial affairs. As such, he was chairman of a fairly newly formed ADL financial issues committee. In quasi retirement, he was happy to have more time than ever before to spend on his efforts to reduce hospitalization costs.

Sarah Fuller spent most of her day, at Burlington, exploring new ways of increasing ADL's Decision Resources general activities in Pacific Ocean markets; specifically, she was wrapping up a contract with an affiliate of the University of New South Wales to augment operations in Australia.

Irwin Miller, whose Opinion Research Corporation in Princeton had substantially enhanced its potential work load earlier in the year by inaugurating a new telephone-interviewing center, was at Acorn Park to sit in on a meeting of ADL's top consumer packaged goods executives.

Kamal Saad, who more often than not was on the road far from his Brussels headquarters, was for a change right there, putting together the final presentation to the board of directors of a chemical company of an assessment of what its capital requirements would be if it decided to expand its area of operations.

John Magee was on an airplane returning to Boston from London. He had gone to England to outline ADL's corporate strategy at the annual planning conference of Cambridge Consultants Ltd., and while he was at CCL had inspected its newest laboratory building. It had been a busy year, and with all the fuss about nerve gases in some respects a harrowing one, but he had nonetheless found time along the way, finally, to finish his model boat.

Index